How to Sell Antiques and Collectibles on eBay®... and Make a Fortune!

Dennis L. Prince
Lynn Dralle

McGraw-Hill
New York   Chicago   San Francisco
Lisbon   London   Madrid   Mexico City   Milan
New Delhi   San Juan   Seoul   Singapore
Sydney   Toronto

McGraw-Hill books are available at special quantity discounts to use as premiums
and sales promotions, or for use in corporate training programs. For more information, please write to the Director of Special Sales, Professional Publishing, McGraw-
Hill, Two Penn Plaza, New York, NY 10121-2298. Or contact your local bookstore.

Library of Congress Cataloging-in-Publication Data

Prince, Dennis L.

  How to sell antiques and collectibles on eBay– : and make a fortune! / Dennis L.
Prince and Lynn Dralle.
    p. cm.
  ISBN 0-07-144569-2 (alk. paper)
  1. eBay (Firm) 2. Internet auctions. 3. Selling—Antiques—Computer network
resources. 4. Selling—Collectibles—Computer network resources.   I. Wilson, Lynn
Dralle. II. Title.
  HF5478.P753 2004
  745.1'068'8—dc22   2004020079

From Lynn

To my awesome parents, Sharon Chase and Wayne Dralle.
I love you. Thanks for everything!

From Dennis

For you, Dad. You'll always be priceless in my eyes.

Contents

Acknowledgments

From Lynn

Thanks to Dennis Prince and Donya Dickerson at McGraw-Hill for being so great to work with! Both of you are amazingly supportive and positive. You made it very enjoyable to write this book.

I would like to acknowledge my friends and family who read what I wrote: Lee Dralle, Kristin Dralle, Wayne Dralle, Sharon Chase, Melanie Souve, and Peter Gineris. I am grateful for having such super kids, Houston and Indy, who put off playing with their mommy while I wrote the book.

Thanks to Sharon Korbeck, editor at the *Antique Trader*, for talking with me and to Kim Esser, University of Southern California Library, for helping me with research. Thanks also to Elaine Henderson at Pattern Glass (*www.PatternGlass.com*) for sharing her knowledge. My gratitude to the Scalise family, Lori, Lou, Hunter, and Paige, who let us photograph their entire furniture collection!

Thanks to my assistant, Maria Cota, who took so many great photos, to Jon Brunk for his super photos, and to my talented brother, Lee at L.A. Dralle Photography (*www.LADralle.com*) for taking more photos and for making them all look fantastic! I also appreciate Susan Thornberg, who did a superb job preediting.

My thanks to Deborah Masi and Lara Stelmaszyk with Westchester Book Group and Pattie Amoroso and Cheryl Hudson at McGraw-Hill. The book looks incredible!

To all my wonderful eBay customers who have bought from The QueenofAuctions—thanks for making it fun and profitable!

And finally, I am indebted to my mom, Sharon Chase, and my dad, Wayne Dralle, who spent the spring and summer taking care of my kids so I could write!

From Dennis

Though only my name is credited on the cover of this book, the truth is that any good book one person writes is made better by the team with which he works. Certainly, my case is no exception and it's my duty—no, it's my pleasure—to extend my sincerest thanks to those with whom I've worked to bring this book to completion.

Of course, I begin with my co-author and collecting compatriot, Lynn Dralle. Although I had hoped to work with someone full of motivation on this project, I could never have anticipated your infectious enthusiasm. Lynn, you're a treasure in this world and a true "find" to all who have the good fortune to get to know you.

Next, at McGraw-Hill, I give my deepest thanks to Donya Dickerson, Project Editor. She a true "rarity" in regards to her unerring vision, commitment, and passion for a new title like this. Donya, you're the tops in my "value guide" and I'm richer for having the opportunity to work with you. Rounding out the McGraw-Hill team are the indispensable Mary Glen, Anthony Sarchiapone, Brian Boucher, and the entire Sales and Marketing team. Thanks to all of you for playing along here. You're all top-notch curators of creative excellence and I thank you for your priceless contributions.

Next, my thanks to Deborah Masi at Westchester Book Group, Production Editor par excellence, for giving this book the rest of the polish and perfecting touches.

And, last but not least, thanks to everyone at eBay, both those who operate the site as well as those buyers and sellers who truly make it work. Thanks to all with whom I've interacted throughout the years. We've written the history of online business and cyber-collecting together and I look forward to continuing our good work together for years to come.

Introduction

OVERVIEW OF eBAY

eBay has changed the way the world does business. If you can believe it, Sears, the Disney Store, and even the Goodwill Industries now have eBay divisions and are selling their overstocks and slow turning inventory.

I, Lynn Dralle, became familiar with eBay about six years ago in a very unique way. My grandmother, Cheryl Leaf, owned an antiques and gift store in Bellingham, Washington, that she started way back in 1950—before people were interested in the antiques and collectibles business! I spent almost ten years—from 1993 to 2002—running her store for her. It was a lot of fun, and under her tutelage I was able to really grow the business. By the time we closed the doors in August 2002 our sales had grown tenfold and we had tripled our square footage. eBay had a lot to do with that growth, and unfortunately or fortunately (however you choose to view it) eBay had a lot to do with our decision to close the actual brick-and-mortar location.

In 1996, *People* magazine had an article about some hot new stuffed toys called Beanie Babies. I immediately found out who the Ty representative for our area was and placed the maximum order allowed—36 of each style per month. It was about a $5,000 wholesale order each month. At that point, this was quite aggressive for our small store, but I like to take calculated risks, and my grandmother said, "Go for it." She was the queen of calculated risks and very successful at it (see Figure I-1).

We enjoyed a great relationship with Ty and made a lot of money from those little critters. Everything was great until one morning in January 1998, when I received a form letter from Ty Inc. They were canceling the accounts of any store that had *antiques* in their name. Ty Inc. had decided that they did not want their product to be carried in antiques stores. I was devastated. We had lost our cash cow.

BEAN THERE: Cheryl Leaf, 85, holds Beanie Babies, one of the hot items to give as gifts this year. Leaf is the original owner of Cheryl Leaf Antiques & Gifts, which she has owned for 47 years.

Figure I-1 Cheryl Leaf holding Beanie Babies in 1997 for a *Bellingham Herald* article.

How was I going to find Beanie Babies to sell and replace those sales figures? Hello, eBay! That same year, I started buying Beanie Babies on eBay in bulk to sell in our antiques and gift store. It took me another 8 months before I started selling on eBay. But we will talk about this later.

Now it's Dennis's turn to talk. I, Dennis Prince, was bitten by the nostalgia bug and developed a fast eBay fever after finding a much-cherished board game (anyone remember Poppin' Hoppies?) from my youthful days available on the fledgling auction site back in December 1995. Driven to acquire more such long-lost treasures of my past, I realized that I could put many of my own possessions up for auction to try and offset the cost of the items I was winning day by day, week by week. Two weeks after finding eBay, I launched my first auction (a promotional set of California Raisin figures) and was $80 richer within seven short days. I've since bought and sold roughly $100,000 worth of collectible goods, and my business shows no signs of slowing.

Back to Lynn. Because we needed to move a lot of inventory from my grandmother's shop I became interested in selling on eBay and realized it could be used for more than just buying Beanie Babies. Within a few months of selling on eBay the store was consistently moving $20,000 worth of inventory a month. It was incredible! For the past five years, I've made a career out of eBay. In addition to buying and selling as a PowerSeller on eBay, I've taught classes on how to run an eBay business, created an auction tracking system for eBayers (*iBuy* and *iSell*), written an eBay newsletter, produced a couple of videos about making money through online auctions, and written an entertaining eBay book, *The 100 Best Things I've Sold on eBay.*

As I mentioned earlier, I am the granddaughter of Cheryl Leaf, an antiques dealer and larger-than-life personality who passed away in August 2000 at age 88. I grew up in the antiques business (see Figure I-2). I started accompanying my grandmother to antique shows at the age of seven and over the years came to depend not only on my grandmother's business insights, but on her wisdom, strength of character, and humor as well.

What Makes This Book Special?

This book will not spend any time on the basics of eBay. For that, we suggest you see Dennis Prince's book that started this series, *How to Sell Anything On*

Figure I-2   A *Bellingham Herald* newspaper article from 1976 that described Lynn's family's antiques business.

eBay . . . and Make a Fortune!, or watch the video series *Trash to Cash with Lynn Dralle. How to Sell Antiques and Collectibles on eBay . . . and Make a Fortune!* delivers much-coveted and immediately practical information about where to find items, how to identify them, and how to get top dollar for them on eBay. We promise that this book won't be boring, because it is written in a personal tone and from the heart.

WHAT'S INSIDE

This book is broken down into three logical and easy-to-follow parts, to help you go directly to the information you need in order to be successful. Each of the sections is described below.

Part 1: Welcome to the Wonderful World of Antiques and Collectibles

The first section will cover the antiques and collectibles industry in general and talk about the great opportunities available to make your fortune. You will learn about five top-level categories of antiques and collectibles in very broad terms: furniture, ethnographic items, glass and pottery, tabletop items, and decorative collectibles. We go into detail about how some of the original antiques dealers did business and how people in the "old days" found their collectibles. You will learn about what types of things were popular and how that has all changed. It seems that most collectors like things that are familiar to them or that they grew up with (we are reliving our childhoods!). The older guard likes Victorian brides' baskets, pickle castors, and cruets. Today's collectors are hot for 1950s Eames-era items. We will get better acquainted with what determines an antique and go over some important concepts like grading and provenance. Finally, we will touch on becoming an expert and discuss where to go for more information and how to network with other antiques and collectibles dealers.

Part 2: Selling Antiques and Collectibles with Success

In the second section we describe the basics of running an antiques business. A business plan is the most important component to getting started. We will touch on etiquette, including bargaining and other important strategies. We will also examine the differences between buying for resale and buying as a collector. Lynn's grandmother used to say, "When you buy for resale, you must leave your personal tastes outside the door." How right she was! We will look at how to determine values before you buy and learn about all the different places to buy antiques and collectibles, including antiques shops, shows, thrift stores, garage sales, and even through online auction! To start you on your way to making your eBay fortune, we will explain how to target specific customers and give tips for boosting sales. Finally, we will talk about your working space and, most importantly, how to handle, store, and ship these fragile items.

Part 3: Becoming an Expert Antiques and Collectibles Seller

This section is the most important section for helping you become a top-notch antiques and collectibles online seller. It is broken down into the five general categories we touched on in Part 1, but in this section we will get into the nitty-gritty: what you really need to know to make a fortune with furniture, ethnographic items, glass and pottery, tabletop items, and decorative collectibles. We will take a look at each of the five markets and discuss where they are headed. To make your fortune you will need to know how to buy these specific items and where to go to find the best sources. You will read about how to research your item and figure out exactly what it is. Most antiques and a high percentage of collectibles are unsigned. This is where research is key! You'll learn how price, presentation, and promotion are so important not only in the real world but also on eBay. You'll also learn what to do with your items if they don't sell on eBay. Unfortunately, this does happen. About 10 percent of things you think you will sell on eBay never do. We will wrap up with how to continue to grow and expand your business.

MAKING A LIVING AS AN ANTIQUES DEALER

As eBay has grown and changed, so has the way people are making their living on the Internet. As an expert in antiques, Lynn has seen thousands of people calling themselves antiques dealers with no formal training or knowledge of the etiquette of old-school dealers. Most of the original guard of antiques dealers are gone. These are the people, like Lynn's grandmother, who used to do 18 antiques shows a year all around the country. This was hard work—loading and unloading vans full of merchandise and being on the road most of the year or, alternately, having to have an open shop seven days a week (or sometimes a combination of both). eBay has made it possible for someone to be an antiques dealer from their home without having to put in the hard time that traditional antiques dealers did. eBay reports that there are over 400,000 people making their living on eBay.

Making a living as an antiques and collectibles dealer is a great vocation. You get to be part detective, part archaeologist, part seller and marketer, part entrepreneur, part treasure hunter, and the best of everything! We hope this book makes your antiques and collectibles experience a better one as you go on your way to make your fortune! Through her classes, Lynn has taught more than 5,000 people how to buy and sell on eBay. She asks her students to keep in touch and let her know how they are doing. Just today she received an e-mail from a former student. It makes life fun and interesting. Please e-mail us and share your stories, your suggestions, and your exciting successes. We'd love to hear from you at *allaboard@mail.com* (Lynn) or *dlprince @bigfoot.com* (Dennis). Let's get started!

PART 1

WELCOME TO THE WONDERFUL WORLD OF ANTIQUES AND COLLECTIBLES

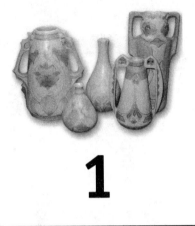

1

Why Specialize in
Antiques and Collectibles?

Did you know that certain collectible cereal boxes can sell for big bucks on eBay? A recent completed-auction search on eBay (which lists all items sold or listed for the past 2 weeks) found a Peter Max–designed Love cereal box from 1970 that sold for more than $450 (see Figure 1-1). It did not even come with the original cereal, and it was flattened for safe keeping. Amazing! Granted, Peter Max is a very famous artist who is well known for his colorful, psychedelic style, and he contributed to the Beatles *Yellow Submarine* album cover, but these prices are still amazing!

Antiques and collectibles cover almost every item imaginable. Anything that someone collects can be termed a collectible. The best part about this category is that antiques and collectibles can be found in anyone's home. You don't have to go out and invest a huge amount of money in inventory to get started. Just look around your house, your garage, your attic, and your storage unit and, while you are at it, spend some time at your parents' home doing the same thing. Voilà—you have taken that first step on the road to making your fortune! But let's not get ahead of ourselves. There is still a lot to learn to be successful with antiques and collectibles on eBay, and this book is going to show you how to get there.

IMPORTANT STATISTICS ABOUT THIS INDUSTRY

The antiques and collectibles industry can present a challenge when it comes to figuring out an annual sales volume. According to Sharon Korbeck, editor of the *Antique Trader*, there is not an accurate number for sales volume, and there are several reasons for this. For starters, it is a fragmented industry and

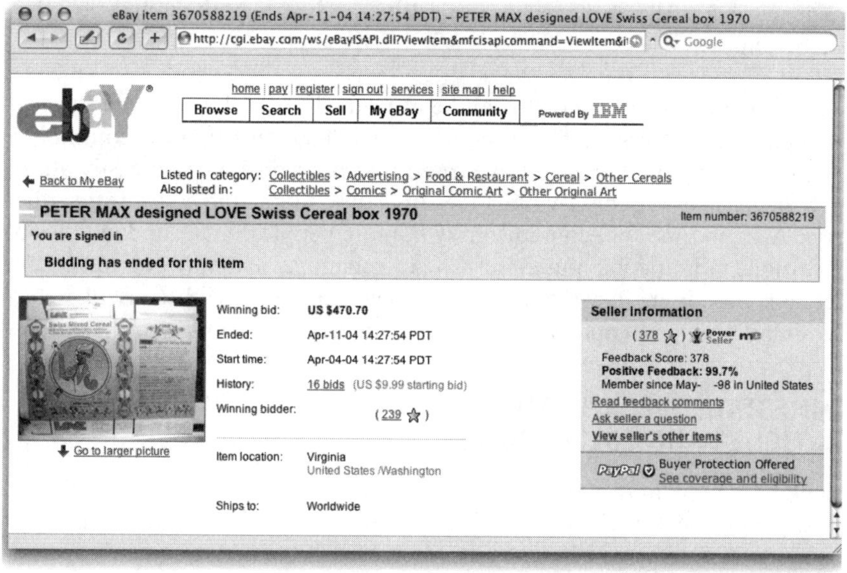

Figure 1-1　Peter Max cereal box sold on eBay on April 11, 2004, for $470.70.

hard to quantify. What this means is that the sales number would need to include sales figures not only from brick-and-mortar antiques stores but from antiques malls, antiques shows, flea markets, garage sales, auctions, thrift and pawn shops, and, finally, online markets, including eBay. Korbeck explains that antiques and collectibles is not a regulated industry like banking, so reporting of sales is not required. For example, she noted that the people who sell as a hobby or on eBay out of their homes would not be reporting under any industry code.

According to Kim Esser, a Research Analyst at the University of Southern California, the industry numbers for SIC code 5932, Used Merchandise Stores, in 2000 indicate that $17 billion was spent in secondhand stores. The National Association of Resale and Thrift Shops reported that resale was one of the fastest-growing segments of the retail industry, with an estimated growth of about 5 percent per year. A growing segment within the antiques and collectibles industry was flea markets, which had grown to a $7.5 billion-a-year business by 2000.

eBay TIP　eBay sold $8 billion in merchandise for the first quarter of 2004, up 51 percent over last year! Based on this figure eBay has predicted that the collectibles category will account for $1.6 billion of its business for the year 2004. Any way you look at it, these are

4   How to Sell Antiques and Collectibles on eBay . . . and Make a Fortune!

huge numbers. The antiques and collectibles industry, both on and off eBay, is growing.

A reason for this growth can be attributed to the 1990s, when the ecologically minded turned to recycling. In the 2000s this trend is continuing. Vintage has become trendy. More and more people who could easily afford new items now purchase vintage because they prefer the styles from other eras. Also, in times of economic growth, more people donate, and in times of recession, more people purchase used merchandise. Anyway you look at it, resale is one of the few recession-proof segments of retail because it is successful in both good and bad times. And that is good news for you!

IMMEDIATE OPPORTUNITIES IN ANTIQUES AND COLLECTIBLES

There are many immediate opportunities in the antiques and collectibles industry. Let's backtrack and spend some time examining the term *fragmented industry*. A fragmented industry has low overall barriers to entry, apparent absence of economies of scale, high inventory costs, diverse market needs, and a highly diverse product line. The diverse product line requires a great deal of user/seller interface on small volumes of product. What this means in layman's terms is that antiques and collectibles favors the small business over the larger one. It also means that it is relatively easy and inexpensive to break into the antiques and collectibles business. And with the advent of eBay, this has never been truer.

Good news for us! With eBay, there are no big start-up costs except for inventory, and another benefit to eBay is that you can turn over your inventory in 3, 5, 7, or 10 days, so even the inventory expenditure does not have to be huge. We will talk more about start-up costs in Chapter 5.

Another great thing about antiques and collectibles is that they have a limited supply. Remember the old saying "The best investment is land, because they are not making it anymore." This is also true for antiques and collectibles but with the difference being that with each succeeding year, the supply of objects diminishes: fewer antiques and collectibles come onto the market because they have found permanent homes in collections, but also because there is the inevitable deterioration and breakage. While the supply is continually decreasing, hopefully the demand continues to increase. Lynn's grandmother used to say that antiques and collectibles are the only inventory that actually gains value as it collects dust in your store! (See Figure 1-2.)

However, all of this good news doesn't necessarily translate into success with antiques and collectibles. Korbeck says that knowledge is key in this business. You have to continually educate yourself, and that is why you bought this book, isn't it?

Figure 1-2 Cheryl Leaf Antiques and Gifts store inventory gathering dust circa 2000. This stock is not like fresh produce in a grocery store or the latest trends in a clothing boutique, which have to be continually marked down and cleared out quickly. Antiques can actually increase in value as the years go by.

AN OVERVIEW OF THE SUBCATEGORIES

Antiques and collectibles is a huge field, encompassing every subcategory imaginable. Vintage clothing is considered collectible, books can be antiques and collectibles, old LPs (records) are desirable, and the list goes on. As we found out earlier, even cereal boxes are bringing in big bucks as collectors battle over them. For the scope of this book we had to narrow the playing field down into a manageable size.

To accomplish this, we did research on eBay, looking at the top categories with the most listings and taking into account that some of these categories would have higher-priced items. We also chose groups of items that would most likely be found in your home or you could easily find at estate and garage sales. From this research, we outlined broad categories and determined which are the most popular. This book will focus mostly on these categories.

Furniture

Of the five areas we selected, *Furniture* had the least number of listings (78,000 items), but this category does have higher ticket prices. This is always good! Also, everyone owns furniture and can easily find furniture to buy and sell. Over the years, china and glassware break and metalware gets melted ("worth its weight in gold") and repurposed (pewter was made into bullets), but furniture has remained and endured.

We will take a look at furniture by room and by eras. It is a huge category with a lot to learn, so we will start with the basics and teach you just enough to be dangerous. Just kidding. You will learn things such as where to look for marks. Even though the majority of furniture was never marked, it doesn't hurt to check, because your piece may be the rare one that was signed! Also, what do you call a certain piece, is it a highboy or a dresser (see Figure 1-3)? What is the primary wood and what is the secondary wood? How was it made—with dove tailing, nails, or staples? *Furniture* is a great category to list and sell, and I have made some of my best profits in the furniture arena.

Ethnographic/Cultural Items

Ethnographic items run the gamut from classical, as in Greek and Roman, to the huge Asian category. Of the 115,000 recent listings in this area, more than 40 percent of them were Chinese and Japanese antiquities. Things such as cloisonné, Imari, and snuff bottles are among the treasures.

This section also includes collectibles from all cultures, such as Russian hand-painted boxes, Hawaiian grass skirts, South Pacific serving bowls, and

Highboy   Dresser

Figure 1-3   Highboy with lowboy, courtesy of Cottone Auctions. Note how different it looks from the pictured traditional dresser.

African masks. It is a fun classification, and we will help you learn some of the rudimentary skills you will need to identify your items or at least get started on the right track. Since no one can become an expert in all of these fields, we will also point you in the right direction for learning more and where to go to get an expert's opinion.

Pottery and Glass

Based on a recent search on eBay, this section had 355,000 listings on one day! Wow! These types of antiques were once termed smalls by the old-time antiques dealers. Smalls are obviously tinier items that are easy to display in a cabinet and easy to package and ship. Smalls would not include furniture, linens, and larger items in general.

We have broken this huge classification into two chapters. Chapter 13 focuses on pottery and Chapter 14 on glass. We will examine items ranging from rustic Watts Pottery to fine Rookwood and from American brilliant cut glass to Tiffany glass. A lot of pottery and porcelain was signed with the maker's mark on the base or underside. This makes it a lot easier for us to do our research. However, most glass was never signed, and we will show you how to start your investigation by identifying shape, color, type of manufacture, and use. Once you have these basics, we will look at where to go for more information.

eBay TIP In this area, condition is very important, and we will talk about chips, cracks, crazing, and flaws done in the making. These are just some of the things you will need to know to become a successful seller on eBay.

Tabletop Items

Tabletop is one of Lynn's favorite categories. (Okay, to be honest, all antiques and collectibles are Lynn's favorites!) China sets, flatware, and stemware are easy to find at garage and estate sales, and you can make some of your highest returns on investment this way. For example, Lynn recently bought a box of dinnerware for $8 and sold the pieces individually on eBay for more than $450 (see Figure 1-4).

The *Tabletop* category includes china, dinnerware, glassware, stemware, and flatware. A recent check of this category on eBay revealed 309,000 items listed (almost as many as pottery and glass). For beginners, this is a great category if you want to test the eBay waters. You will find a lot of these items right in your own kitchen or dining room!

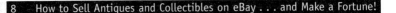

8   How to Sell Antiques and Collectibles on eBay . . . and Make a Fortune!

Figure 1-4 This photo shows a few of the Cornishware China pieces that Lynn bought a box of for $8 and sold in 15 auctions for $482.95. That's what you call a huge return on investment!

Decorative Collectibles

Decorative Collectibles is the biggest category we will be covering. This one is the granddaddy of them all—a recent look on eBay showed more than 452,000 listings in this category alone. Decorative collectibles are another big faction of the "smalls" world. These are things that you will find in your parents' or grandparents' hutch. Things like a collection of Lladro, Bing & Grondahl, or even Hummel figurines. Maybe your brother had an elephant collection. Now is the time to sell it! *Animals* is a subcategory in *Collectibles* on eBay, comprising approximately 25 percent of decorative collectibles. There is a huge following for all types of animal-related collectibles particularly dog items, such as bulldogs and spaniels. This is also the place where a lot of name brands come into play—Enesco, Precious Moments, Boyds Bears, Dept. 56, and the list goes on and on. Luckily, almost all of these items are signed with the maker's mark. It makes our job of describing the pieces so much easier. Since these items are usually commodities and not as unique and rare as others, we will focus more on strategy in this section to help you get top dollar.

In Chapter 2, which covers the history of selling antiques and collectibles, we get going on our road to fortune.

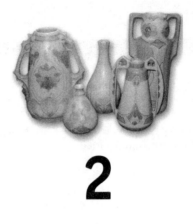

2

The History of Selling Antiques and Collectibles

Antiques and collectibles have been bought and sold since the beginning of time. Early antiques such as jugs, tables, and other utilitarian items were originally traded or bartered for food and other necessities of life. In the seventeenth century, Japan got into the game with beautiful porcelains like Imari, and the decorative antiques and collectibles market was on its way.

HISTORY OF ANTIQUES DEALERS: THE ORIGINAL MARKET

In the more recent past, say 50 years ago, this industry was dominated by small mom-and-pop shops. The old-time antiques dealers worked hard at their craft, spending hours hunting for bargains, cleaning, repairing, pricing, dusting, and displaying their wares in their stores. Research was next to impossible. There weren't a lot of reference books, and the dealers would have to check what other dealers were selling, read trade magazines, and sometimes PFA to price their goods. PFA was what Lynn's grandmother called one of her pricing techniques: pulled from air.

These dealers usually had to keep set store hours, and that meant spending many hours tied to your business location, which didn't leave much time for finding stock.

Many antiques dealers sold at shows each year to broaden their market base beyond their small towns. It was typical for a dealer to do 12–18 antiques shows a year. It was a ton of work. Lynn knows about this first-hand: her grandmother started dragging her along to antiques shows when she was only seven! The preparation for these shows was intense. They would spend two weeks prior to each show picking out which items to take, making sure they were clean, in good repair, priced, and that there was a nice mixture of goods. Then they would pack each item very carefully in divided boxes filled with tissue. They had "snowboys, fatsies, finish feeders, plates, and tinies" boxes. These were their funny terms for the different-sized and -shaped divided boxes. Packing was a science, and it would take 2–3 hours to pack the van with the shelves, risers, display cabinets, extra tables, tablecloths, utility box, lights, electric cords, and, at last, all the fragile antiques.

The shows typically ran three days, plus an extra day for setup, which was a full day's job. The tables were provided, but the dealers had to set up everything else, including the electrical cording, spotlights, shelving, and drapes (see Figure 2-1).

What does this mean for you? With eBay, you can make the same profit without all the extra work. You should by now have a feel for how much work this industry used to be, and for such small financial returns. Now let's take a look at how this industry has continued to evolve since the 1950s.

HOW HAS THIS INDUSTRY CHANGED AND EXPLODED IN THE PAST 50 YEARS?

Generally speaking, the 1950s and 1960s were dominated by small shops and antiques shows. In the 1970s, mail-order and the collectibles businesses really took off. The *Antique Trader* was a huge source of buying and selling opportunities. It was truly a shopper's periodical. Starting in about 1970, collector's plates became the rage, as popular then as Beanie Babies were in more recent times. Bing & Grondahl and Royal Copenhagen had owned this market since the 1890s, but suddenly everyone wanted a piece of that pie. Frankoma in 1968, Imperial Glass in 1970, Goebel Hummel entered in 1971, Metlox in 1973, and the list goes on. The Bradford Exchange took it to a higher level in the late 1970s. The plate business thrived throughout the 1970s and made a lot of money for the dealers who dealt in these items by mail, in person, and at shows. Lynn's antiques shop used to advertise collectible plates every other week in the *Antique Trader* and would sometimes sell $2,000 worth of them from one ad. It sure beat all the work that an antiques show required!

Some of the more traditional antiques dealers would not be caught dead with a newer collectible in their stores, and they missed out on a huge opportunity. However, some of these dealers did advertise their antiques in the popular magazines (*Antique Trader*, *Hobbies*, etc.) and did supplement their sales figures.

The plate business in the 1970s was the basis for many of today's popular decorative collectibles such as those from Enesco, Franklin Mint, and Boyds Bears. You will learn more about this category in Chapter 16.

Figure 2-1   Cheryl Leaf in an antiques-show booth circa 1975.

The 1980s brought us the antiques mall, which became a great opportunity for a part-time hobbyist to make a little extra cash. The part-time antiques dealer did not have to keep an open shop and could pay a small percentage to the owner of the mall. Antiques malls typically charged a flat rate for booth rental—$50 to $500 a month depending on size—and then a small percentage of sales, 10 percent or so. Because the dealer didn't have to invest a huge amount of money, the number of new dealers entering the business increased. The antiques mall was a great concept for the buyer also. Instead of having to drive to 20 different shops looking for one item, the antiques collector could find many items under one roof. The downside was that the dealer wasn't there to explain the history or to share his or her knowledge. Antiques malls are still around today and seem to be surviving.

The 1990s definitely was the decade of the Internet. Antiques stores moved online, and suddenly it wasn't so hard to comparison-shop or purchase hard-to-find items. At first, it was a great boom to the antiques business. Again, an antiques dealer could be a part-timer without a huge capital outlay. They could sell in an antiques mall, have a Web page, and never have to meet their customer face-to-face in their own shop or at a show. It really took the antiques business from the personal to the impersonal.

Lynn launched her Web page *www.antiquesandgifts.com* in 1995, and it was a huge success. She sold Royal Copenhagen and Bing & Grondahl collector's plates and other items. But the Internet was becoming glutted toward the end of the 1990s. It seemed that everyone had a Web page and it was becoming confusing for both buyers and sellers. As a buyer, it was difficult to shop because you had to go to too many sites and spend too much time surfing to find what you were looking for. It was a problem for the antiques dealers because no one was finding their sites. eBay seemed to answer this problem by offering both buyers and sellers a great alternative. Collectors could quickly find everything they were looking for in one location, and the seller could place their items up for sale and be guaranteed customers.

eBAY'S EFFECT ON THE WAY PEOPLE BOUGHT AND SOLD ANTIQUES AND COLLECTIBLES

eBay has definitely affected this business category and in a big way. It is even easier now, more than ever, to become an antiques and collectibles dealer by selling on eBay. According to Sharon Korbeck, editor of the *Antique Trader*, antiques collectors will still want to touch and feel the higher-end items. The person who will pay $5,000 for a Stickley bookcase will want to see it in person. They are most likely not going to pay such a high price for it on eBay. Figure 2-2 shows an eBay auction for a Stickley bookcase with an original estimate of $3,000 to $8,000 that only sold for $1,000.

eBay TIP On more expensive items, use a hidden reserve to protect your investment. If this seller had used a hidden reserve of $3,000, he or she would not have had to let it go for only $1,000, and could have relisted it again in the Fall, when prices tend to be higher, and would have had a better chance to sell it for the reserve price.

However, we believe the smaller items, smalls, have moved to the Internet. The brick-and-mortar antiques store will always be around, but the Internet is here—eBay in particular—and it must be dealt with.

Much like *Personal FX* and the *Antiques Roadshow* have brought antiques and collectibles into the mainstream, eBay has also helped to deliver more collectors. A person will see something on eBay, buy it on eBay, and become hooked—in other words, they become collectors.

What has eBay done to prices in this category? Some antiques and collectibles are selling for a lot more on eBay than we could ever expect to get in an open shop or at a show. On the other hand some are selling for a lot less. In 1999, Lynn sold a chintz side teapot for $1,000 on eBay; in her brick-and-mortar shop she would have been lucky to get $500. The eBay market has

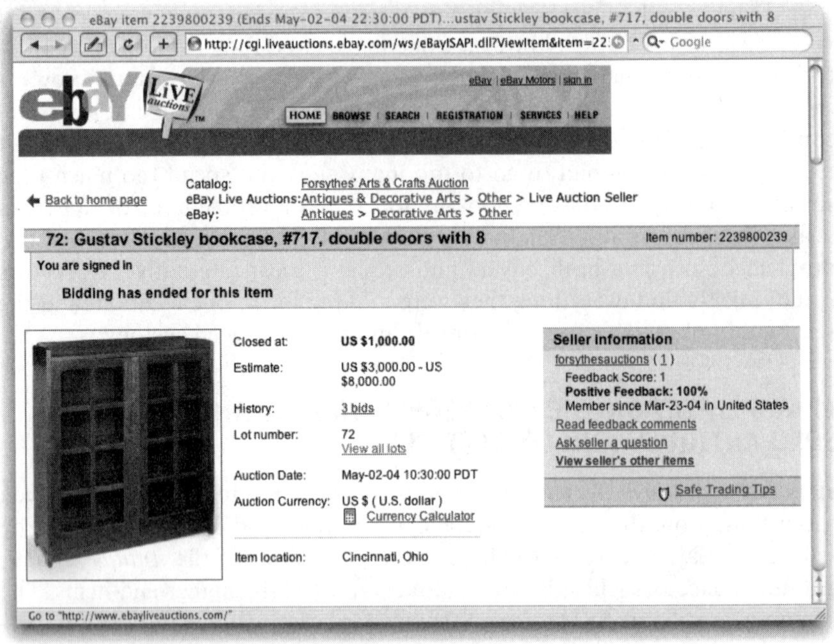

Figure 2-2 A Stickley bookcase sold at an online auction for $1000 on May 2, 2004.

become a leveling force and for the most part has been positive by opening up antiques and collectibles to the world. There is now a worldwide market for you to buy from and sell to.

TODAY'S TRENDS: PEOPLE ARE BUYING THEIR CHILDHOODS

There are two major trends in the antiques and collectibles marketplace— home decor and reliving our youth! Following the gross overconsumption of the 1980s there has been a return to home and hearth since the 1990s. People are looking to the past to decorate their homes, and antiques are a very popular choice. Also, collectors are looking to their past for what is valuable. What they want is often what they remember from and treasured in their childhood. Pong, yellow smiley faces, and vintage lunch boxes are all in demand. This is what is known as the millennium effect. Everything seems older now that we are in the year 2000. Because technology progresses so rapidly, things invented or popular in the 1960s to 1980s now seem ancient. Vintage technology such as the hefty Texas Instruments calculators from the 1970s are bringing close to $400 as long as they work. Just who is the antiques and

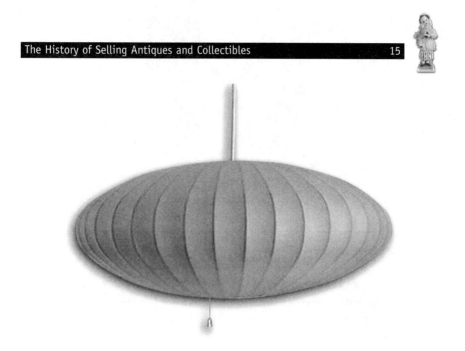

Figure 2-3 People love items from their childhood. This Eames-era bubble lamp sold on eBay for $231.

collectibles customer? Typically, the collector has been characterized as being between 35 and 55 years old and someone who wants good quality. They are also known for being affluent and well educated. This puts the consumer's childhood back about 30 to 50 years. This corresponds exactly to what we are seeing as being very popular on eBay right now. Items from the 1950s to 1980s are in great demand.

As an example, the Eames style is super-hot right now and encompasses space-age and sleek modular items. Please see Chapter 9 for more information on these pieces. Many of us grew up with these furnishings, and now they are selling for huge dollars! Just listing an item with "Eames era" in the title can get your item ten times more views than if you did not mention the Eames name. Lynn recently sold an Eames-era bubble lamp for $231 that she had picked up at an estate sale and only paid $20 for (see Figure 2-3).

The antiques industry has changed from consisting mostly of brick-and-mortar shops to hundreds of thousands of dealers selling on eBay. The range of what is considered antique and collectible has also changed from being very strict to now including items that are only twenty years old! What all this means is that you can do great on eBay with a huge range of products. You don't have to just sell your typical "antique." We will discuss this in more detail in the next chapter.

3

Becoming Better Acquainted with Antiques and Collectibles

An antique is defined as "an object of ancient times" or "a work of art, piece of furniture, or decorative object made at an earlier period and according to various customs laws at least 100 years ago." Most antiques dealers generally consider items 100 years old to be true antiques. That means that items made in 1904 and earlier would now be considered antique. However, recently some customs laws have changed this definition and only require 50 years for an item to be considered antique. That means anything made 50 years ago could be called an antique in your selling description. This takes us right back to the middle of the Eames era.

For the purpose of this book we will still consider an antique to be more than 100 years old—but we do have a little leeway when using the word *antique* in our titles and descriptions. In general, Lynn uses *antique* for anything made in 1940 and earlier—that is, about 65 years old. If it's not an antique, it's . . . vintage. Vintage is considered by the dictionary to be "a period of origin or manufacture and characterized by excellence and enduring appeal—classic." To antiques dealers, *vintage* is a term used for something that is not antique but still has some age to it. You can use the word *vintage* in your auction titles and descriptions when an item was made between 1940 and 1980.

Okay, 1980 doesn't sound very vintage, but it is about 25 years ago! Also, remember the millennium effect that we touched on in the last chapter. Now that we are in the year 2000, everything made in the 1900s, even as recently as 1980, seems ancient. A big cause for this is the field of computer technology, where objects become obsolete in a matter of months and are

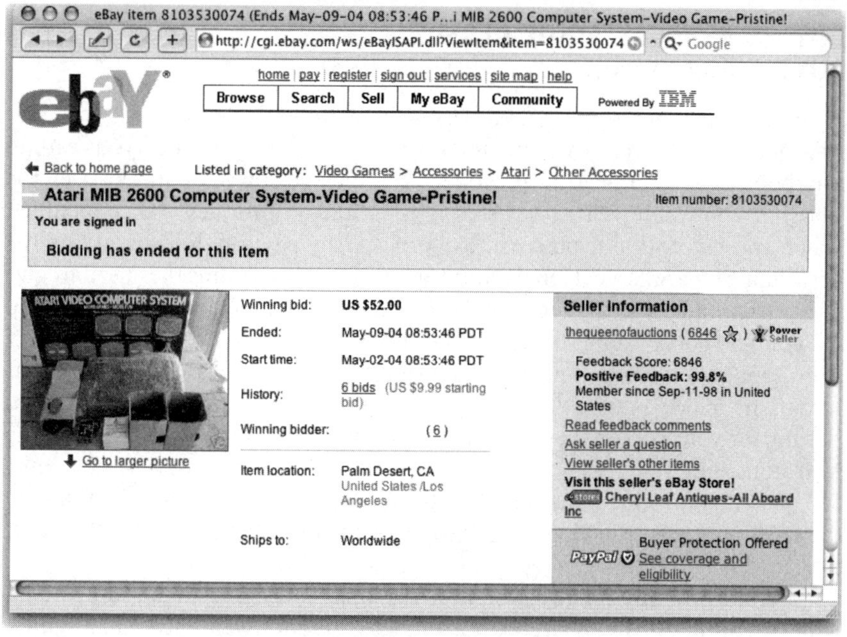

Figure 3-1 Vintage is hot! This Atari video console sold on eBay for $52.

quickly replaced, boosting the rarity of earlier models, and a relic can be something manufactured as recently as a generation ago (only 20 years). We like to call these items vintage and not antique. *Vintage* wraps it up very nicely without misleading our customers on eBay. Lynn was recently lucky enough to find an Atari MIB (mint in box) video console game from 1980 at a rummage sale. She paid $5 for it and was thrilled when it sold for $52 (see Figure 3-1). Vintage at it's finest!

Now all of this doesn't mean that we can only sell items from the beginning of time to the 1980s on eBay. Not at all. What about modern merchandise, say from this year? These items are collectibles, decorative collectibles to be exact. A collectible is described as "that which is accumulated or worthy of being collected." This spans almost every item imaginable, because the human race is so diverse and we each decide what we think is worthy of being collected. Collections can be as unusual as matchbooks or hot salsa bottles or grains of sand! In this book, we will be focusing on the more traditional brand-name collectibles. These conventional decorative collectibles, such as collector's plates, Cabbage Patch Dolls, Longaberger Baskets, and Hummel figurines mainly date from the 1970s to now. This is a growing and expanding category, and in Chapter 16 we will get into more detail about this huge dollar opportunity.

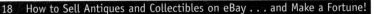

18   How to Sell Antiques and Collectibles on eBay . . . and Make a Fortune!

BUYING AS A COLLECTOR VERSUS BUYING FOR RESALE

When you are building your inventory, keep in mind that buying for your collection is very different from buying for resale. We know most of you reading this book have a collection or collections that you have acquired over the years, or you wouldn't be interested in the topic of antiques and collectibles. When you buy for your personal use you usually pay top dollar and buy the best examples available. Here is some advice Lynn's grandmother used to give to her customers and students when she taught classes about antiques. If you are going to collect something, first, continually educate yourself, second, buy from reputable dealers, and third, always buy the best example you can afford. This makes your collection not only fun, but a very good investment. Buying for your personal collection on eBay is a blast. Lynn started collecting Marmorzellan vases when she was 13 years old. Her first vase cost only $13.50. Marmorzellan was made by the Galluba and Hoffman Company in the 1890s and it is considered to be some of the most beautiful porcelain ever made (see Figure 3-2).

When you buy on eBay for your personal collection, make sure you do your research. Always search the completed auctions and see what similar items have actually sold for before you bid. To do this, click on "Search," then "Advanced Search" and then type in your title—for example, "Marmorzellan." Make sure that you click the box that says "Completed Items only." The

Figure 3-2 eBay now makes it much easier to find rare collectibles such as this Marmorzellan collection.

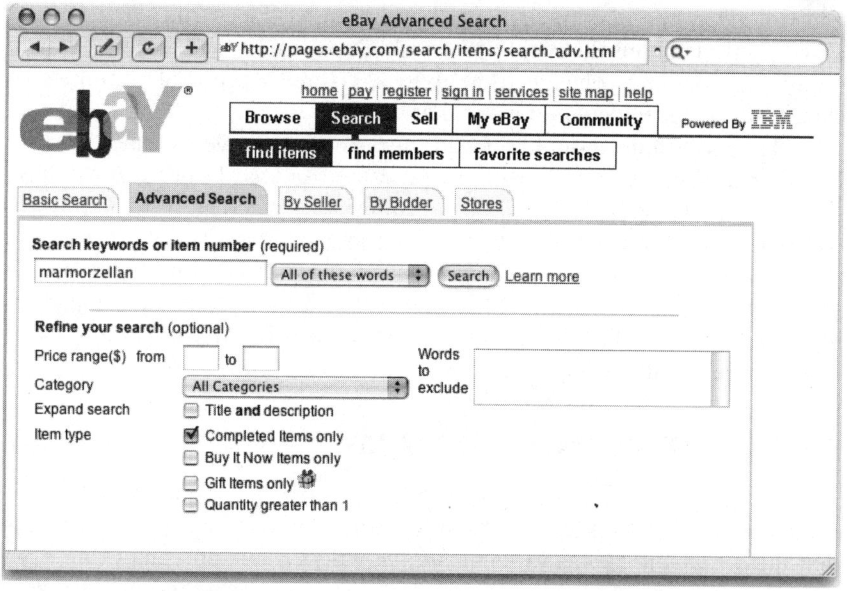

Figure 3-3 Advanced Search page showing the "Completed Items only" box checked for Marmorzellan.

last two weeks of items listed, relisted, sold, and not sold on eBay is public record. This information is extremely valuable.

When the list of completed auctions comes up, it is a good idea to sort by highest price. In this case there were only three items listed in the last 2 weeks. Take note of anything that is similar to what you are collecting. One of the vases was almost identical to the ones that Lynn looks for, and it sold for $76.89. Keep a notebook of dates and prices that pieces sell for. This information is invaluable. You will be able to start tracking what time of year will be the best for you to buy, and what you can expect to pay. The $76.89 also gives a good starting point. Do not bid much higher unless it is a really rare example. Try not to get caught up in the auction frenzy and get carried away, because a similar item, even if not the exact same one, will come up again. Also, you should check out the seller before bidding. Make sure that they accept the payment method you want to use, that they have good positive feedback, and that they are not charging too much for shipping.

When you are buying for a collection you are usually very focused and have the freedom to shop around and wait for a bargain. Buying for resale is different. You will need to buy fresh inventory continually. New stock is exciting, and it sells! As a buyer for your eBay online business you will definitely still want to shop for bargains. As Lynn's grandmother used to say, "You make your money in the buying." She was right. If you buy low and sell high

20   How to Sell Antiques and Collectibles on eBay . . . and Make a Fortune!

you will always be making a profit. Keep in mind the $5 rule. If you don't know anything about the item, you shouldn't pay more than $5 for it. If you know a fair amount, you can spend up to $20, and if it is one of your areas of expertise, go higher, depending on what you know about the item.

The great thing about buying antiques and collectibles is that it is a very broad area. When you go out to garage, estate, and yard sales you will have the opportunity to buy such neat and unusual items! The most important things to look for when shopping for antiques and collectibles are brand names, signatures, original high quality, good condition, and a reasonable price. Remember, too, that just because something isn't your personal style, someone else might be willing to pay big bucks for it. We will get into all of this in more detail in Chapter 6.

HOW TO IDENTIFY FAKES AND FRAUDS

There is a big difference between reproductions and frauds or fakes. When a company has gone to great lengths to reproduce an item, this generally means that the original item was valuable and very desirable. Sometimes they even sign it as a reproduction, which is nice, but this is not always the case. Broadly speaking, these companies weren't out to mislead—they just saw an opportunity and demand and went to fill it. An example of a reproduction would be the milk-glass covered hens made by many companies including Westmoreland and later reproduced and distributed by AA Importing. A lot of glass coming out of China is a reproduction and is usually not of the same quality as the original. The mold marks are heavy and the glass often has a greasy feel to it. The great thing about a reproduction is that even if you overpay, thinking it is an antique, there will still be a market for it. Collectors of covered hens may not care if it is a newer example. Just make sure that when you do list it on eBay, you make it very clear that it is not an original old piece. In this example, watch out for reproductions, because milk glass is one of the most-reproduced glass types and one of the hardest for which to determine old from new.

The best way to identify a reproduction is to do your research:

- Start with eBay. As you do your completed-auction research and read the descriptions you'll find that there are usually telltale signs of a reproduction. For example, the newer nesting hens do not have the WG signature embossed on the base (see Figure 3-4).
- Google what you're researching. Google is a great search engine on the Internet. Most browsers will have a tiny box at the top that says "Google." Once you get the page, just type in what you are looking for, and within seconds thousands of Web site links will appear, leading you to vast quantities of information you need for your antiques

Figure 3-4 Milk-glass hen signed "WG" for Westmoreland Glass, on the base.

and collectibles business. E-mail someone in a collector's club and see if they can help you. Names of some of these organizations can be found in a Google search.

- Read all of the reference books you can get your hands on.
- Consult a specialist. We will discuss reproductions in more detail in each of the five categories in Chapters 11 through 16.

Frauds or fakes are made or sold by someone who intentionally sets out to deceive. Frauds are much harder to identify because their makers usually go to great lengths to mislead consumers. As an example, a piece of furniture may be reproduced as a fake. The maker may use period hardware, distress the wood to look aged, and even sign it with a false name. If you have an expensive piece that really looks antique and authentic but you still can't be sure, we highly recommend that you pay for a professional opinion.

GRADING, PROVENANCE, AUTHENTICATION, AND APPRAISALS

Paying for a professional opinion from a specialist is a smart idea because you can't be an expert at everything and you may have a really valuable item. You will only want to pay for an appraisal, however, if the item is going to be worth enough to cover it. There are some online appraisal companies that don't charge a whole lot. You may want to start with one of these, and if your item appears to be very valuable, get the written appraisal from a dealer in person. These written appraisals can be referred to in your description to help

Figure 3-5 When NGC grades coins, such as this gold coin, they return the items encased in a plastic cover. Besides being tamper-proof, the covers will protect your investment from damages.

get big bucks for your item on eBay. They will give your hesitant buyers the added security to go for higher bids. There are dealers who devote their studies to one category, and their opinions can be invaluable.

Grading

Grading is used for commodity items like baseball cards, Beanie Babies, stamps, and coins. It is not used for many of the items we are discussing in this book, but it is good to know about. If you do have an item that can be graded and it is a valuable example, paying for the grading is a good idea because your item will usually sell for more when you list it on eBay. First, find out who is the grading leader for your field. To do this, search on eBay by your item and find out which company most sellers are using to grade their items. For example, Lynn had a lot of valuable gold coins to sell and was not an expert on condition, so she shipped off about 50 coins to Numismatic Guaranty Corporation (NGC)—one of the leading coin graders (see *www.NGC.com* for rates and information)—and paid about $12 for each coin in grading fees. The coins came back in about a week, encased in plastic covers for safekeeping, with the grading written right on the front, which made it easier to sell because shoppers on eBay could see proof of their authenticity (see Figure 3-5). The 50 gold coins sold for over $12,000, which more than covered the $600 Lynn paid in fees. They never would have sold for so much without the NGC grade. Grading is a great way to protect yourself as a seller and let your buyers know that you have a quality item.

Provenance

Provenance is the history of ownership of a particular item. For example, was it owned by Abraham Lincoln? Did it belong to your grandfather and do you remember him using it? All of this is interesting to both the buyer and seller. This is where the detective-work aspect of selling antiques comes into play. Sometimes, you may actually receive authentication with the item you have bought for resale. Whenever we buy something we always ask the seller where it came from. Adding such tidbits of history into a listing on eBay can make the item more valuable to prospective buyers.

Authentication/Appraisal

Authentication, or an appraisal by an expert, is often a smart way to go because it puts a stamp of approval on your item. The written appraisal or authentication will then accompany the item when it is sold, but make sure you spell this out in your description: "This appraisal will be shipped with the item. It will be important to keep for insurance and investment purposes." This helps put bidders in an investment mind-set, and they may bid higher.

There are many registered appraisers around the country. Just to point you in the right direction for getting more information, here are a few Web sites of appraisal organizations to help you find an appraiser in your area:

- *www.appraisers.org* (American Society of Appraisers)
- *www.isa-appraisers.org* (International Society of Appraisers)

Also, keep in mind that many companies are now offering valuations online. eBay recommends several online authentication and grading services on its site. If you go to eBay's home page, click on "Services," then click on "Options," you'll see a button for "Authentication & Grading." This page contains much valuable information on this topic. How handy! Generally speaking, people at valuation companies have trained, practiced, and been tested in their areas of expertise. And their appraisal can be used on eBay to help garner more bids and send you down the road to your eBay fortune.

CARE AND STORAGE

Antiques and collectibles are usually fragile and need special care. Make sure that you treat them with respect and handle them well. For example, antique glassware does not react well to sharp changes in temperature, so if you take a piece from a warm place and place it in a very cool area, or vice versa, it can crack. Lynn used to store glass lampshades in a concrete room in the basement at her store. It was called the tank, and it was freezing. If a shade was brought into the store too quickly—taking it from 30°F to 70°F in a matter of minutes—it would sometimes crack. Be very careful and keep your antiques at a constant temperature.

It is often best not to polish, clean, or repair your antiques until you have done your research. Some types of antiques are worth more in their original state. Patina is a very important concept and refers to the sheen on a surface caused by years of handling. Pieces of antique furniture can bring more

Figure 3-6 Art nouveau lamp minus its patina.

money with the patina—which is sometimes just the buildup caused by dirt, polish, and wax—left as is. For example, Lynn had a beautiful signed bronze lamp that her dad started to clean and polish. He ended up taking off the original patina and rendered it almost worthless (see Figure 3-6).

If you are selling on eBay from your home, as we are, strongly consider having a designated corner or entire room to house your inventory. Make sure that it is out of the way of traffic and that you don't let your seven-year-old son practice his pitching in your office. Also, consider storing and working with fragile valuables in a carpeted area instead of on cement or hard wood, in case you do drop that precious piece. Believe us, this does happen! We will talk about your work-space in more detail in Chapter 10.

4

How to Become an Expert in Selling Antiques and Collectibles on eBay

To be successful selling antiques and collectibles on eBay you will need to be engaged in active and continual learning. The good news is that there are many ways to educate yourself, and a lot of them do not cost any money. Amazing! Let's get started.

REFERENCE BOOKS, CLASSES, AND WEB-BASED RESEARCH

It is a good idea to begin building your reference library before you actually start selling on eBay. Reference books are actually a smart business investment. The $20 you spend for a book can more than make up for losing money by mistakenly selling an item at a bargain price just because you aren't knowledgeable.

First, invest in a few general price guides. A few favorites for antiques and collectibles are *Warman's*, *Kovels'*, and *Schroeder's*. These general reference books will usually have a paragraph or two about a type of antique and then list current prices. Keep in mind that these prices can be outdated by the time the book reaches you and that prices do vary in different parts of the country. However, they are still a great learning tool and give you a good handle on price ranges.

 eBay TIP These reference tools can be picked up at any major bookstore or on any online bookstore's Web site. Take some time flipping through them to figure out what items interest you, to see what items sell for more than you would have imagined, and just to get a feel for many of the antiques available in the market.

Once you have familiarized yourself with these general books, buy books that focus on your specific areas of interest. Do you love glass? Are you a furniture buff? Does Eames-era design appeal to you? Whatever you have a passion for is what you should specialize in. Unfortunately, we have a passion for any and all antiques and collectibles, so our personal libraries of reference books are quite large. This is never a bad thing! You don't have to spend a lot of money doing book research. Most local libraries carry a comprehensive set of books on antiques. You can check out these books or put aside a day each month to stop by the library and catch up on current antique trends.

You can also learn a tremendous amount by subscribing to monthly or weekly antiques publications, and their appearance in your post office box is a great reminder that it is time to continue your education. Three of the largest publications are the *Antique Trader*, *Kovels' Newsletter*, and *Art & Antiques*.

Another great way to learn about antiques is to sign up for a class. Many local colleges, community colleges, or antiques dealers offer classes on antiques. There are even Web-based classes that you can take from the comfort of your home.

Finally, spend some time searching the Web. The Internet is such a wealth of information, and it is literally all right there at our fingertips. For example, if you are interested in cookie jars, go to a search engine (such as *www.google.com*), and type in "antique cookie jars." You'll be amazed by what comes up. You'll likely find several fantastic articles that contain information you can use as you sell your cookie jars on eBay. For example, did you know that the English biscuit barrel or cracker jar was the precursor to the cookie jar? These older items will likely sell well on eBay, and you can color your listing with the history of the item. Cookie jars are also typically American, and they really took off in the 1930s. Did you know that Andy Warhol collected cookie jars, and when he died one sold at auction for $3000 (and its book value was only $250)? You can see that provenance (an item's history—see Chapter 3) made this specific cookie jar worth much more just because of who owned it! When all was said and done, Warhol's 136 cookie jars sold at auction in 2002 for over $198,000!

It took two minutes on the Internet to learn all this information on cookie jars. What a great world we live in!

LEARN FROM eBAY

Another great place to learn for free is on eBay. eBay maintains a 2-week back history of listings for public record, and this can provide a tremendous

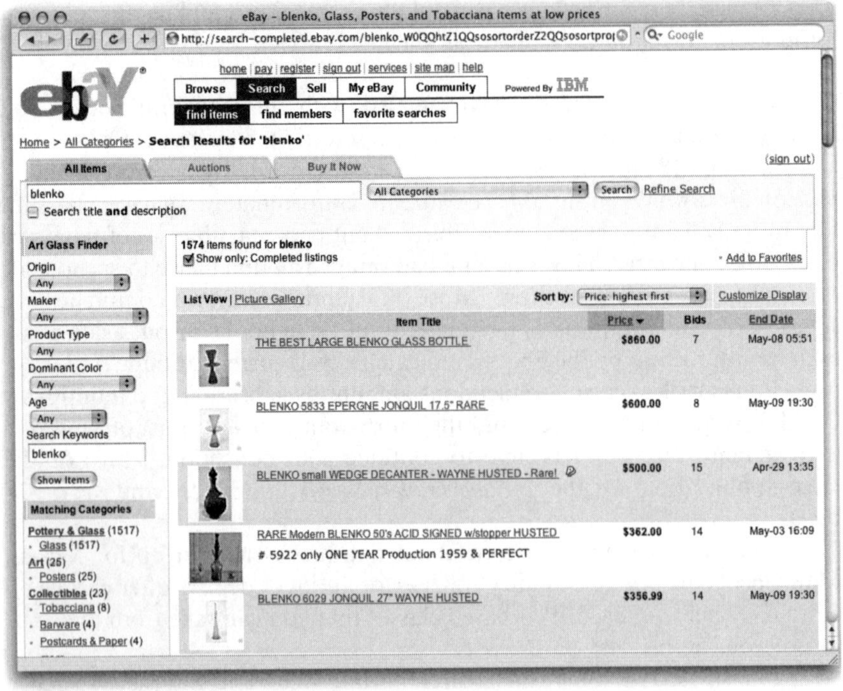

Figure 4-1   Blenko completed-auction listings, April 2004. Note what shapes and colors are selling for the most money. The large Blenko bottle sold for almost $900!

amount of information. If you are interested in Blenko art glass, for example, do a completed-auction search to bring up the last 2 weeks' worth of listings and sales (see Figure 4-1). A recent search for this specific item yielded the information that in a 2-week period 1574 Blenko items were listed. Sort by highest price first to learn the highest price people are willing to pay for a specific item. To do this, click the box on the right that says "Sort By" and select "Price: Highest First."

Reading the auction descriptions will tell you a great deal about an item, including what people are looking for and what colors or styles bring the highest price. Keep in mind that not all the information may be accurate, but, regardless, you should use eBay to gage prices and see what is hot!

To supplement your learning, hop over to a site specifically focused on your item. To continue our example we went to the Blenko Web site (*www.blenkoglass.com*) and found some very useful background information, including that Blenko is art glass made in the United States and that the company started in 1893 in Kokomo, Indiana. Their pieces are all blown glass and always have a rough pontil (not polished; we will discuss pontils in Chapter

14). The majority of pieces were never signed, and you will be lucky to find a piece with the original label. All that from the Internet! Fascinating and free learning!

EXPERIENCE IS THE BEST TEACHER

Another great way to learn more about the antiques and collectibles business is to get a part-time job helping out at one of your local antiques shops or antiques malls. This hands-on learning is invaluable, and if the shopkeeper can't afford to hire you, you may want to volunteer your services.

Spend time browsing at antiques shows, around flea markets, and in all the shops you can find. It is also fascinating to see what is selling in your local antiques market as compared to other markets you visit when you travel. (And since you are working while you are traveling, all of a sudden your vacation may become a tax write-off!) You may find things both in local and out-of-town shops that aren't selling in that market but that you know there is a large demand for on eBay. At antiques shows and flea markets, take note of which booths have the most customers in them. Determine whether it is the booth's pricing strategies or if they are selling items that are in demand. Lynn was recently at the Pasadena Rose Bowl Flea Market and noticed that the booths with kitschy 1950s Eames-era items were the ones moving the goods!

eBay TIP Hands down, experience in antiques and collectibles is the best teacher. There is no lesson as well learned as the one where you make a mistake and lose money. It happens to all of us. No matter how much you know, you will still buy something that just isn't ever going to sell on eBay. Don't sweat it! Just look at it as a learning experience and don't make that same decision again.

NETWORKING

Antiques dealers are a nice bunch. For the most part, they love to talk and share stories. You'll likely find that it is not a competitive business. No one has exactly the same item in exactly the same condition to sell at exactly the same time. Instead, antiques dealers are a loyal bunch and are more than happy to refer clients to other dealers. The act of referring clients yields credibility to the consumer and also paves the way for referrals from other dealers. While this has changed some since the advent of eBay, you will still find it to be true to a great extent. So get to know your local dealers. Spend some time in their stores browsing, buying, and chatting. It is a great place to learn.

Another way to network is to join an antiques association or collector's

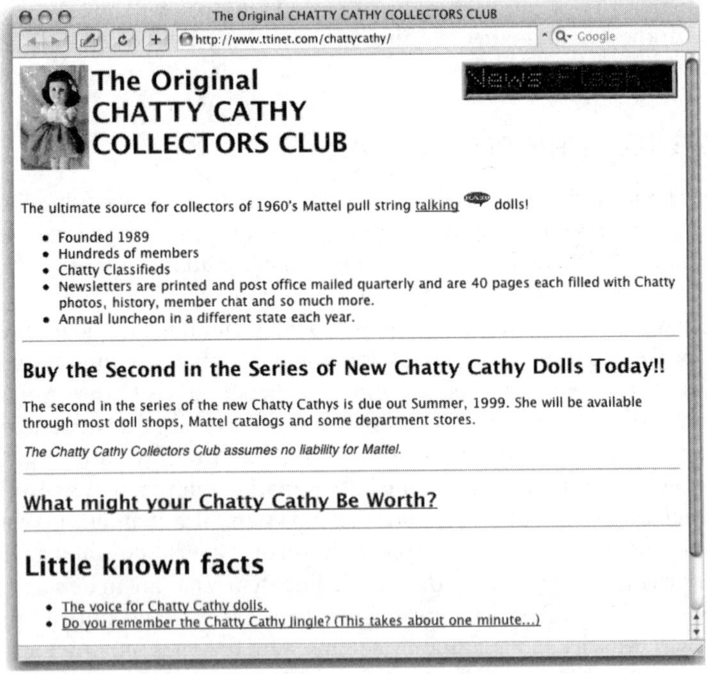

The Original CHATTY CATHY COLLECTORS CLUB

http://www.ttinet.com/chattycathy/

The Original CHATTY CATHY COLLECTORS CLUB

News Flash

The ultimate source for collectors of 1960's Mattel pull string talking dolls!

- Founded 1989
- Hundreds of members
- Chatty Classifieds
- Newsletters are printed and post office mailed quarterly and are 40 pages each filled with Chatty photos, history, member chat and so much more.
- Annual luncheon in a different state each year.

Buy the Second in the Series of New Chatty Cathy Dolls Today!!

The second in the series of the new Chatty Cathys is due out Summer, 1999. She will be available through most doll shops, Mattel catalogs and some department stores.

The Chatty Cathy Collectors Club assumes no liability for Mattel.

What might your Chatty Cathy Be Worth?

Little known facts

- The voice for Chatty Cathy dolls.
- Do you remember the Chatty Cathy jingle? (This takes about one minute...)

Figure 4-2   There is a collector's club for pretty much anything, including the Chatty Cathy doll, which was very popular in the 1960s. Look for it online at *www.ttinet.com/chattycathy*.

club. Some of the top antiques associations are the Associated Antique Dealers of America (AADA) and the Antiques and Collectibles Dealer Association (ACDA). There are also collector's clubs for everything imaginable (see Figure 4-2), and the *Antique Trader* lists many of these clubs in their publication. Do a Google search and look for one that's a match for your interests. Many of these clubs will let you post a picture of an item and ask for help identifying it, which can be very useful.

ETIQUETTE AND HONESTY

Honesty is very important, and it ties in with becoming an expert. The only way that antiques and collectibles dealers can continue to be successful is if they operate honestly and ethically. "Antiquity with Integrity" was the motto of the National Association of Dealers in Antiques (NADA). One rule of thumb is that you should never intentionally misrepresent an item. If something is damaged, list it as such in the auction description. If you don't know what an item is, say you don't know. Explain that you have searched eBay, the Web, and all your reference books and that you still can't figure it out.

In the case of an unidentified item, try asking for help in the title of your listing. It is amazing how happy fellow eBayers can be to share their knowledge. Lynn has had great experiences with the eBay community pitching in to help. She recently bought a jug at a charity sale, and it was marked with a stamp that said "North Carolina" and that was all. In the listing title she mentioned how it was signed and asked for help in the description. Within an hour a nice eBayer had identified the year and the maker and even sent her a link to a book containing more information. The jug was made by Sam Propst in 1930 and ended up selling for $610! (See Figure 4-3.) Asking for help not only got Lynn the information she needed to sell this jug, it also added to her credibility because she didn't give incorrect information.

As an antiques dealer, all you have is your reputation to keep your customers coming back. This will show up in your feedback rating on eBay. Strive to keep your feedback positive by guaranteeing what you sell and being honest and ethical in all of your dealings.

Never stop learning as long as you live; it will serve you well in business and in life. It will keep your mind active and interested. Buy lots of books, take classes, and surf the Web for knowledge. Join Web-based clubs, local organizations, and network with other dealers. Experience is the best teacher, so spend as much time as you can out in the field. Don't forget to have fun!

Figure 4-3 This Sam Propst pinch jug, unmarked, sold for $610 after a fellow eBayer helped correctly identify it!

PART 2

SELLING ANTIQUES AND COLLECTIBLES WITH SUCCESS

5

Creating a Winning Business Plan for Your Antiques and Collectibles Business

---

Always take the time to strategically formulate a business plan and then follow it. Keep in mind that at any point you can make adjustments to your plan, but as they say in scuba diving, "Plan your dive and dive your plan." Your life depends on that plan in diving, and the same is true for your business's life and longevity. A business plan will keep you on course, help you stay profitable, and steer you in the right direction if you need to make changes. It will also help you make important decisions, such as when to hire extra help.

GETTING STARTED

The first step in creating a business plan is to answer some important questions. From this information we will formulate a working plan and mission statement that will keep us moving in the right direction. You'll formulate answers to questions like: Is this business going to be a hobby, seasonal, part-time, or ultimately your full-time profession? How much do you want in gross sales each week? If you would be happy with $200 in gross sales per week (which works out to a nice $10,400 per year), you will have a different strategy than the person who wants to do $1,000 in gross sales per week, or $52,000 per year.

Plan How Many Items You Need to Sell

eBay is a numbers game. The more items you list, the more money you will make. On average, each item we sell on eBay will gross between $10 and $20—

obviously some are much higher and some are lower. You can get to the upper end of this spectrum once you gain more experience and develop a knack for what sells. We are going to use a conservative $10 for the purposes of this book. You can adjust this figure as you get a sales history for the type of items you plan to sell. If you are selling higher-ticket items you will need to adjust for that also. Keep in mind that this does not mean that every single item will sell. It does mean that during one week, if you have 20 items up for auction, maybe one will sell for $125, four will sell for $9.99 each, 10 will sell for $2.99 each, and five just won't sell. That comes out to $194.86 divided by 20, which yields an average gross of $9.74 each—right at our $10 estimate.

Determining how many items to list each week is easy if you start with how much money you'd like to make. Let's say that you are the part-timer who wants to bring in $200 gross per week. Then, using these numbers, you will need to consistently put 20 new items up for auction on eBay each week. If you want to make $1,000 a week (as a full-time job), you will need to put 100 new items up for sale each week (see Figure 5-1).

eBay TIP Let's talk about the time commitment required here. eBay is very time consuming. Don't kid yourself that it isn't. Keep in mind that you are finding the items, writing a description, measuring and noting condition, researching, photographing, listing, collecting the money, and finally shipping them. And all the while you're answering a slew of e-mails. That said, it is also extremely rewarding. You will have the luxury of working for yourself, and the sky's the limit as far as your potential income. You will be able to set your own hours and be your own boss!

We find that it takes about 50 hours a week to manage 100 to 200 auction items. That works out to a conservative half hour per item. Lynn has an assistant who works 25 hours a week, helping with photography, answering e-mails, logging payments, shipping items, leaving feedback, and troubleshooting. If you are going to be managing 20 auctions a week, plan on working 10 to 15 hours. The good news is that if you do list more items, the time required per item goes down slightly because of economies of scale.

WHAT IS YOUR FOCUS?

Now that you know the time required and rewards expected, take a look at what areas you want to focus on. Do you have certain areas of expertise? Are you interested in furniture generally, or specifically midcentury modern? There are many benefits to having a specialty: it's easier for you to become an expert in that area, and you'll have an easier time targeting customers who buy in that area. You may want to wait until after reading Chapters 12–16 to

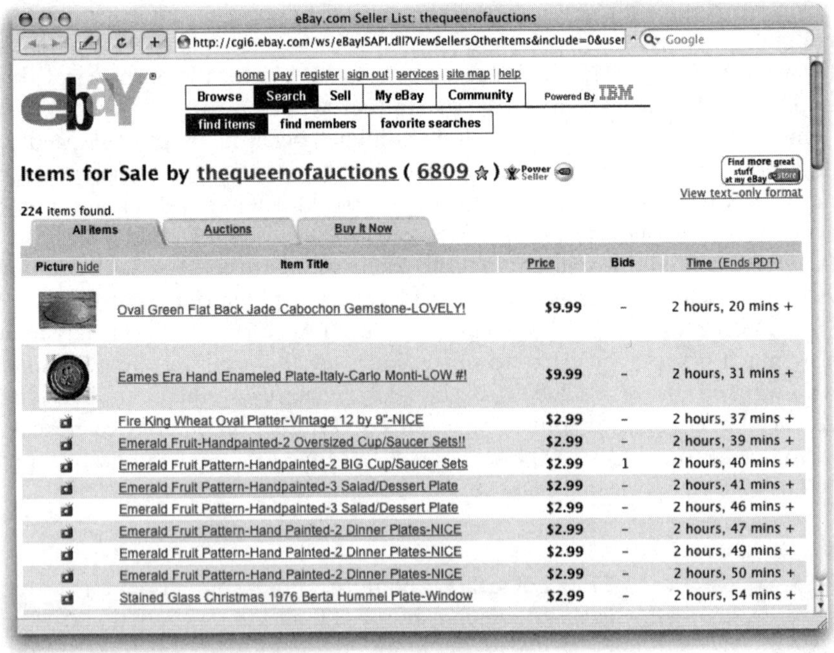

Figure 5-1   Here is a list of Lynn's auctions for just one week. If you want to make a full-time living on eBay, you must constantly list new items to sell.

decide which of the five areas is for you. At this point, you should also decide where you are going to get most of your inventory. Are you going to be a live-auction shopper? A garage and yard saler? Or a combination of several? We address buying strategies in Chapter 6.

YOUR WORKING PLAN AND MISSION STATEMENT

Once you have answered all these questions about your eBay business, it's time to formulate a working plan. A working plan is a commitment to a particular work ethic. As an example, here is Lynn's working plan.

> I am committed to spending 50 hours per week total (myself and my assistant) doing eBay. It will produce approximately $2,000 per week in gross sales. I will specialize in glass, pottery, and table-top. My inventory will come from wanted-to-buy advertisements and from garage, yard, and charity sales. This will be my primary source of income.

The next step is to devise a mission statement, which puts your vision and core values succinctly into two or three sentences. When the going gets tough, a clear mission statement is a great thing to read! It will help you focus and give you a sense of purpose. It should have three components. What will you be doing on eBay? What do you hope to accomplish? What benefits will it yield?

Your mission statement should put into words what makes you want to jump out of bed in the morning and get right to work! When Lynn first started selling on eBay, she would wake up in the middle of the night to check her auctions—and she still does this on occasion! Here is Lynn's mission statement.

> I will sell high-quality, unique items on eBay to customers from all over the world as my full-time profession. This business is exciting to me because I enjoy treasure hunting and finding bargains. Family is very important to me, and eBay enables me to keep my grandmother's memory and business alive while spending all day at home with my young children.

CREATE A CATCHY NAME

Now the fun begins! It is time to pick out a name for your business, and more importantly your user ID, for selling at online auction. eBay reports a total of 104.8 million registered users as of March 30, 2004. This is an astounding number. Keep in mind that when you do go to register your clever user ID, it may already be taken. Lynn started out selling as LA Wilson in 1998, and this was not very catchy so she changed it to TheQueenofAuctions. Be creative.

Your user ID should be something that ties in with your mission statement and working plan. It should be easy to remember, because your goal is to have repeat customers who can find you easily by searching for your user ID. If you are going to be very specialized you could have a handle like FurnitureNut or GlassGuru. If you will be selling a little bit of everything it is good to have a more general name like AddictedtoAntiques.

Once you have your user ID, decide if that will also become your business name. If so, you will need to register it as an assumed name with your county government. Write to the secretary of state's office in your state and get the details. It's perfectly fine to have a separate business name. Lynn, for example, sells as "the queen," but her business name is still Cheryl Leaf Antiques, in honor of her grandmother.

After you have a business name, create business cards with your business name and the items you want to buy. Take these with you everywhere you go. One antiques dealer Lynn knows takes piles of business cards with him to garage sales, and he hands them out to every single person he meets. Imagine how many people call him with antiques they want to sell—it's a fantastic way to build up your inventory of items to sell on eBay.

eBay TIP   It is better to not mention on this business card that you sell on eBay, because eBay is still intimidating to some people. If you mention eBay, it may scare the seller away, or they may decide to cut out the middleman and sell it themself.

What should you print on your card? Just your business name, what you want to buy, and a telephone number and/or e-mail address. It is also nice to have a logo or photo to make your card stand out.

You should also consider having a business card for your eBay business. You can enclose it with every item you ship, to help advertise your business and to help your customers remember your name. Be sure to include your user ID on your card if it is different from your company name (see Figure 5-2).

START-UP COSTS AND CASH FLOW

A great benefit about running an antiques or collectibles business on eBay is that your initial investment in this enterprise can be next to zero! It's very easy to keep your overhead low, and we highly recommend that you defer as many expenditures as possible. The best part of eBay is that you will most likely be doing it from your home, and you probably already own most of the expensive equipment (a computer and digital camera, for example) that you need to get started.

Legal and Tax Advice

You will want to speak with your accountant or attorney to determine how to set up your business. Will you be a sole proprietorship or a corporation? You will also need to apply for a sales tax permit if you live in a state that charges sales tax. This will act as your business license and enable you to buy inventory without paying sales tax because it is for resale. It will also require you to collect sales tax on items delivered within your state. This means that if you sell a vase to a woman whose address is in a state other than your home state, you do not collect sales tax. However, if you sell a painting to a man in your home state, you must collect sales tax (regardless of whether you ship it to him or he picks it up) because the item is being used in your state. This amount will likely be such a low figure that you will only be required to file forms once a year. Your local Small Business Administration (SBA) office can help you get started.

Initial Investment and Cash Flow

To figure out initial investment, it's helpful to use a notebook or a spreadsheet on your computer (see Figures 5-3 and 5-4 for initial investment forms,

Figure 5-2   Here are Lynn's two separate business cards, one for Cheryl Leaf Antiques and one for TheQueenofAuctions.

and Figures 5-5 and 5-6 for cash flow forms). Your initial investment consists of the items you need to purchase before you ever sell anything on eBay. This includes the research books and periodical subscriptions that are important to make sure you are as informed as possible about the items you sell and their potential value. Business cards, business licenses, and tax/legal advice are also mandatory initial investments. Take a look at the example initial-investment form in Figure 5-3. This form shows various types of investments you may want to make as you start your eBay business. As you see, there is a space for you to add any costs for setting up your office, such as a shelf to store inventory on. You may not need to remodel your work area, but you should include a small amount of money here just in case you have these expenses. We will discuss your work space in more detail in Chapter 10. Finally, if you don't already own a working computer and digital camera, you'll have to factor these items into your start-up costs as well, since it's essential to have these for your eBay business (see Figures 5-3 and 5-4).

The samples in Figure 5-3 and Figure 5-4 didn't include any inventory costs in the initial investment form because with eBay items move so quickly (3, 5, 7, or 10 days) that inventory doesn't become a start-up cost.

A	B	C
1		
2	**Start Up Costs**	
3	**Sample**	
4	What you will spend before you even sell an item	
5		
6	Research Books	$98.00
7	Periodical Subscriptions	$55.00
8	Business Cards	$45.00
9	Remodel Work Area	$100.00
10	Digital Camera	
11	Computer	
12	Licenses	$25.00
13	Legal/Tax Advice	$100.00
14	Misc.	
15		
16	Total	$423.00
17		

Figure 5-3 Here is a sample initial-investment form that has been filled out.

E	F	G
1		
2	**Start Up Costs**	
3	**Blank**	
4	What you will spend before you even sell an item	
5		
6	Research Books	
7	Periodical Subscriptions	
8	Business Cards	
9	Remodel Work Area	
10	Digital Camera	
11	Computer	
12	Licenses	
13	Legal/Tax Advice	
14	Misc.	
15		
16	Total	$0.00
17		

Figure 5-4 This blank initial-investment form can be used for your own needs.

Next, you should complete a cash-flow chart by month, based on your experience and your estimated monthly sales. Since you will continually need updated books for research, this is an ongoing expense. Inventory also shows up here. Packing supplies are a big expense, so be sure to take this into account, as well as any money spent on advertising, such as a flyer to send with each package advertising your other sales items or your Web site. We will discuss packing in Chapter 10.

For your cash-flow chart, you must also enter what you'll spend on eBay fees. eBay charges a fixed insertion rate plus a percentage when you actually sell an item. These fees run an average of 7.5 to 10 percent of total sales for Lynn's antiques and collectibles business. PayPal, the best way to collect money, costs her about 3 percent per transaction and only 75 percent of her customers use PayPal. Your percentages may differ, but this is a great starting point until you have some established tracking. As you grow your business, you'll learn what other costs you'll incur, such as batteries for your camera and other, similar items.

	A	B	C
1			
2		Cash Flows--Ongoing Expenses	
3		Sample	
4		What you will spend on an ongoing basis per month	
5		Based on $8,000 in Sales	
6			
7		Research Books	$20.00
8		Inventory	$800.00
9		Auto Expense	
10		Packing Supplies	
11		Bubble Wrap	$50.00
12		Tape	$25.00
13		Packing Peanuts	$105.00
14		Tissue	$20.00
15		Boxes	$135.00
16		Flyer/Business Card	$40.00
17		eBay Fees 7.5%	$600.00
18		Paypal Fees 3.0%	$180.00
19		Batteries	$4.00
20		Shipping Fees	
21		UPS	
22		USPS	
23		Overhead	
24		Electricity	
25		Internet Access	
26		Heat	
27		Telephone	
28		Water	
29		Garbage	
30		Insurance	
31		Repairs	$12.00
32		Supplies	$35.00
33			
34		Misc.	
35		Help	
36			
37		Total	$2,026.00
38			

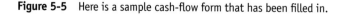

Figure 5-5   Here is a sample cash-flow form that has been filled in.

E	F	G	
1			
2	**Cash Flows--Ongoing Expenses**		
3	**Blank**		
4	What you will spend on an ongoing basis per month		
5	Base it on your projected Sales		
6			
7	Research Books		
8	Inventory		
9	Auto Expense		
10	Packing Supplies		
11	Bubble Wrap		
12	Tape		
13	Packing Peanuts		
14	Tissue		
15	Boxes		
16	Flyer/Business Card		
17	eBay Fees 7.5%		
18	Paypal Fees 3.0%		
19	Batteries		
20	Shipping Fees		
21	UPS		
22	USPS		
23	Overhead		
24	Electricity		
25	Internet Access		
26	Heat		
27	Telephone		
28	Water		
29	Garbage		
30	Insurance		
31	Repairs		
32	Supplies		
33			
34	Misc.		
35	Help		
36			
37	Total	$0.00	
38			

Figure 5-6   Use this blank cash-flow form for your business.

eBay TIP   If you run an eBay business from your home, remember that you can do an income tax write-off for repairs and supplies (i.e., windex, goo-gone, paper towels, and printer paper). Other expenses such as utilities may also be deductible. Please check with your accountant.

INVENTORY

When the subject of inventory arises, the best place to check first is your own home. This is a great way to declutter your life while at the same time raising the money needed for start-up costs. Make a list of things you are interested in selling, or fill boxes with items you don't need or use anymore. Look for brand names, good condition, and items that don't have sentimental value. If it belonged to your grandfather and you are on the fence about parting with it, keep it!

Check your attic, basement, clothes closets, bathrooms, and kitchen cupboards. Dinnerware and flatware, for instance, sell really well. Don't leave any stones unturned. Once you have sold these items on eBay, it is time to venture out into the real world and spend real money—cold, hard cash.

We will get into building your inventory in more detail in the Chapter 6, but for the purposes of your business plan, think about how much money you plan to spend on your inventory versus how much you hope to make from it. For example, you might spend about $200 each weekend on inventory that will turn into $1,000 to $2,000 during the upcoming week.

TRACKING PURCHASES AND SALES

Keeping track of your purchases and your sales is a very important part of the equation. You must keep good records not only of your monthly expenses, as we saw in the monthly cash flow, but of every item you buy and sell. A simple ledger system, a computer spreadsheet, or Lynn's recordkeeping notebook system *iSell* (available through *www.TheQueenofAuctions.com*) all work well.

To keep records in a simple ledger, just mark the date and the item purchased with the price paid. It is best to do this the moment you return from making your purchases, while it is still fresh in your mind. Otherwise, all the items start to look alike. Make columns to record price received and direct expenses such as eBay and PayPal fees.

eBay TIP When Lynn started selling on eBay five years ago she realized she needed a way to get organized to keep track of what she bought and sold. She invented the *iSell* three-ring binder looseleaf tracking system. Each sheet contains a place to fill in the date an item was purchased, from whom it was purchased, and the price paid. There is even a profit/loss on the back side to list direct costs. This system has been a lifesaver! Check it out at *www.TheQueenofAuctions.com*.

Whichever method you use to keep track of your inventory, make sure it is simple *and* effective (see Figure 5-7). It is so important to keep track of your progress, and later you can use this information to figure out ways to improve your bottom line.

GETTING PAID

Let's touch on getting paid. Most of you already know the drill. You can use PayPal or your own merchant terminal to accept credit cards, you can take personal checks (with a 10-day wait on shipping merchandise to buyers, to make sure checks clear), money orders, or even cash.

eBay TIP   One note about PayPal. You may receive charge-backs if you ship to an address that hasn't been confirmed on the PayPal page. If the credit cards turn out to be stolen and the ad-dresses weren't confirmed, you won't be covered by PayPal's protection policy. This can be costly if you are dealing in valuable antiques. Protect yourself and never ship an expensive item to an unconfirmed address.

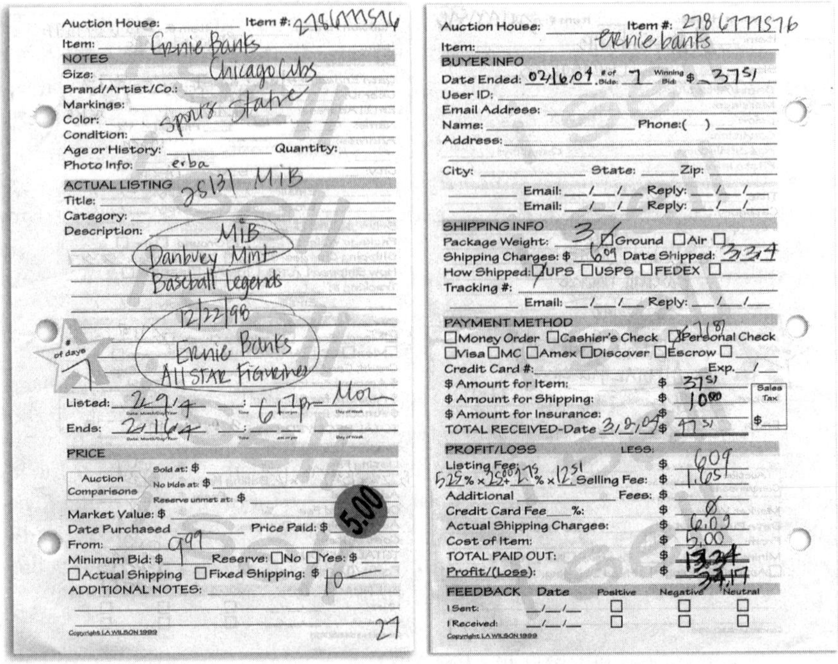

Figure 5-7   This sample *iSell* sheet is a convenient place to keep track of sales information.

When it comes to payment, PayPal is not cheap. It costs about 3 to 4 percent of the purchase price, and this cuts right into your bottom line. If you get a merchant terminal, your cost is reduced to approximately 1.9 percent per transaction. Nevertheless, most customers prefer the convenience of Pay-Pal and do not want to phone you with all their personal information. There are other hidden costs in taking charge-card information over the phone, including the time spent on the phone with customers.

For higher-priced items, escrow also becomes an option. Escrow works this way: the escrow company will collect the money from your buyer. Once they have verified the funds, they tell you to ship the item. Once the buyer receives the item and is satisfied, the buyer notifies the escrow company to release the funds to you. It is a great system that protects both the buyer and the seller. There are several good escrow companies recommended on the eBay Web page.

Now that money details and business planning are out of the way, let's get to the exciting part: going out and finding treasures! It is like an adventure every day. You never know what you will uncover. Could it be a unique desk that is worth $20,000? Could it be a rare jug that sells for $1,000? Let's get started and find out!

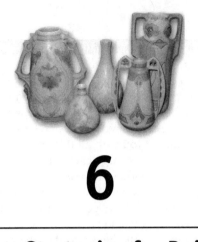

6

Buying Strategies for Building Your Inventory

At this point, we will assume that you have already cleaned out your entire house, scoured your garage, and probably even hit up your friends and relatives for anything worth selling on eBay. Good for you! Now, however, it is time to actually purchase inventory. Buying antiques and collectibles can be both exciting and intimidating. It's fun to see the wide range of items that are available in the world. At the same time, it can be nerve-racking to be unsure about whether or not you are getting a good price. Of course, if you are worried that something is too expensive, remember: there will always be more merchandise available to purchase somewhere else.

eBay TIP Remember, you don't have to sell everything you buy. Lynn's Grandmother frequently said, "I have never regretted anything I have purchased, but I often regret things I have sold." If you buy something you love when shopping for your business, you don't have to sell it. Keep it for your own home or collection.

ETIQUETTE IN BARGAINING

As a bona fide antiques dealer with a sales tax number and business cards, you are in a great position to bargain for a better price. It's a tradition of long standing that antiques dealers give discounts to their peers, and it is considered a common courtesy in the industry, even if your policies on discounting for the general public are a different story.

For many of you, bargaining may be something you've never done before. Here are some key rules to remember. First, upon entering an antiques-show booth, antiques shop, or antiques mall, find out what their policy is for other dealers, and identify yourself with your business card. You will be asked to fill out a resale tax form; some dealers make photocopies of these forms and fill them out in advance so when they're out buying the forms are ready to hand to sellers. If the standard discount is 10 percent but you are interested in a large quantity of items, it is fine to ask politely if they would offer an additional volume discount.

Keep in mind that you should never insult a dealer or seller. Always ask questions politely, not condescendingly, and please don't react even if their prices are too high. Some people feel they should make a disparaging remark or sound when a dealer gives a price that is too high. Instead, consider saying, "Thanks, I will think about it" and put the item back on the shelf.

Always ask the seller what they know about the item. Knowing provenance (see Chapter 3 for more information) will help you get more money for the item when you resell it later. There may be some key information you are missing that could be the reason for the higher price. If you notice a defect, like a chip or missing piece, ask them if they realized it was damaged? They may not have known and will adjust the price accordingly. As a side note, any item that is damaged should be marked "as is" by the seller with a specific note telling what is wrong.

The same bargaining etiquette holds true at garage, estate, and yard sales. Someone went to the trouble of pricing their items. Please don't insult them. You can say things like, "That's more than I wanted to spend" or, "I really like this piece, but it is out of my price range." Most of the time they will work with you to find a price you are both happy with. Remember, people have a limited time to sell their items and generally want them gone by the end of the day.

eBay TIP   Remember the old saying that "You attract more bees with honey." It is true: you will get more when bargaining if you ask sweetly. Try complimenting the seller on their taste by saying something such as, "Wow, you have such beautiful things. I really like this bowl that you have priced at $25. It's lovely. Would you consider taking any less?" More often than not, they will say, sure, how about $10. Sold!

BARGAINING STRATEGIES

The number-one rule for bargaining is to let the seller name the price first. There's a famous saying that "Whoever names the first price loses." This is

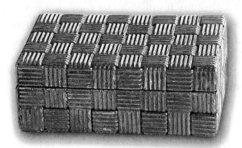

Figure 6-1   This signed Tiffany pillbox was purchased as part of a box of 80 items that cost $400. Just this one item from the box sold for $123 on eBay.

true in all aspects of business and negotiating. If you can hold your tongue and wait the seller out, they will usually throw out a number that is less than you would have offered. Once the price is stated either verbally or on a price tag, the negotiating can begin.

eBay TIP   One negotiating strategy is to buy items by the box or by the table, or even the whole shop. This is absolutely the best way to get merchandise for the best price. Put all the things you want in a box or together on a table and ask for a deal. This works great! Buying in numbers gives you an advantage—the law of averages. You know that one or two items will be worth more than you think (see Figure 6-1).

You don't necessarily have to tell the seller at a garage sale or yard sale that you are a dealer. However, most of the time they will figure it out. Once the transaction is completed, hand them a business card and ask them to call you if they have anything else to sell that you would be interested in. You have already proven to them that you are serious, pleasant to deal with, and willing to pay cash. It is a good bet that they will call you if they run across any other items or have some better things that they didn't put out that day.

At estate sales, when you are dealing with a family member or an antiques dealer hired to run the sale, it is a good idea to let them know you are a dealer. Because estate sales are usually held when a person has passed away, the family members or the professional hired to handle the sale will be very motivated to get rid of everything to the walls in a few days. If they know you are a dealer they will understand that you have money and are serious about buying. Give them a card and let them know that you would be interested in buying everything that is left once the sale has ended.

As a final strategy, remember to take your time if you find a great sale or shop. Slow down and always take one last look around, checking for things you may have missed. A great place to double-check is under tables to see what is on the floor. This is where you can find great dinnerware sets and other treasures. Lynn recently found a mint Atari video game in its box on the floor under a newer Play Station steering wheel. She paid $5 for it and *it* ended up selling for more than $50! (Refer back to Figure 3-1.) By sticking it out and taking her time, she found some hidden treasures. Just think what you can find.

eBay TIP   Take a kit in your car to assist in your buying trips. Your kit should contain a black light, magnifying glass or loop, flashlight, reference book, empty boxes, rope, and packing supplies. The black light can be used to test for vaseline glass, which will glow under the light, and also to spot glue or cement from repairs that otherwise may escape notice. The magnifying glass is to help read signatures, and the flashlight is great for looking at items in dark corners or to use at garage sales that are held early on a dark morning. The rope is very handy for tying a car trunk shut or to secure items you have found.

WHAT SHOULD YOU LOOK FOR?

When you are building your inventory, look for items that are underpriced or undervalued. Before you go shopping, check on eBay to see what is hot, then look specifically for those items (see Figure 6-2).

eBay TIP   eBay publishes a hot sheet, which you can find by going to "Services," then to "Seller Central," and clicking on "What's Hot." It is an invaluable tool! Get out your general price guide and before you go buying read up on companies that make the hot items list.

Keep up on your periodical reading about which antiques are up-and-coming trends and about where the market is headed. Then, when you go shopping look for these items, as well as for unique and unusual items, because weird and wacky consistently sells on eBay. We will discuss current market trends specific to each of the five merchandise categories later in the book. As you shop, always try to buy the best example you find, and make sure it is in good condition. Follow our $5/$20 rule until you become more comfortable with a particular category.

If you are somewhere that you can't get to a computer or reference

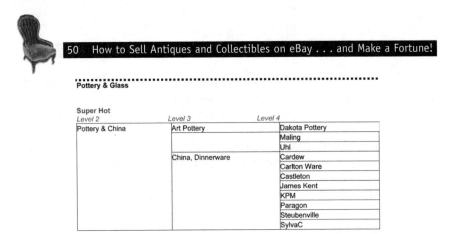

Figure 6-2   In this *Hot Categories* report from eBay, Dakota pottery and Maling are the most popular items in the *Art Pottery* subcategory.

book and you need to make a quick decision, call a friend with Internet access and ask them to look up prices of similar items. Doing this will protect you and keep you from making too many mistakes! You can also get Internet access on some cell phones now. Consider purchasing this service so you can check the value of items while you shop. It may be money well spent.

WHERE ARE THE BEST ITEMS?

You can find great items almost everywhere you go. Lynn always looks for what she calls sleepers, or items that are undervalued and just collecting dust as they wait for you to pick them up and sell on eBay. Lynn's grandmother always said that there are sleepers in every store in America and in every store in the world. You just have to be smart enough to smoke them out. The following section lists great places to go to find these hidden treasures.

Antiques Shops, Shows, and Malls

Antiques malls and antiques shows allow you to see a lot of merchandise in a short time frame without spending the day driving around. However, shopping in antiques malls can be confusing. Some are large and overwhelming.

Any time you go into an antiques shop, mall, or show, remember to identify yourself as a fellow dealer when you enter. Ask them to point you in the direction of items that interest you. Ask them about their discount policies for other dealers. As you are building your inventory, spend time in your local shops once a month and get to know the owners. Let them know what you are buying, and learn from them. As they get to know you better, they will call you first when something you like arrives.

To find the shops in your area, check the yellow pages in your phone book. The *Antique Trader* (*www.AntiqueTrader.com*) and *Maine Digest* (*www*

.MaineAntiqueDigest.com) are great resources to locate shows in your area. When traveling on vacation or for business, always make time to visit the local antiques shops. It is a great learning experience to see what items are selling and for what prices in other parts of the country. Hand out your business card, and look for bargains. A great resource for finding shops in other areas are the Mapbooks of Antique Shops (there are other mapbooks listed online: do a search on *Google* to find them), or try contacting the chamber of commerce or visitor's bureau in the cities you plan to visit. They can recommend some of the better shops. Before your trip, spend some time calling to figure out which shops and malls will have the things that interest you most.

Antiques shows are a fantastic way to see a lot of quality merchandise in a short time period. Hand the dealer your business card if you are interested in purchasing an item. If, at a show, you see something that is authentic, and the dealer is reputable and the price fair, go ahead and purchase it. When shopping in an antiques mall, if you see something that looks intriguing, pick it up and carry it with you or have them hold it at the front counter until you decide. If you try and go back later, you may not be able to find it because the malls are usually large and spread out.

A good tactic for getting bargains at antiques shows is to show up for the last hour of the show and negotiate for better prices. Dealers often do not want to pack items up and haul them back to their respective stores.

Flea Markets and Thrift Stores

Flea markets are a lot of fun and allow you to find a multitude of junk or treasures all in one place. Make sure you get there early, and be prepared to walk a lot. You might not find much, but you'll see what's selling. You just never know what will be collectible. Use your time at the flea market to find bargains and learn.

eBay TIP Consider getting a booth at a flea market. Take along a pal to set up your items for sale while you scout around for bargains before any of the buying public is let inside.

Thrift stores are another great place to check on a regular basis. Many wealthy or very busy people choose not to host their own garage sales and instead donate their items directly to charities such as the Goodwill, the Salvation Army, the American Red Cross, or their local church. These stores can be a gold mine. The best thing to do is to get to know the people who work there. If you go into your favorite thrift store on a weekly basis, the employees will start to recognize you and show you things you may have missed.

Store Closings/Closeouts

Read your local newspaper and watch for store closings and closeout sales. Many businesses don't last for long, and this type of sale is a great place to pick up bargains at pennies on the dollar. Even if it is not an antiques store, you never know what they were using for fixtures and display—these pieces can turn out to be great antiques. Also, you may find collectibles if the store dealt in newer items, such as those from Swarovski, Hummel, or Precious Moments. Don't pass up these items; collectibles are hot on eBay!

Garage, Yard, Charity, and Estate Sales

These sales are Lynn's favorites because she only has to spend four hours on a Saturday to find all the items she needs for selling on eBay the next week. It's smart to do your research the night before. Look for advertisements in the classified section of your newspaper or online that say *estate, charity, antiques, collectibles,* and *furniture* (see Figure 6-3). Pass on the ones that list a lot of children's clothes or toys. Always be at the charity or church rummage sale when it first starts. These are the very best! Plan your strategy so that you have your route figured out and will be at the best-sounding sales right when they start, if not a half hour before. Garage-sale etiquette really requires you to not show up before the listed time. However, it is a jungle out there, and some dealers show up an hour ahead of time. Fortunately, at the best sales (charity and church) they will not let anyone in early.

Survey the sale quickly when you arrive. You don't want to waste precious time at a mediocre garage sale when the next one on your list could be incredible. Are the items overpriced? Is everything marked "Made in Taiwan" or "Made in China"? If yes, this should tell you that the person does not care for quality, and you probably won't find much at that sale.

However, if all the items are higher quality, antique, fairly priced, and in great condition, then you may have found a super sale. Remember, a good technique here is to grab a box and fill it up quickly. Throw anything that looks unusual or unique into the box. You can always edit later. Use the $5 rule. If it's $5 or less, take a chance. Some of these turn out to be the best items! Don't forget to hand your business card to the seller when you are finished.

eBay TIP If you show up at a sale and the seller mentions eBay, as in, "I looked that up on eBay and it goes for $60, and I am only asking $20," you should walk away. It is a good bet that they have checked most of their items out online and you won't find much that would be cost-effective for you to sell.

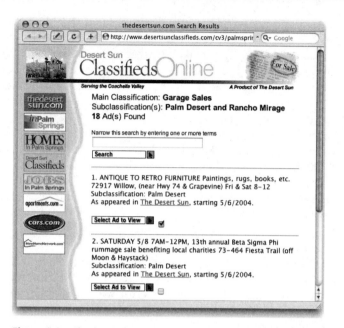

Figure 6-3 Check your local newspaper online for a list of classified ads. This one gives key information about area garage and yard sales.

eBay TIP Another good tactic is to show up after the rush is over. Make it close to the end of the sale. Lynn has been given a lot of items for free this way and purchased others at a great discount. For example, on the last day of an estate sale most items are marked down by at least 50 percent.

Live Auctions and eBay

Live auctions are a blast, and you can learn a lot about what people are willing to pay top dollar for. On the other hand, they can be serious time wasters. You can end up at an auction for several days and never get anything great. On the other hand, you can stumble across an auction where there are great box lots and you can make a fortune. Some of the best auctions are in the country, not in the city. Check the Internet, your local paper, and the trade magazines to see when and where they will be held.

When you do attend live auctions, make sure that you are there for the preview. This will give you a chance to mark down the lot numbers and the maximum that you are willing to pay. Keep in mind that the action house usually charges a buyer's premium that can add 10 percent to the cost. As in both live auctions and on eBay, make sure that you do your research and find out appropriate price ranges. Mark the maximum on your card and do not go over it. It is very easy to get caught up in the auction frenzy, which is one reason eBay has been so successful. Don't let overzealousness ruin your chances of making your eBay fortune.

When it comes to buying on eBay, a great strategy is to buy by the lot. One of Lynn's acquaintances buys large lots of postage stamps on eBay. He then sorts them out, grades them, and sells them individually—and he's doing a great business. Another idea is to purchase complete sets of china and flatware. Break them out into mini-packages of twos and fours and sell them this way to make a profit.

eBay TIP   Watch for misspellings on eBay. Since Lynn collects Marmorzellan, she sometimes searches by "Marmorzelan." You just never know when a spelling error will mean a bargain for you! Search by general terms such as *glass* or *pottery* to look for something that was not identified correctly.

There are plenty of bargains to be found at live auctions and on eBay. This is especially true on eBay in the summer months when sales drop off. You will find that not as many people are inside their homes using their computers, so you can pick up some steals because there is not as much buying competition.

Classified Ads for Both Wanted-to-Buy and For Sale

Browse the classified section of your local newspaper for individual items for sale. You can usually phone the person and get more information before you actually make an appointment to view the merchandise. When you call on the phone, ask specific questions: What exactly do you have? How many pieces? What are the prices? Where did you acquire these items? Do your weeding out before you agree to meet. It is always a good idea to take someone else with you for safety reasons.

Keep in mind that these trips can be time wasters also. You could spend hours driving to someone's house to view their items, only to find just a bunch of junk. These people may have just wanted a free appraisal. Asking the right questions will help prevent this scenario.

If the seller expects you to name the price, don't do it. They should have an idea of what they want to get for their goods. You may find that if you name the price, the person will say they will contact you and then use your bid to get $10 more from the next dealer. Do not let yourself become part of a bidding war. Instead, try saying, "When you have decided on a price, please give me the opportunity to purchase your things."

eBay TIP   Keep in mind that buying stolen property is a serious consideration in this field. You do not want to aid and abet a criminal. Do your due diligence to make sure that the items you are purchasing are not stolen. Usually, you will get a funny feeling if the items are stolen. Something just doesn't add up. The person will not answer all your questions and will skirt the issues. If you feel uncomfortable, play it safe and trust your instinct.

Placing a want ad in your local paper and in one of the nation publications like the *Antique Trader* can be a lot of fun and less work than answering advertisements. People will be answering yours! Try to catch trends before they happen. For example, Lynn's grandmother saw a trend in the 1970s and knew that stretch glass would become popular. She ran a wanted-to-buy ad in the *Antique Trader* consistently and bought stretch glass from all over the country for $1 to $2 per piece and resold it several years later at a great price. You can also advertise to buy entire estates. If you have the capital to do this, it is a great opportunity. Just don't overpay. Remember, you will need to handle all the items numerous times before you make any money!

We hope you realize the incredible opportunity waiting for you when you start buying inventory. Your money will be made by finding unidentified treasures, buying in bulk, or by bargaining for the best price. Now that you know where to go for merchandise, how to bargain, and what to look for, it is time to determine the value of goods before you purchase them. We will explore this in the next chapter.

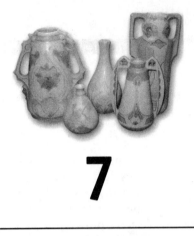

7

Determining the Value of Your Antiques and Collectibles

As you build your inventory by going to garage sales and antiques malls and all of your other sources, there will be times when you have five seconds to make a decision and times when you have five weeks. Hopefully, it will be somewhere in between these extremes. If you only have five seconds you should use the $5/$20 rule, which we've discussed previously: spend $5 on a whim, $20 if you are somewhat knowledgeable, and don't go over $20 unless you have a reference book or quick access to the Internet. Keep in mind that even if you do check eBay and the item looks like it will sell for a lot, this is not a guarantee. On the flip side, if there aren't any sales on eBay it could just mean that there may be no sales history on your particular item in the last two weeks—it could actually be a very sought-after item.

Lynn's rule for purchasing smaller goods is to try and make ten times what she pays for an item. If something costs $1 at a yard sale, you should expect on average to sell it for $10. On more expensive items, when you spend above the $20 ceiling, a good rule of thumb is to shoot for three times what you pay. If you pay $30 for something, it should sell for close to $100.

When you don't follow that rule, it can come back to haunt you. As an example, Lynn was recently at a garage sale and found an adorable wicker baby carriage and remembered seeing it sell years ago at antiques shows for close to $500. It was marked $125, and she bargained the price down to $100. She bought it without consulting anything or anybody about *current* trends (as opposed to her memory of years ago)! (See Figure 7-1.) After listing the baby buggy on eBay with a starting price of $99, it did not sell. Lynn re-listed it several weeks later and only made $99—one dollar less than what she paid.

Figure 7-1 Just because something once sold well—like this wicker baby stroller—doesn't mean it is still a hot item. Make sure you are up-to-date about what an item is worth.

There was no return on investment here, and it ended up taking a lot of Lynn's precious time. It was a good learning experience, and now Lynn always checks eBay for current values.

Knowledge is key when you are buying. So, how do you come by this crucial knowledge? Let's take a look at where to go for prices when you are purchasing.

WHERE TO DO YOUR RESEARCH: PRICE GUIDES, eBAY HISTORY, TRENDS, AND OTHER SOURCES

Price Guides

We mentioned in Chapter 4 that price guides are a must-have building block to your eBay business library. Always keep an up-to-date price guide in your car so that if you are at a sale, in a shop, or at a show, you can ask the seller to hold the item while you run out to your car and check prices. Buy the new issue every year. Some of our favorites:

- *Schroeder's Antiques Price Guide*, Collectors Books, $14.95
- *Kovels' Antiques and Collectibles Price List*, Random House, $16.95
- *Antique Trader Antiques & Collectibles Price Guide*, Krause Publications, $17.99
- *Warman's Antiques & Collectibles Price Guide*, Krause Publications, $19.99

Remember that these guides gather prices from all over the country and that condition is very important. Keep in mind, too, that because of the constantly changing nature of the antiques business, the prices are probably a bit

58   How to Sell Antiques and Collectibles on eBay . . . and Make a Fortune!

outdated by the time the book goes to print. However, the guides are still an invaluable tool and will likely prevent you from making many expensive mistakes.

Learning from eBay History

eBay is one of the best ways to check an item's value before you purchase it as well as an invaluable resource to use when you are ready to price the item for resale. eBay is where you are going to be selling your items, so there is no better place to check for current pricing conditions. eBay used to publish the last four weeks as public record in a completed-auction search. Now a completed-auction search makes available only two weeks of information. This has made research a bit trickier and not as thorough. To see what a completed-auction search looks like, please refer back to Figure 3-3.

Unless you have a computer with a wireless connection, it can be difficult to access eBay when you are driving from garage sale to garage sale and antiques mall to antiques mall. If you find a potentially great item when you are away from Internet access, consider calling someone you know who is at home and who can quickly access eBay. Recently, Lynn was at an estate sale looking at a set of 60 dishes that was priced at $150. They were Johnson Brothers England in the Old Britain Castles pattern done in brown with color hand tinting, and they were in perfect condition. She knew her brother was at home, so she called him, and he provided the crucial eBay research she needed. By doing a completed-auction search, he learned that just the soup tureen alone in that pattern and color had recently sold for $80 and that plates typically sell for about $10 each. By breaking the set up into 16 individual auctions Lynn made a $400-plus profit (see Figure 7-2).

If you go to a sale that you know will have great buys, you may even consider having someone sitting and waiting for your phone call so you can quickly do research. Of course, you may want to give this person a percentage of the money you make for their help.

eBay TIP   As you determine what a product is worth, look to see if you can break the item up into multiple listings. China sets do very well broken up into auctions of two to four pieces. They are really quick and easy to list, and because you're offering so many pieces in someone's pattern, they will usually buy multiple auctions to save money on shipping.

As an ending note to checking prices on eBay, keep in mind that this is just 2 weeks' worth of records. Your item may sell for more and it may sell for less. In some cases you may see the end price of two people battling it out over a specific item that drove the cost up. Lynn sells the same 1971 Berta Hummel

Figure 7-2 By splitting up this set of Johnson Brothers England Old Britain Castles dishes into multiple auctions Lynn was able to make a more than $400 profit.

Christmas plate week in and week out on eBay. Some weeks she gets $2.99 for it, but she has gotten up to $54 for that same plate. It is all about who is looking for your item on that particular day and on the condition of the piece. The rule is often the exception on eBay. The best solution is to continually monitor the eBay sales history of items you frequently sell. You will likely notice trends in when your item sells the best and when it doesn't sell at all.

Researching the World Wide Web

Web-based research is also a very important pricing tool. If you can't find your particular item on eBay, try looking on a search engine, such as Google. You will more than likely find many Web sites with fixed pricing. Keep in mind that even though one Web site lists a certain price, it does not necessarily mean that your item is going to sell for that price.

One valuable Web site for gauging prices on tabletop items is *www .replacements.com*. They list almost every pattern imaginable. Some of their prices are high, but you should usually expect to get about 25 to 30 percent of their list price for an item when you sell it on eBay. For example, Replacements sells the Johnson Brothers England Old Britain Castles dinner plate for $23.99. On eBay, these dinner plates sell for an average of $8, or about 33 percent of retail.

Pricing with Periodicals

Another place to look for pricing trends is by reading your periodical subscriptions and watching shows like the *Antiques Roadshow*. If you can spot trends for items that are just starting to take off in popularity, you can pick up items for a bargain and wait for the rest of the country to figure it out.

Melmac, plastic from the 1950s, is becoming very collectible. Couroc is

Figure 7-3 Watch for items that are starting to become hot collectibles. This Melmac Couroc Black Tray with Dolphins cost only $2, but as Melmac became more popular, Lynn was able to sell it on eBay for $39.

a company from Monterey, California, that makes high-quality Melmac pieces, usually black with shells, stones, rocks, and sand used in mosaic designs. These pieces can be picked up quite inexpensively at yard sales and in thrift stores (see Figure 7-3). This is one example of something worth stockpiling. Try to find what other items are getting ready to surge in popularity.

Most periodicals contain articles and columns on items that they think are becoming more valuable. These are the pieces you want to read about and start looking for when you are hunting. Lynn had read about Couroc, as part of the growing Melmac trend, in a back issue of one of her magazines and knew to watch for it.

Paying for an Appraisal

If you have found something that you think is very rare and you can't find out anything about its value, *please* pay for an appraisal. If you find something you aren't sure about at an antiques show or in a shop, ask the owner if you may take the item on approval. If the item was inexpensive enough to purchase and you still can't find out any information, once again an appraisal is a great way to go. When you do hire an appraiser, he or she may ask you how you want the appraisal written. There are appraisal values written for insurance purposes (these are typically at the highest end of the price range), appraisal values written for division of property (typically in the middle, at retail price), and appraisal values written for what you could expect to sell it for quickly (typically the lowest value, at wholesale price). You may want to have your appraiser give you a range so that you can use the higher insurance value in your auction description but still know realistically what you could hope to sell it for quickly. To find an appraiser in your area, please refer back to Chapter 3.

CONDITION: REPAIR AND RESTORATION?

Before you buy anything, check its condition carefully. Condition is very important when you go to sell your item. Chips, cracks, crazing, wear, nicks, splits in wood, and repairs will all detract from the price you will hope to receive. Replaced hardware and marriages will also take away from your sales price.

A marriage is when two originally separate antique pieces are put together; for example, the top, high portion of a highboy being placed on a nonmatching low portion. In a marriage, the types of wood may be different or the design a little off. Pay close attention to see that they match perfectly.

Marriages happen frequently with cruets, perfume bottles and decanters, and their stoppers. Often the original stoppers were lost or broken. How can you tell if you are getting the original stopper? When the original antique pieces were made, the maker would sometimes hand paint the same number on the stopper and on the base, ensuring that when the item left the studio it had the correct stopper (see Figure 7-4). This is a great way to check antique glass and make sure that the stopper and base are original.

Use a black light to go over any piece that you are considering for purchase and look for hidden glue and repairs. If your piece is "as is," decide how much you will have to spend to repair it or if you will sell it as a "fixer" on eBay. If you are considering repairing the item, get an estimate from the repair shop to help you figure out your costs. There are glass grinders; resilvering companies; furniture, china, and doll repair shops; and the list goes on. Check online and in your local phone book for these services. "As is" pieces do sell on eBay and sometimes using "fixer upper" or "needs TLC" in the title actually draws people looking for projects.

You should always take condition into consideration when deciding what to pay. Work backward from what you can expect to sell your piece for.

Figure 7-4 This antique perfume bottle has a number 13 hand-painted on both the stopper and the base, which proves that it's a matching set.

Let's say you are going to buy an oak dresser that needs to have a leg replaced. You know that a perfect antique oak dresser will sell for $150 on eBay. Using the three-times rule, you would only want to have $50 total sunk into this piece. If the dresser is priced at $25 and you know that it will cost you $35 to get the leg repaired, this is not a good investment. If the seller will take $15, then you should buy it and spend the $35 to get it repaired. However, if a fixer-upper antique oak dresser will still bring $100 on eBay, you may opt to pay the $25 and not put any money into repairs. You will learn to look at each piece on a case-by-case basis.

DEAL WITH REPUTABLE DEALERS

One final concern with pricing is making sure you get what you pay for. In other words, you want to be certain the seller isn't unscrupulously selling you a reproduction of something but calling it an original. The best way to protect yourself from dishonest people when buying at antiques shows, flea markets, antiques shops and malls, auctions, and on eBay is to deal with a reputable seller.

How can you tell if they are reputable? First, they will have been in business for a while. Secondly, they will stand behind their merchandise. For example, at Lynn's antiques shop, if she accidentally misrepresented an item in any way, such as giving a wrong age or not marking where something is damaged, she takes it back for a full refund—no questions asked. Most reputable dealers will give you a written guarantee if asked.

A reputable dealer will most likely belong to a professional organization such as NADA or their local chamber of commerce. Lastly, they will be happy to share their knowledge with you, have clearly marked store policies, and answer your questions quickly. On eBay, a reputable seller will most likely be a PowerSeller and have a high number of positive feedback points by his or her name.

It is still okay to buy from a relatively new seller on eBay. Practice your due diligence by reading all their feedback and asking questions in advance about their return policy. If it is an expensive item, you may want to ask for the seller's phone number—sometimes questions are more easily asked and answered over the phone than through e-mail. Remember to pay for a purchase from a new eBay seller with a credit card or PayPal, instead of sending a money order or personal check.

One of the best parts about the whole eBay process is figuring out what things are worth! You'll find that as soon as you come home from a morning at garage sales, you'll want to turn on your computer, open your reference books, and start valuing your items. This detective work can be so much fun. The first time you realize that your item is worth a lot of money, is one of the best feelings in the world! Please let us know about your success stories. Our e-mail addresses are in the introduction to this book.

8

Targeting Customers Interested in Your Antiques and Collectibles

---

Believe it or not, you can actually find a loyal bunch of customers on a site as big as eBay. Although eBay does have a lot of users, if you consistently offer high-quality merchandise, accurate descriptions, fair return policies, and quick service, you can maintain a loyal customer base. So how do you build your loyal customer base? Let's find out!

eBay TIP Since *Antiques* and *Collectibles* are two of the most popular categories on eBay, there are a lot of people who sell in these areas. In order to have your listing stand out from the crowd, it's important to use the targeting strategies in this chapter.

USE YOUR eBAY STORE TO GET CUSTOMERS

If you have been selling on eBay for a while you probably already have an eBay Store. An eBay Store is a part of the eBay Web site and allows you to list things for 30, 60, 90, or 120 days at a fixed price. You must put a Buy-It-Now price on all your goods, but the listing fees are much lower than for an auction item. Your customers can view what is in your eBay Store by searching for your seller name or by clicking on your eBay Store logo when they find your other auctions. There is also a feature on the eBay Search page to search by store instead of searching the auction listings. This is a very useful tool for targeting customers. There are several benefits to having your own eBay Store. For starters, it allows you to list a large quantity of merchandise at a very low listing fee. The final value selling fees remain the same as in an auction format. It also allows you to categorize your items into 20 different categories that you define. If you specialize in a wide range of antiques and collectibles, you can use a broad range of categories, such as:

- *Antiques*
- *Books/Catalogs/Paper Items*
- *Clothing*
- *Collectibles*
- *Collector's Plates*
- *Dinnerware*
- *Flatware*
- *Furniture*
- *Jewelry*
- *Lamps & Lighting*
- *New Gift Items*
- *Trade Beads & Loose Gems*

If, on the other hand, the types of items you sell are highly specialized, you can break categories down by the year created, by brands, or by some other characteristic. The best feature of these Store categories is that when buyers find one of your auctions, the auction page automatically shows them four current auctions you have for similar items. This feature allows you to target customers who are shopping for similar items to the one in the listing they are looking at (see Figure 8-1). If you don't have an eBay Store, we recommend that you start one!

TECHNIQUES FOR FINDING YOUR CUSTOMERS

As you post your antiques or collectible items on eBay, you may be worried that people won't be able to find your goods because there are so many other antiques and collectables listed. Luckily, there are several ways you can drive customers to your eBay auctions. We will discuss four of them in this chapter: key words in your listings, banner ads, links from other Web sites, and other sellers who sell similar items.

Using Key Words for Success

Most of us know something about how key words work in eBay listings. Basically, when someone enters a search word or string of words on eBay's Search page, eBay brings up all the auctions that have this word or words in the title. In addition, eBay allows shoppers to do a search by title and description, which also will search for key words in your description.

The key to success is to always have the right key words in your title and

Figure 8-1 An eBay Store such as this one allows you to easily target customers who are looking for the types of antiques and collectibles you are selling.

listing. As you are first getting started selling antiques and collectibles on eBay, it may take some time to determine which words or keyword phrases will bring the most shoppers to your individual listings (in Chapter 9 we discuss strategies for doing this in detail).

You can also use an auction tag in every auction description. An auction tag is information that you want to be in all of your descriptions, and it usually doesn't change. For example, it could say:

> Save on shipping with multiple purchases. Good luck bidding! We owned Cheryl Leaf Antiques & Gifts in Bellingham, WA. Our Grandmother was Cheryl Leaf, and she owned and operated her store for 52 years and was highly respected in the antiques, vintage, and collectibles business. She was a charter member of the National Association of Dealers in Antiques and wrote many articles for their journal.

You should include key words or search terms that your buyers will likely use, such as *antique, vintage, collectible,* and other terms specific to your category. This tag will make your listings come up every time buyers include one of these words in their title and description searches.

A paragraph in your description about your eBay business and your areas of specialization will also encourage shoppers to keep coming back for more. If you specialize in vintage children's books, you would want to have something like this in all of your listing descriptions:

> I specialize in vintage, antique, collectible, and rare children's child bedtime stories storybooks storybook and books book.

Please check my auctions frequently as I am always listing fresh merchandise.

See how this will encourage customers to keep coming back and will also bring up your listings in the search if someone types in any of your key words or string of words.

Banner Ads

As you have probably noticed on eBay, whenever you enter a key word and place a search, a banner advertisement, and its accompanying auction link, shows up directly above the results. If you click on this banner ad you will be directed to the advertiser's auctions, Store listings, or About Me page. Very nifty. eBay charges for these in an auction format, of course! The company that runs the site will place your Cost per Click (CPC) bids for you based on your maximum bid. You can set a maximum price, such as 55 cents, and the site will determine how much you are paying for each of the key words you use (each key word will have a different price based on its popularity). The best part is that you only pay when a user actually clicks on your ad.

The banner ads are ranked based on what the seller's bid for a particular key word is. The higher the bid for that key word, the more times that ad will be displayed in rotation with other banner ads.

eBay TIP   eBay occasionally offers promotions, such as a $50 credit toward a keyword banner promotion.

Since the banner ad process is a little confusing, the best place to get started is on the Web site. To check out these banner ads on eBay, go to *www.ebaykeywords.com*. It will walk you step-by-step through the process and make it easy to understand. The first step you need to take is to design your banner. For ideas on how to do this, look at some of the other ones that pop up and above all, design the banner ad with your customer in mind (see Figure 8-2).

To ensure success with banner ads you must select the right key words. Sometimes keyword phrases work better and will have a lower bid than just a single word will. Finding that target customer is very important, and using a

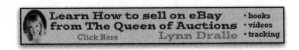

Figure 8-2   A sample banner ad for eBay's "Keyword Banner" promotion.

longer string of words can help bring someone who is serious about buying directly to your items.

You will find that longer strings of words are not as popular and are quite reasonably priced. The lowest price for any click-through is ten cents. You will need to set your maximum bid price for your campaign, and the site will bid for you, just like eBay does. The site shows you exactly what other banners you will be competing against and each of their top bids. Try choosing one and two words, such as *antiques* or *furniture* or *vintage kitchen* to ensure more hits. You will also find out how many times the ad is viewed and how many times someone has clicked-through on it. You can also link the banner to a category in your eBay Store. For more information, check out the Web site for banner ads at *www.ebaykeywords.com*.

There are many other search engines out there that will charge you for key words that link to your Web site or eBay auctions. If the eBay banner ads work for your auction business, check out Google and Yahoo! for more options. Just make sure that it is within your advertising budget and that it really drives sales and adds new customers.

Links from Other Web Sites

Linking from other Web sites is another way to drive traffic to your eBay Store and auctions. If you have your own Web page, you can add a button that asks viewers to "Click Here" to see your eBay auctions. This is a great way to target customers interested in exactly what you are selling.

You can pay for and place ads on many other, similar Web sites. Remember to do your research first and stay within your budget. First, find the Web sites you are interested in linking to. Next, contact them to find out what they charge. They will most likely charge by click-through. Here is a link to the advertising rates on Tias.com, one of the world's largest online antiques malls and definitely worth checking out: *www.tias.com/makeashop/index .cgi?page=bannerad.html*. They charge 30 cents per click for a banner ad. Tias.com also has a great free, e-mailed newsletter, and you can also buy ads to put in their newsletter for $1 per 1000 readers.

You may also want to set up an online store in one of these larger online antiques malls. This is a great way to meet other dealers and get exposure for fixed-price goods. You could also link from that Web site to your eBay auctions.

Networking with Other Sellers

Another way to target customers who will be interested in your antiques and collectibles is to network with other sellers who are selling similar items. There are many ways to do this. You can trade links on your Web sites or set up a referral system. Other dealers selling on eBay can become your friends and colleagues. eBay Live is a convention held every year and is a great place to mingle with other sellers. There are also many chat rooms on eBay itself.

Strike up friendships with other dealers: it will bring in more paying customers for you in the long run.

ANTIQUES WITH INTEGRITY

The number-one way to keep your customers once you have found them is to run your business with integrity. We touched upon this in Chapter 4, but since this is an important topic, we feel it is worth going into in more detail. Remember that the customer is always right, and bend over backwards to make your customer happy. For example, we both have a policy that no matter who is at fault we always take the high road and offer a full refund, including shipping both ways. Be honest and have clearly spelled out customer policies. Keep your customer informed at every step of the eBay process. If you do all of these things, you will ensure high positive feedback for yourself and keep your good customers coming back for more and more of your items. They may even recommend you to their friends!

Honesty in all your dealings is another must. If you know that something is not antique, never list it as an antique. If your piece is damaged or has a defect, note this in your description. If you make a mistake in a listing, fix it or end the auction early and then re-list the item. If you accidentally ship the wrong item to a customer (yes, this does happen), get on the phone immediately and explain the mix-up. Do everything you can to ensure that the customer feels safe dealing with you. Remember that eBay is still an intimidating place to a lot of your customers, and you must take extra care to make them feel secure.

Take a moment and jot down your customer policies. These should be clearly listed in all your auctions. Do you wait 10 days for personal checks to clear before you ship? Do you only ship on Tuesdays and Thursdays? If you let your customers know these things ahead of time you won't run into any surprised and unhappy customers. What is your return policy? Who pays the shipping to return an item? Do you pay the shipping if it was your mistake? What if the buyer just changes his or her mind and wants a refund, who will pay the shipping? Make sure these policies are all clearly stated in your auction listing.

Keeping your customer informed throughout the eBay process is a necessity. It will lead to better feedback for you and save you from many headaches. Let them know immediately after the auction ends what your policies are and what payments you accept. PayPal will automatically send out an e-mail like this for you. Use this automated feature because it will save you time. Once a payment is received and the item shipped, notify the buyer. The United Parcel Service (UPS) will automatically e-mail your customer with the tracking number. This is another fantastic service. If there is going to be a delay in shipping, let the customer know.

BUILD A FOLLOWING FOR YOUR AUCTIONS:
REPEAT CUSTOMERS ARE THE BEST!

Once you have found these great customers, ones who actually pay, it is a great idea to keep them. Lynn has a customer in Las Vegas who buys several items from her each week. Not only does he actually purchase a large quantity, but whenever he bids on items it helps drive up prices.

A good way to keep your customers returning for more is to add a personal touch to what can be a very impersonal way of doing business. Lynn sends out a personal note with each package that gets shipped. It is a newspaper article about her grandmother and her antiques business (see Figure 8-3). At the bottom is a printed message with a blank for the customer's name and a blank for the shipper's name, as well as a link to Lynn's Web site to keep the customer coming back for more.

You could also enclose an order form, which lists other items that are available for purchase. If you don't have a newspaper article or other item to include in each package, even writing a simple "Thank You" on the back of your business card will do nicely.

Almost daily someone e-mails us asking if we have a certain special item. We keep a detailed database of these requests, because we never know when something will become available. You can also actively look for these items for your customers on other Web sites, in antiques stores, and any time you are out buying.

In addition, we keep e-mail addresses and mailing addresses of all of our customers and frequently send out an e-mail to everyone on the list notifying them of a special promotion or other offer.

eBay TIP   Be very careful with the e-mail addresses, because eBay has specific rules about mass e-mails. You should only send to people who have been your customers in the past, and you need to make this very clear in the first sentence of the e-mail, with a sentence like, "Hello, you are receiving this e-mail because you have purchased from us in the past." At the end of the e-mail you must give people an opportunity to be deleted from your mailing list, and then honor their wishes.

Another idea is to mail postcards to your customers. In the Internet age it is fun to get a piece of real mail, and this stands out from the many e-mails people receive every day. Because postcards do incur costs (as opposed to e-mails, which are free), wait until you have a large advertising budget before you plan extravagant promotions. Another promotional idea is to provide free shipping for a month for any auction win. If you work hard to keep your customers happy it will pay off in your bottom-line profits.

IO The Bellingham Business Journal • August 2000

SURVIVOR: CHERYL LEAF ANTIQUES
A closer look at a Bellingham business that has stood the test of time

Ability to change has kept business afloat

Store's founder passed her love of antiques
on to her granddaughter, who now runs
the 50-year-old business

by Jennifer Hayes

Like many 50-year-olds, Cheryl Leaf Antiques & Gifts isn't showing its age. The business is still expanding and adding new products, even though newer antique stores have since come and gone, and the industry has faced increased competition from online auction houses such as eBay.

Lynn Wilson attributes the shop's vitality to her grandmother, Cheryl Leaf, who lived for buying and selling antiques.

"It's amazing. She never slept much. She would string beads and price postcards until midnight. It's great to find something you love that much," said Wilson, who manages the store for the 88-year-old Leaf.

Wilson, who picked up Leaf's enthusiasm for selling old glassware, sculpture and collector plates, has also had a hand in growing the business. Since she took over as manager, Wilson has brought in more gifts, increased revenues by selling antiques online and written books for tracking Internet auction sales and purchases. All of the changes have helped the business increase sales, despite a drop in walk-in traffic to the antique store. Still, Wilson doesn't take the store's success for granted.

"It's getting tougher. We're always going to have to come up with ways to reinvent ourselves," Wilson said.

The real Antiques Road Show

Leaf started collecting antiques when she was eight years old. She found a discarded handcarved beer stein at a neighbor's yard and she got hooked on collecting.

Wilson said Leaf, who was 18 months old when her mother died, probably adored antiques because it created a connection.

"I think she looked for ways to tie her to the past and to her mother," said Wilson.

Those items Leaf's mother owned,

such as a salt dip and a crystal tumbler, Leaf never got rid of.

"With family things, you don't want to sell them," said Wilson.

For years, Leaf acquired items from Hill's Antiques, then located in the Alaska Building (presently occupied by Key Bank) on the corner of State and Holly streets.

Opal Kale, whose mother, Rachel, started Hill's Antiques, said Leaf used to walk from her bookkeeping job downtown and come to the store every payday to make a new purchase. Over time, Leaf learned more about antiques and became good friends with Hill.

"My mom liked her — and she was always a good judge of character," said Kale.

After Leaf amassed a collection of antiques, she decided she wanted to open her own store. She picked a house on Northwest Avenue — then old Highway 99 — and wrote a letter to the city asking for permission to convert some of the rooms into a storefront.

"She used 'Mrs. Elmer Leaf' (her husband's name) in the letter, because she thought the application would go over better," said Wilson.

Leaf's application was approved, and she opened the shop in 1951.

Wilson said the business attracted attention since her grandmother always stocked quality merchandise. She went on buying trips to Europe and Asia, searching for the best items to bring to the store.

However, she refused to buy things that were old just because they were popular. Leaf never understood the reason household items such as cereal boxes and cola bottles gained antique status.

"She always said if something was junk when it was made, it would be junk 100 years from now," said Wilson.

After years of buying and selling, Leaf developed a strong awareness of

the difference between junk and treasure. Using that knowledge, she wrote columns on antique reproductions for the National Association of Dealers in Antiques.

"She is highly thought of in the industry," said Wilson.

However, according to Wilson, Leaf's true talent could be her business acumen. Leaf's father, a former banker, told her early on that the secret to business survival was keeping overhead low. Leaf followed that advice religiously, said Wilson. As the business grew, Leaf avoided hiring staff, added on space to accommodate growing inventory, and always paid cash.

During buying trips around the world, she also kept her eye out for a bargain. Wilson remembers her grandmother buying 1,000 duck decoys on one trip, 100 lamp shades in another.

"If one was good, 100 was better," said Wilson, with a smile.

Summers in Europe

Wilson developed a love of antiques herself after working in her grandmother's store as a 13-year-old. Leaf often took her granddaughter on her European buying trips, and to antique shows across the United States during

→ ONLINE, page 11

Lynn Wilson, the grandaughter of Cheryl Leaf, now manages Leaf's antiques store. When she was younger, Wilson accompanied her grandmother on buying trips to Europe every summer, instilling in her the same love of antiquing.

Dear_____,

We have packed your item with care and want you to be satisfied. If you are happy, please leave us positive feedback.

We recently closed our physical location on August 2nd, 2002 to help serve you better with our on-line business that continues to grow.

Thank you so much for you business!

_____
at Cheryl Leaf Antiques

Email: ldralle@dc.rr.com
www.antiquesandgifts.com
www.queenofauctions.com

Figure 8-3   A personal touch, such as this article about Cheryl Leaf's antiques business, is a great way to stand out from your competition.

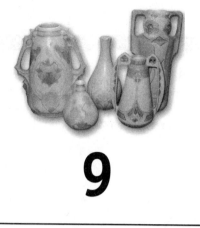

9

Tips for Boosting Sales

Selling antiques and collectibles successfully on eBay depends on you presenting each and every one of your auction listings perfectly. To reach your final destination—making a fortune on eBay—having a sales strategy is very important. This chapter provides the successful tactics we've learned from our own experiences, but for your own sales strategy, you still will have some trial-and-error learning. eBay is constantly changing, and as it changes we must constantly adapt. As in any successful business, change is a certainty. Always evaluate how each tip works for you, and adjust as you go.

USING THE RIGHT KEY WORDS IN YOUR TITLE AND DESCRIPTION

One of the most, if not the most important, selling features on eBay is your listing's title. You have only 55 characters to sell your item, and you should always use each and every character. Do not leave a stone unturned. Why? Because most buyers search only by title instead of by title and description. The more words you have in your title, the more customers you will drive to your listing.

Think about every title from the buyer's perspective. Say you have a purple pansy Winton English bone china plate to sell. If a buyer wanted a purple plate to decorate their kitchen, think about what words they would use to search: purple, plate, pansy, pansies, floral, antique, chic, vintage, bone china, English, decorative, hand-painted, lovely, Victorian, fancy, ruffled, mint. If, on the other hand, they collect Winton English bone china, they will find your listing in your search as well. Because of this, you should pick out the words that you think would most likely be used in a buyer's search. You may also want to include an adjective at the end, like *lovely*. Why? If 125 purple plates come up in the buyer's search, you want something about yours to stand out. If you don't believe it is lovely or unique or rare, why would anyone else?

As a seller of antiques and collectibles, you should always try to include the following in your title:

- Maker
- Era
- Shape
- Origin
- Year
- Best feature
- Color
- Size, if necessary

Our example, "Antique Winton Plate English Purple Pansies Chic Lovely!" covers most of these areas by using all 55 letters: maker: Winton; shape: plate; era: antique; origin: English; best feature: pansies; color: purple; and the fact that it is chic and lovely. The more titles you write the better at it you will become. Practice makes perfect!

PRICING STRATEGIES

Pricing for an antiques store, for a garage sale, or for selling on eBay is a tricky business. It has to do with price elasticity of demand, which is a basic economics model that shows how the consumption of certain goods is more sensitive to a change in price than other goods. For example, a 50 percent increase in the price of cigarettes would make an impact in demand, but not by a great deal because people have difficulty quitting smoking. This is called low elasticity of demand—demand will not change by much. On the other hand, a 50 percent increase in the price of the meals at McDonald's, would reduce their business significantly because there is a lot of competition that offers similar products at lower prices. This is termed high elasticity of demand, which means that demand will change a great deal with a price increase. Why do some items have different elasticities of demand than others? The most important reason is the availability and closeness of substitutes. The more substitutes there are for the product, the higher the elasticity. There aren't any close substitutes for cigarettes (even though there are a lot of different brands), but there are a lot of substitutes for McDonald's—Carls Jr., Burger King, and Jack in the Box. Let's apply this to antiques. If you have a 1971 Royal Copenhagen Christmas plate (there were probably 50,000 made) you have an item with high elasticity of demand. If you charge too much on eBay it will not sell, because there are a lot of available identical substitutes on the same site. So we will price this item very competitively. However, if you have a rare and unique World War II Purple Heart, it will have low elasticity of demand and you will be able to price this item higher.

Another important consideration with antiques is perceived value. Some customers feel that if an antique is priced too low, it is not a good piece. On the other hand, if it is overpriced, customers will walk away and not give your auctions another chance, thinking that you have overpriced all your items.

As an expert in selling antiques and collectibles, Lynn has gone through many pricing strategies during her eBay career. In the beginning, she priced items at the price she wanted to receive. While this protected her from giving anything away, it did not encourage the auction dynamic to kick in—in other words, she rarely had a bidding war that would drive the price higher.

Next, she went through a 99-cent phase, which did not last long, because she found that too many of her things were selling for only 99 cents. A lot of money was lost at this pricing technique.

She now has a happy medium in her pricing strategy (although remember, these are her guidelines and this system might not work for you). The majority of her auctions start at $9.99. At that price point, auction dynamics take over and people start to bid against one another. The $9.99 price makes good business sense, too, in terms of eBay fees. There are price changes in listing fees at 99 cents, $9.99, $24.99, $49.99, $199.99, and up (see Figure 9-1 for listing fee tier). At $9.99, with its associated listing, or insertion, fee of 35 cents, the price is high enough to make money even if it sells only at that list price.

If the item is a rare antique, consider pricing it higher to let the buyers know that it is a "worthy" piece. For example, if it is worth less than $100, the starting price should be anywhere from $24.99 to $99.99 to get the most bang for your listing buck. Keep in mind that there is a big difference between a 35-cent insertion fee for a $9.99 item and a $2.40 insertion fee for a $99.99 listing. This may not sound like much on a single auction, but if you have 100 to 200 auctions up each week the fees can start to add up.

If you think your piece is worth over $100, consider using a hidden reserve, with a low starting price to get the auction going. That way you can ensure you get at least a minimum of what you want to receive. Plus, the $1 to $2 and up extra charge for a reserve-price auction will be refunded if your auction reaches reserve and sells.

When it comes to pricing, be careful about how many fees you are paying, and find out what works for you. Only price your items high if they are rare, have low elasticity of demand, or have sentimental value. If you are selling something that has sentimental value, do your research and find out what it is worth. If it is worth $200 and you are happy with receiving that price, then start the auction at $199 or set a hidden reserve for that amount. If you protect yourself you will make the most money.

Starting Price, Opening Value or Reserve Price	Insertion Fee
$0.01 - $0.99	$0.30
$1.00 - $9.99	$0.35
$10.00 - $24.99	$0.60
$25.00 - $49.99	$1.20
$50.00 - $199.99	$2.40
$200.00 - $499.99	$3.60
$500.00 and up	$4.80

eBay Picture Services Fees

Feature	Fee
First picture	FREE!
Each additional Picture	$0.15
Preview Picture	Free
Slide Show	$0.75
Supersize Image	$0.75
Picture Pack	$1.00 (a $1.75 value)

Listing Upgrades Fees

As a seller, you can choose several optional features to help promote your listing. Please note that these fees are **non-refundable**.

Listing Upgrade	Listing Upgrade Fee
Home Page Featured	$39.95 (single quantity) or $79.95 (quantity of 2 or more)
Featured Plus!	$19.95
Highlight	$5.00
Item Subtitle	$0.50
Bold	$1.00
Listing Designer*	$0.10
Gallery	$0.25
Gallery Featured	$19.95
List in Two Categories	Double the insertion and listing upgrades fees (excluding Scheduled Listings and Home Page Featured).
10-Day Duration *The longest listing duration available*	$0.20
Scheduled Listings	$0.10
Buy It Now	$0.05
Gift Services	$0.25

* No Listing Designer fee for Selling Manager Pro subscribers.

Return to top

Additional Reserve Price Auction fee (fully refunded if item sells):

Reserve Price	Reserve Price Auction Fee
$0.01 - $49.99	$1.00
$50.00 - $199.99	$2.00
$200.00 and up	1% of Reserve Price (with a maximum of $100.00)

Final Value Fees

Closing Value	Final Value Fee
$0 - $25	5.25% of the closing value
$25 - $1,000	5.25% of the initial $25 ($1.31), plus 2.75% of the remaining closing value balance ($25.01 to $1,000)
Over $1,000	5.25% of the initial $25 ($1.31), plus 2.75% of the initial $25 - $1000 ($26.81), plus 1.50% of the remaining closing value balance ($1000.01 - closing value)

Figure 9-1　This chart shows eBay's current fees. If you are listing multiple antiques and collectibles, you can play with the price point until you find what is most cost-effective and profitable.

LISTING FEATURES

eBay has many extra features that they would love for you to pay for and use. When it comes to selling to the antiques and collectibles market, there are extra features that are worth the money and others that aren't.

The first place eBay wants you to spend your money is to list your item in two categories, such as both *Antiques* and *Collectibles*. Use this feature very selectively, because it actually doubles your listing fees without a whole lot of benefits. If, for example, you were to list 400 items at a starting price of $99 and put each item in two categories, you would spend $1,640 before you actually sold anything!

eBay claims that listing in two categories will bring more people to see your auction, but most buyers do not buy by category, they find their items though title searches. The only reason to list in double categories is if both categories are super-specific. Please see the example in Chapter 12 of a Vienna bronze inkwell bird that was listed in two specific categories, *Inkwells* and *Bronzes*. But even so, it may not be the best use of your money.

The next added feature to consider is whether or not to include a subtitle. The subtitle costs 50 cents, and the words that you use in the subtitle will not be picked up in an eBay title search but is instead used to further explain your item once a buyer is looking at the auctions that his or her search pulled (see Figure 9-2). Because of the extra cost, this feature works best on very expensive items that the first 55 characters just can't completely identify.

The Buy-It-Now feature is worth the 5-cent fee if you have duplicates of one item and can set a fair price that makes you money. This feature doesn't work as well with antiques, but for some common collectibles that you have a lot of, it will allow you to sell items faster.

eBay TIP If a buyer e-mails you and asks you to end your auction early by adding a Buy-It-Now price, *do not do it*! This is a great indication that you have a very rare item and that your customer is trying to save money. Politely explain that it is your policy to never end an auction early, because most bidders wait until the last seconds to place their bids and you don't want any angry customers.

Scheduling an auction to start at a date and time that is not exactly 3, 5, 7, or 10 days from when you list it is a great feature. For only 10 cents, you can

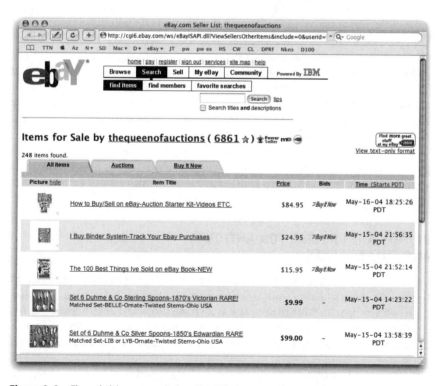

Figure 9-2 The subtitle appears below the title in an auction search.

schedule your auctions to start at any time up to 3 weeks out. Use this feature when you are out on an antiques buying trip or on vacation. We don't recommend paying for Designer Themes at 10 cents, Bold at $1, or Highlight at $5. You can make your own listings look great with simple html. See Dennis Prince's book *How to Sell Anything on eBay . . . and Make a Fortune!* for more tips on this. The reviews are mixed on Featured Plus for $19.95 and Home Page Featured for $39.95. You may want to try these, but make sure you have all your ducks in a row and really understand what you want it to accomplish for your business, because $39.95 is a big price. These expensive features may work great if you have a very rare and desirable antique piece of furniture. Gift Services, at 25 cents, is basically a waste of money. Most buyers know that if they ask, you will ship directly to a gift recipient, and most antiques and collectibles purchases are personal anyway, not for gift giving. There is one feature that is free on the listing page. "Free?" you ask. "It can't be." It probably won't stay that way for long, but for now the Andale Page Counters are free, and we love these. Use them in all of your auctions. They count the number of visitors to your auction page. You can have the counter showing or hidden. Counters that show are great because when you get a lot of visitors to your auction it makes other bidders nervous about bidding. Antique collectors are a very competitive bunch, and this will drive them crazy! The more views your antique auction shows, the higher they will want to bid. The counters can also be used to measure how the auction title is working and to see how interested people are in the item. If your item doesn't sell the first time out and 20 to 100 people looked at it (this is a lot of people for an antique or collectible item), then the price is probably too high. If it was a $9.99 item, maybe lower the starting bid to $2.99 and try again. If it was a $99 item, lower it to $49.99, a $49.99 item to $24.99, and a $24.99 item to $9.99. You will still be following the price divisions in the listing-fee chart and getting the most for your money! If 20 people or less looked at the item, then your title may need work. If your title has hit all the key points, then this may be an item that isn't in much demand and may never sell.

PHOTOS ARE CRUCIAL FOR ANTIQUES AND COLLECTIBLES

Selling antiques and collectibles requires photos. If you are new to selling in these areas, you probably want to know how many photos you need and what photos must be with your listing. If it is a straightforward auction, such as for a single plate, then one picture will do. If it is an expensive item, such as a large antique dresser with a matching mirror, then two to six pictures is a good idea.

If a piece of glass, pottery, or china has a signature, it is a good idea to

Figure 9-3 By inserting a smaller photo of a signature on your original photo *before* posting it on eBay, such as with this dinnerware, you can save money on each auction you list.

show the signature or you may be asked to e-mail extra photos later, which will take up a lot of your valuable time. You can actually show the signature and the item using just one photo by taking a photo of the signature and placing it in the corner of your main photo. It works great and will save you 15 cents (in additional photo charges) every time (see Figure 9-3).

Using the Gallery Photo feature is important for antiques and collectibles as well. For those of you who do not know what a gallery photo looks like, refer to Figure 9-2. These are the little photos to the left of each listing that automatically come up in an auction search. It costs 25 cents but is well worth it, especially because people are very concerned with how items in these categories look. Because so many people use this feature now, you lose the competitive edge, but one of Lynn's students recently told her, "I only search auctions on eBay that have gallery pictures," so it's expected. Nevertheless, if your item does not sell the first time out, consider removing the gallery photo to save yourself 25 cents.

For items such as antique furniture that require photos from a lot of angles and that will likely sell for more than $100, consider putting up four to six pictures and paying for the Picture-Pack option. You will find that with more expensive items your buyer will want to feel that he has actually seen and touched the item, so photos of antiques and collectibles must be clear and focused. Thus, make sure that your digital camera has a good zoom lens and can take excellent close-up photos of patterns and signatures.

England: Periods by Reign	
Gothic	1000-1600
Elizabethan	1558-1603
Jacobean	1603-1688
William and Mary	1689-1701
Queen Anne	1702-1713
George I	1714-1726
George II	1727-1759
George III	1760-1819
Regency (approx.)	1810-1820
George IV	1820-1830
William IV	1830-1836
Victorian	1837-1901
Edwardian	1901-1919

England: Periods by Designer	
Chippendale	1750-1780
Adam	1760-1790
Hepplewhite	1770-1800
Sheraton	1795-1815

United States: Periods by Common Name	
Shaker/Primitive	1620-1900
Pilgrim	1630-1690
William and Mary	1690-1725
Queen Anne	1725-1750
Chippendale	1750-1780

Federal	1780-1820
Classical/Empire	1815-1850
Victorian and Renaissance Revival	1837-1901
Eastlake	1870-1890
Anglo-Japanese	1880-1910
Art Nouveau	1895-1910
also known as	1890-1914
Colonial Revival	1880-1925
Mission/Arts and Crafts	1895-1920
Golden Oak	1890-1930
Art Deco	1910-1930
Eames/Midcentury Modern	1945-1969

France	
Louis XIII	1610-1643
Louis XIV	1643-1715
Louis XV	1715-1774
Louis XVI	1774-1792
French Country	1790-1940
Directoire	1795-1800
Empire	1800-1815
Louis XVIII and Charles X	1814-1830
Louis Phillipe	1830-1850
Second Empire	1850-1870
Louis XV and Louis XVI Revivals	1870-1930

All years are approximate

Figure 9-4   Use this chart as a general guideline for the dates of different eras.

ERAS AND THE McKINLEY ACT

One of the most important details you can feature in your listing title, besides the date or year, is the era that your item comes from (see Figure 9-4). Many buyers search by era; for example someone may type in the key words "Eames era," because he is furnishing his entire vacation home in midcentury modern.

A very important concept in the marking of antiques came about because of the McKinley Tarriff Act of 1891. It was an American act that required foreign-made imports to be stamped or labeled in English with their country of origin, using "Made in _____." If a piece is marked "Made in England" or "Made in China" you can be relatively certain that it was made after 1891. If it says nothing, or just "China," you can assume that it was made prior to 1891, but this gets tricky. The item may have been marked with a paper label that has fallen off, or the item may not have been made for export to the United States, in which case, it did not have to be marked. Nevertheless, this is a very useful piece of information to help you date your items.

In Chapters 11 through 16, we will discuss in detail how each era affects different categories of antiques. But for now, just remember that including specific eras in your listings is a key selling strategy. Refer to Figure 9-4 for some dating ranges for eras, but keep in mind that these years are just guidelines and you will find varied date ranges in different research books. We discuss some of the more recent and popular American eras here: Victorian, Art Nouveau, Mission, Art Deco, Eames, and the 1960s, 1970s, and 1980s. Items that you have a good chance of coming across in your buying trips will most likely be from one of these eras.

Victorian, 1837–1901

The Victorian era is named after Queen Victoria, who reigned from 1837 until 1901. Known for its overornamentation, this was a time of intense creativity, nostalgia, exaggeration, and experimentation. During this period, many artisans turned to past styles, such as Gothic, rococo, Byzantine, Romanesque, and reworked designs of earlier eras. These revivalists and their wares all became lumped under the heading "Victorian." Some examples include the use of garnets, cameo jewelry, gaudy furniture, and elaborate vases.

After Prince Albert died in 1861, Queen Victoria went into mourning for the rest of her life. She wore mostly black, and this influenced much of the art and antiques of that later time period. Victorian mourning pieces are quite collectible and include things such as hair jewelry and ornate, lavish funeral-remembrance pieces (see Figure 9-5).

Figure 9-5 Victorian mourning jewelry: a locket made from the dearly departed's hair. A very collectible item!

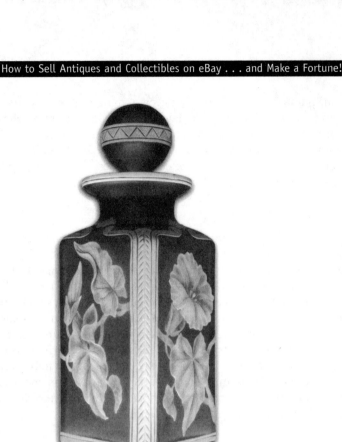

Figure 9-6   Art nouveau cameo glass perfume bottle, unsigned but attributed to Webb.

Art Nouveau, 1895–1910 or 1890–1914

Art nouveau was established as the first decorative style of the twentieth century at the 1900 World's Fair in Paris. Its style is decorative, characterized by curving lines, and influenced by nature, especially flowers. It was developed by a brilliant and energetic generation that sought to form a new fashion trend. As the Industrial Revolution sparked new ideas based on new technologies and lifestyles, some people retreated into the past, embracing the spirit world, fantasies, and myth. Art nouveau was in direct opposition to mass production and was aimed at taking decorative arts to the highest level. These talented artists brought high standards and unique craftsmanship to everyday items. The pieces can be creative, colorful, and artistically daring. Some famous makers of this period include Daum Nancy, Tiffany, Galle, Steuben, and Webb Cameo, and pieces from this era continue to be in demand (see Figure 9-6).

Figure 9-7 Arts and Crafts oak chairs: lady's rocker (left) and gentleman's chair (right), both of mortise-and-tenon construction and in the Stickley style, 1908.

Mission/Arts and Crafts 1895–1920

Out of all the excess came simplicity. This movement turned against the overly ornate and bulky Victorian styles and went back to basics. Plain, honest lines that showed workmanship were common.

It was an intellectual movement that led to new architecture and new interior designs. Gustave Stickley and Frank Lloyd Wright were architects who also designed furniture. Stickley's designs were in radical opposition to Victorian froufrou (see Figure 9-7). His style was bold, angular, and reminiscent of the rustic furniture of the Southwest American style (Spanish-American), which is where the term *mission* comes from. These designers used massive oak boards and mortise-and-tenon construction, with the tenons often pegged and passing through the mortise as a design element. The furniture design crossed over into pottery, metalwork, and other decorative pieces of the period. The lines were sleek, the workmanship apparent (think hand-hammered copper vases), and elements squared off. It was much less fluid than art nouveau, and if you did see elements from nature such as a pine cone or a poppy flower, they would be stylized. This era is hugely popular in the general population and on eBay. Many homes are decorated strictly in the mission style, and using "mission" or "Arts and Crafts" in your title can bring you many bidders.

Figure 9-8 The Chrysler Building in New York City is a famous example of art deco style.

Art Deco, 1910–1930

Art deco is often confused with art nouveau; in fact, they are very different. Art deco was a mix of modern decorative-art styles and drew from the avant-garde painting styles of the early twentieth century. It was a bit cubism, Russian constructivism, and Italian futurism, all ending up with simplification and geometric shapes. The aesthetic included intense colors and celebrated the rise of technology and speed, which art nouveau was protesting against.

This geometric style permeated almost every facet of life during this time frame, including architecture, clothing, jewelry, home furnishings, and even appliances. The name came from the Exposition Internationale de Arts Decoratifs Industriels et Moderenes, held in Paris in 1925. This exposition celebrated life in the modern world. Keep in mind that the eras that affect art

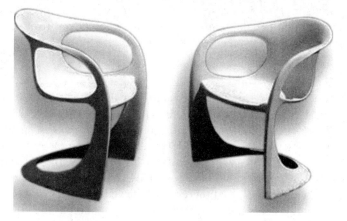

Figure 9-9 Pantone-style, sleek, Eames-era chairs such as these are in high demand and worth in the $300–$400 range.

and antiques are the very same that influence all aspects of our lives, including our architecture (see Figure 9-8). This is important to remember when we are trying to spot new trends.

Art deco is a very sought-after era on eBay. There are people who collect just deco items. A recent completed-auction title search on eBay using "art deco" yielded 32,913 items. Now that is big business!

Eames/Midcentury Modern, 1945–1969

Eames-era items are very sleek and modern. This type of design was a response to the end of World War II, when Americans and the rest of the world needed a radical change. Steel, plywood, and plastic were used to meet the demand for more multipurpose, space-saving, and affordable objects. Charles Eames (1907–1978), an American industrial designer and architect, is famous for the now-classic, prize-winning chair that is constructed of molded plywood on metal. His designs span the period from 1945 to 1969, and his and other pieces from this time frame are referred to as Eames era. Items from this era are consistently hot on eBay (see Figure 9-9).

Peace and Love: Op Art, 1960s

This book would not be complete without touching on newer eras in collectibles. The 1960s are being termed op art (optical art), for the art that was all the rage in 1965. Highlights from this era are the 1964 New York World's Fair, miniskirts in 1965, *Star Trek* in 1966, and Woodstock in 1969—and collectibles related to these topics are constant favorites on eBay. The first man on the moon in 1969 was also an important event. The peace-and-love-decade collectibles include items as diverse as lunch boxes, toys, televisions (technology), and wild psychedelic furnishings.

Disco Decade, 1970s

There isn't a specific term used consistently on eBay for the 1970s yet, but there are great collectibles from this era. This decade brought us *The Godfather* in 1972, *American Graffiti* in 1973, and *Saturday Night Live* in 1975. The 1970s were famous for Pet Rocks and Mood Rings. Technology reached new heights with the VCR in 1975. Disco fever hit in 1977 with *Saturday Night Fever*, and 1978 brought us punk rock. This could definitely be called the disco decade! Collectibles from this era include yellow smiley faces, turquoise jewelry, and bulky Texas Instrument calculators (technology again).

Total Excess, 1980s

The 1980s was a decade of total excess. Sony Walkman debuted in 1980, and everyone was wearing designer jeans. Princess Diana and Prince Charles were married in 1981. The aerobic-video craze began in 1982, and compact discs came out that same year. The year 1983 brought us Cabbage Patch Dolls. The big movie of 1987 was *Fatal Attraction*. People wanted more expensive houses, cars, and clothes and a more extravagant way of life. Collectibles to consider from this decade are Rubik's Cubes, designer clothes, and Atari video games.

RECAP OF TIPS TO BOOST SALES

There are many ways to increase your sales volume on eBay. Some of the easier ones are pricing correctly, using the best eBay listing features, and having the right photos. Don't overlook how important your title and description can be, and definitely select your key words carefully. "Era" is one of the most important key words that people search by. Study your eras and *always* include your item's era in your title. Remember the 32,913 items with "art deco" in the title! That's amazing!

10

Packing and Shipping

After the fun of hunting for treasures, doing your research, and actually selling your items on eBay for big bucks comes the reality of packing and shipping! Packing and shipping with great care is a crucial way to ensure your customer's continuing happiness. In this chapter, we'll discuss the specifics of packing and shipping valuable and often fragile antiques and collectibles.

YOUR WORK SPACE

The first step in this whole process is to set aside a dedicated work space. Most of you probably already have an office or desk area that houses your computer and is probably where you work when you list on eBay. The work area we are talking about in this section is an area set aside for the receipt, photography, storage, care, and packing of your goods. You don't need one whole room devoted to this. You can use several different areas to meet the varied requirements.

If you are lucky enough to have an entire room devoted to your eBay activities, then set up a large table for the receipt of goods. A nice 3-by-8-foot table is perfect for when you haul in all your garage-sale finds on Saturday morning. If you don't have an entire room, then set aside a part of your garage, the utility room, or an unused closet to house the new merchandise.

It's a good idea to keep a shelf next to your work table for storing items before you mail them. The storage area is the most important area, because this is where your goods will sit unattended and unwrapped for at least one week if not an entire month. Why that long? It can take some buyers up to three weeks to pay, and this added to a seven-day auction makes for a month.

This shelf can be in a corner of your eBay room, or it can be shelving in

Figure 10-1 Here is a sample storage shelf that protects items and keeps them readily accessible.

your garage or that linen closet that you aren't using. The main thing is that it be safely out of the major traffic paths in your house. Also, because so many antiques and collectibles are breakable, make sure your shelving is sturdy and that it is attached to the wall in case of an earthquake or another disaster (see Figure 10-1).

eBay TIP Place your items on these shelves once their pictures have been taken. Keep in mind that you may have to find them again to help you respond to the inquiries you will receive and the questions the buyers will ask. Often, potential buyers will ask, "Can I please see a close-up of the signature on that chess set?" If the items are accessible, it makes it easy for you to answer their questions and most likely improve your chances of making the sale!

When it comes time to ship the sold items it is wonderful to have another work table. You can use the same table that you use for receipt of goods and as your staging for photos, but we recommend having a different one if you have the space. Look for a table with shelves underneath it, which allows convenient storage for shipping supplies. Because shipping can be messy—the packing peanuts you will be using can stick to everything—consider having a packing area outside your house.

Another key item to have in your packing area is a large packing-peanut dispenser (see Figure 10-2). This can hang from a garage ceiling and

Figure 10-2 This packing-peanut dispenser allows you to pack quickly and helps protect delicate antiques and collectibles.

makes it easy to dispense packing peanuts. These run about $150. They are worth the expense, but make sure you are making a solid profit before you buy one.

PACKING FRAGILE GOODS

Most antiques and collectibles are fragile goods. There is nothing that makes a customer angrier than having their one-of-a-kind item—which they spent years searching for, weeks bidding on, and days waiting for—arrive broken. Make sure you always pack these items well, regardless of whether they are worth $1,000 or $2.99. Especially fragile items include glassware, pottery, china, plastics, and some metalware. Most people don't realize that metal and plastic can be breakable, but these pieces can easily be dented or bruised. If in doubt about an item, consider it fragile and pack it as such.

Fragile items must be either double boxed or bubble wrapped (see Figure 10-3). To double box an item, first wrap it in tissue and then place it in a box that fits very snuggly around it. If you use bubble wrap instead of a box, wrap the bubble wrap around your item and secure the wrap with packing tape. Next place either the box or the bubble-wrapped item inside a box that will allow for two inches on all sides. Fill the empty spaces to the top with packing peanuts.

eBay TIP   Remember to put a note or your business card inside the box to help you build a strong base of repeat customers.

After you have everything in the box, secure it with packing tape. Write the customer's name on the outside of the box, especially if you aren't going to ship it that day. If you forget to do this, you will spend hours opening up already-packed items, trying to figure out what is what.

SMALL NONBREAKABLES

Nonbreakable items are wonderful to ship, which makes your life so much easier. Examples of unbreakable items would be paper goods, linens, rugs, quilts, books, and stamps. Really tiny unbreakable items can even be packed in a hard, small box and still fit in a flat envelope.

Unbreakable items can often be sent in flat, strong cardboard envelopes or mailers. Flat-rate priority envelopes from the United States Postal Service (USPS) are great for many of these items, and no matter what they weigh, the cost is only $3.85. Just wrap a piece of tissue around the item, enclose your thank-you card, and drop it in a cardboard envelope or mailer.

Figure 10-3 Vase packed with bubble wrap and packing peanuts and ready to be shipped.

SOURCES FOR SHIPPING SUPPLIES

Now let's discuss the items you will need for your shipping station. If you ship via UPS you will need to purchase all of these supplies. If you ship USPS priority you will not need to purchase the boxes; they are provided free of charge, which makes for a significant savings.

- *Bubble Wrap.* This is a must. It runs about $30 a roll.
- *Packing Tape.* Also a necessity, you can buy it by the case to save money.
- *Packing Peanuts.* These are good, but not cheap. A 14-cubic-foot bag should run you $15 wholesale.
- *Tissue Paper.* This is nice to have on hand but you'll likely find that you don't have to go out and purchase it. You'll get enough when you buy items at garage sales, auctions, or from other dealers.
- *Boxes.* These are a necessary evil. Expect to pay between 15 and 50 cents for each box.

Shop around and try to find a wholesale shipping supplier in your area. U-Line, for example, is a great place, with locations in Los Angeles, Chicago, Atlanta, Dallas, Minneapolis, and Newark, New Jersey. Check their prices at *www.uline.com.* There are also companies selling packing supplies on eBay. Check it out!

HOW TO CHOOSE THE BEST CARRIER

There are many choices for shippers these days. UPS, FedEx, and the USPS are the most common for items that are not oversized and are under 70 pounds. Lynn uses UPS for fragile items going to the 48 continental states and the USPS for international shipments, for packages going to Alaska and Hawaii, and for all nonbreakables.

Shipping Internationally

UPS and FedEx are not viable options for shipping overseas or to Alaska and Hawaii. They both charge too much and only ship by air. UPS also requires all sorts of customs forms to be filled out, and your international buyers will not be happy about the duty charges. Most international buyers will request USPS service anyway. When Lynn first started selling on eBay in 1999, she shipped a carton of book binders to Canada by UPS. It not only cost a fortune to ship—$28—but the buyer phoned to say he had refused the package because UPS had placed customs forms on the package and was requesting another $25 in duty. It was an expensive lesson to learn. Again, stick with the post office for shipments to Alaska, Hawaii, and overseas.

Consider charging buyers a handling charge in addition to the USPS price because there are so many forms to fill out and someone may have to wait in line at the post office to complete these shipments. Most overseas buyers will not request insurance because then they must pay duty on the declared insured amount.

Domestic Shipping

The two biggest companies for shipping are UPS and the USPS, but FedEx is becoming more competitive because of their expanded ground service. There are pros and cons for these companies. UPS picks up from any home-based business—for about $8 to $10 a week for a regularly scheduled daily pickup, and for about $1 to $5 per package for individually scheduled pickups. This service can save a lot of time!

UPS has online record keeping, allowing you to print out great labels, and processes automatic e-mails to your customers with their tracking number. They also issue a free tracking number with each package, and insurance up to $100 is automatically included. Also, UPS is very quick to pay a claim if an item is lost or damaged. Not so with the USPS. You can spend a lifetime trying to get a claim processed and paid from the government, which is why it's best not to use them for breakables.

The downside of UPS Ground Service is that you must supply your own boxes, and that it takes a lot longer for goods to reach their destination. It can take seven to eight working days from coast to coast. UPS rates are competitive with USPS once you add the additional cost of tracking and insurance to the Priority Mail price.

DETERMINING SHIPPING AND HANDLING FEES

Consider setting a fixed price for all your UPS shipping fees. From years of experience we have found that we break even by doing this without spending all day e-mailing shipping rates back and forth based on certain zip codes. Here is a breakdown of the fixed prices we use:

- For small breakables, charge $7, shipping, handling, and insurance.
- For medium items $8, shipping, handling, and insurance.
- If items are much larger, charge $10, $15, even up to $35, based on the size and weight.

eBay TIP   Remember, UPS does charge by volume (dimensions) or weight, whichever is greater. Don't get burned with this. One seller we know started out selling on eBay with a large picture frame 24 by 36 inches. He quoted $8 for shipping, handling, and insurance. The volume turned out to be greater than the two pounds he thought he would be charged on it and he ended up paying $30 in volume shipping charges on a $10 sale.

For nonbreakable items, it works well to ship by the USPS. They provide free boxes, flat cardboard mailers, and labels as long as you ship via Priority Mail. They have super-quick delivery that usually takes just 2 or 3 days. By the time you e-mail your customer that their items have shipped by this method, they usually have already received the item. The USPS charges an additional 40 cents for tracking, and insurance is also additional, $1.30 for the first $50, $2.20 for up to $100, and it increases from there. This can get pricey. Lynn ships a lot of jewelry, paper goods, flatware, and books using the $3.85 flat rate priority envelope (see Figure 10-4) and charges $5 for shipping and handling. She doesn't pay for insurance on these items but if someone requests it she'll switch the item over to UPS and ship that way with the included insurance.

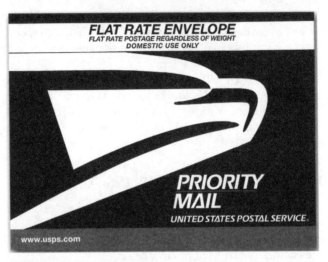

Figure 10-4   The USPS free, flat-rate Priority Envelope is perfect for nonbreakable items. Shipping cost for this envelope is a flat $3.85.

Craters and Freighters

If you are shipping large items, like antique furniture, Greyhound is a great alternative. They will take pieces of furniture that weigh up to 100 pounds. For about $50 you can ship a chair, small dresser, or trunk cross-country. Check with your local Greyhound office for rates and requirements. Craters and Freighters, *www.cratersandfreighters.com*, will come to your location and pack up large pieces of furniture and arrange for their shipping. This service is expensive, but it is an option. You can also contact your local freight companies and get quotes. This means that you would have to prepare the piece of furniture for shipment. Crates, large cardboard boxes, and/or lots of padding are required. We will go into more detail on this in Chapter 11.

Shipping is one of the most important building blocks on the road to your eBay fortune. It will be what keeps your customers coming back for more or what turns them away forever. Spend the extra time to ensure a happy and successful transaction by packing with care. Take a look sometime at feedback comments for different sellers. Almost 50 percent of feedback refers to shipping—how fast the package arrived, how well packed it was, and how well-informed the seller kept the buyer. Be a winner and build a strong foundation for your eBay business with a well-thought-out shipping system.

PART 3

BECOMING AN EXPERT ANTIQUES AND COLLECTIBLES SELLER

11

Making Your Fortune with Furniture

Furniture is a great category, and one that is often overlooked and ignored by many dealers because of the sheer size of the pieces. If you have chosen furniture as one of your areas of expertise then you will have tremendous opportunities to make your fortune. To be successful in this category, you will need to think and work outside of the box. You will need a can-do attitude to sell furniture on eBay. Instead of thinking, I can't possibly move that huge piece of furniture to my home, repair it, restore it, refinish it, and then pack and ship it! you must think, I can move that big piece of furniture and make it look lovely. I can ship it across the country for a reasonable price, and because I am willing to try, the monetary rewards will be all the larger. Remember, furniture is typically higher priced than the rest of the smalls we discuss in this book. Instead of having to sell 100 items a week to make a living, you may only need to sell four or five. Now doesn't that sound great!

THE BREAKDOWN OF SUBCATEGORIES

The *Furniture* category is made up of a few subcategories on eBay. We will be discussing architectural parts such as keys, drawer pulls, locks, doorknobs, and other hardware, but we will look mainly at pieces of furniture as a whole. This is a big category with many different eras and influences, and because of the vastness of this topic, we have to be very general to fit within the scope of this book. We will discuss American furniture from 1650 forward. The chances of you just happening across really old "period" pieces is not that great. If you decide to specialize just in furniture from this era, you will need to do a lot more research than we provide here. This book places a special emphasis on the eight areas that eBay recognizes to describe the style of your furniture piece—Gothic, French country, Empire, rustic/primitive, Victorian,

Art Deco, Mission, and midcentury modern. The shapes, woods, and styles will transcend eras, however, and we will cover the basics here so that you will be able to identify these three things. If you can identify the shape, wood, and style of a piece of furniture it is very easy to do Internet and eBay research.

WHAT ARE PEOPLE LOOKING FOR?

Furniture is great because it actually gets used. Furniture accommodates basic household functions such as sitting, writing, sleeping, eating, and storing things. Many people find that antique furniture is less expensive than new pieces and that it is also a good investment. Lynn's grandmother's frequently taught, even in the 1950s, that "antique furniture is the best value today, as the value of antiques remains far more constant than that of new furniture." This is still true today.

The demand for furniture is as varied as the different tastes in home decor. Some people prefer French Empire, some Amish plain, and others over-the-top Victorian. It is hard to say who the best artisans, brands, and manufacturers are since it really is a matter of individual taste. Most furniture was not signed, which can cause some difficulties for the seller. When you are looking for pieces to purchase, you can't go wrong with good-quality materials, good craftsmanship, and the unique and unusual. A good rule of thumb is "Always buy the best example you can afford." Customer demand remains constant for high-quality, functional pieces. Chairs, dressers, and desks are popular pieces because most people need them. Also, smaller pieces of furniture are always nice because they don't take up as much space and are easily moved around.

WHAT'S HOT ON eBAY

To learn what's selling on eBay, a fantastic resource is their *Hot Seller* report. You can find this by going to "Services," then on "Seller Central," then to "What's Hot" (see Figure 11-1).

A look at the *Furniture* category shows that it is not broken down into really specific categories. It is very general. A current "super hot" subcategory in antique furniture is *American 1800–1849*, which would include Classical/Empire and Victorian styles. Another "super hot" category is *European Pre-1800*, which includes so many styles it is almost impossible to name them, but the list includes, from England, Chippendale, Adam, Heppelwhite, William and Mary, Queen Anne, and, from France, Louis XIV, XV, and XVI, and so forth. *Post-1900* furniture that is hot includes anything from mission to Eames-era. And finally, *American furniture 1850–1899* that would still encompass late-Victorian styles is also a hot area.

These trends are constantly changing, so it is a good idea to check this

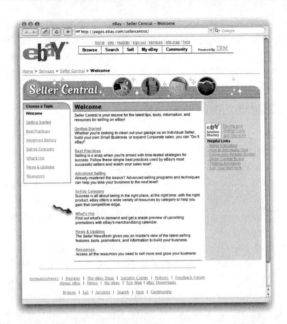

Figure 11-1   Click on "What's Hot" on eBay for a pdf file download of helpful information about what is selling.

invaluable tool on a monthly basis. eBay updates this report approximately once every two months. It's smart, too, to keep a current copy of the report handy to refer to each time you go out buying.

BUILDING YOUR FURNITURE INVENTORY

Where to Find Inventory

You will need start-up inventory to sell furniture on eBay, and the best places to start your hunt are antiques shops, consignment shops, classified ads, live auctions, and eBay itself. Furniture is actually priced very differently in different parts of the country, even more so than small goods. The reason for this disparity in pricing is that furniture is much harder to transport, so there has not been the same leveling of prices that one sees in small glassware and dinnerware items. A Victorian marble-top table that is for sale in a sunny Southern California antiques store will not sell for as much as it would in an East Coast store. The flip side of this is that an Eames-era plastic dining set will not fetch as much in Kansas as it would in San Francisco. There are definite trends in prices in different parts of the country, based on supply and demand. You can use this to your advantage when buying furniture to sell on eBay.

When you start to build your inventory, look for items in your local market that are undervalued because of low demand. Antique furniture can still be found at reasonable prices in America because it is not easy to throw a large piece of furniture on eBay like it is to sell china or dinnerware. It does take effort, but if you want to make your fortune selling furniture on eBay, then specialize and go the extra mile.

Lynn has found great buys on furniture in local stores, in consignment shops, and at auctions. Furniture seems to sell for very low prices at most local auctions. Spend some time sitting through a weekend auction and you will be surprised by how easily you can pick up some bargains, especially if you know your stuff.

Another great idea is to take a camper and travel around the country buying furniture. You will be able to use your knowledge about the items that are selling in your neck of the woods for big bucks but that may not be selling in the Midwest. For example, Lynn (who lives in California) looks for Eames-era plastics and mission oak when she travels to the Midwest, where it can sell for much less. Back in California, the demand is higher because the customer base interested in these types of items is closer and can drive to pick up the items.

Classified advertisements are another great place to look for furniture. You wouldn't believe how much furniture is sold in this manner. When you see an ad, simply call up the advertisers and ask exactly what they have and for what prices.

Finally, get on eBay and search for good buys in furniture. The summer is quite slow on eBay, and this is a great time to pick up some bargains. You can spend the summer months repairing, refinishing, and getting your items ready to sell in the fall. Search on eBay by region and buy things that are close to you so that you don't spend any money on shipping (unless, of course, you get a great deal and can factor the shipping costs into the total price).

Other Sourcing Options

To keep a steady stream of furniture coming into your business it is nice to set up some deals with stores or manufacturers. Visit local consignment shops and dealers in your area and let them know that you are willing to buy good-quality items that have sat around for a while. If you can establish a good relationship with these dealers, they will call you first when they get ready to mark down their items. These can be invaluable relationships to have. Of course, always do your research first and know what you can afford to pay so you know when you are getting the best bargains.

Placing a want ad in the local paper is a great way to keep merchandise flowing. Make a note that you will buy entire households of furniture. There is usually a lot of furniture at garage and yard sales, and it is usually very reasonably priced because the sellers need to clear it out by the end of the day.

eBay TIP Be sure to hit the garage-sale circuit later in the day, when people are ready to bargain. Be prepared to haul away what you purchase right then and there. Invest in a good truck or van. You can pick up a used truck or van for a good price, and it is a necessity if you'll be selling furniture.

Another place to look for both antique and vintage furniture is overseas. Lynn's grandmother actually brought containers of furniture over from Europe in the 1960s, before it became so popular. And today, there are still some bargains to be found if you plan ahead and do your research. Consider specifically looking in some of the developing areas of the world, such as Russia, South America, and Bali, where unique pieces can still be found for reasonable prices. It sounds like a lot of fun, and the whole experience can be a tax write-off.

Furniture Fakes and Frauds

Furniture is divided into several categories: antique, reproduction, period, and vintage (used). Antique furniture is anything that was made 100 years ago or more; however, antique furniture can still not be as valuable as its modern counterpart. Why? Because there was poor craftsmanship 100 years ago just as there is today. This is a valuable lesson to keep in mind as you build your inventory: just because it is old does not always mean that it is valuable. An antique can also be a reproduction, which is a copy of an earlier style. As an example, a Duncan Phyfe chair that was made in 1900 would be considered antique but also a reproduction, since the style was originally made in the time period of 1801 to 1825. A Duncan Phyfe chair that was made in 1820 would be a period piece because it was made during the original period. Period furniture is the pinnacle of the antique-furniture category. It is considered period if it was made new in the period when its design was first introduced. For example, a Chippendale bureau that was made in 1750, the beginning of that era, is considered period.

Finally, there is used, or vintage, furniture. This category includes favorites, such as art deco, mission, and Eames-era styles, which are not quite 100 years old yet. We will discuss eras and periods in more detail later in this chapter in the Eras section.

WHAT ABOUT CONDITION AND REPAIR?

When you look at a piece of furniture to buy, ask yourself some questions:

- What condition is it in?
- Has it been repaired?

- How is the craftsmanship?
- How old is it?

Keep in mind that even though you found the piece of furniture in your great aunt's attic it may not be antique. She could have bought it yesterday and had it hauled up there. Don't make your judgment about a piece of furniture's age from any one of these tips. Take a look at the big picture, which includes condition, repair, craftsmanship, and hardware.

eBay TIP Carefully noting the condition of a piece is very important both when you are analyzing a piece to buy and when you are listing it on eBay. If you don't take the time to go into great detail about the shape of affairs for your particular piece, you will get hundreds of e-mailed questions, and you risk having to take a piece back as a return. You absolutely do not want to have to do this with furniture. You could end up paying hundreds, if not thousands, of dollars in shipping fees for a return. Take your time and note everything about the condition of a piece, even if you don't think a particular detail is important.

There are several things to watch for in antique furniture that differ from other antique merchandise. Always note the following:

- Is the hardware original?
- Is it brass or cast iron? (You can tell it is brass if it will not allow a magnet to stick.)
- Is there wear or tarnish/rust to the patina? If so, tell your buyer.
- Do the hinges have any problems?
- Is it missing any hardware—screws, nails, and so forth?
- How does the wood look?
- Are there scratches, dings, or other marks?
- Are there wormholes?
- Has the wood shrunk?
- If it has drawers or doors, smell inside and describe the smell. Take the drawers out and look at the sides, base, and back.

In the next section, "Craftsmanship," we will explain how to answer these questions. But for now, remember to measure everything and put this in your description. Measure the doors, drawers, legs, seat, and so forth. Look your piece over from top to bottom, noting any and every little item. It's okay to put something in your eBay listing that says "Needs cleaning" or "Sold as is." As long as you cover yourself from the left, right, front, and back, you will greatly minimize the number of returns you get.

eBay TIP   Lynn sells all her furniture "as is." Here is her reason: "I am not an expert in repair and refinishing. Most buyers won't want you to touch the original patina or finish. To begin with, I recommend that you do the same." To learn more on this topic, two great resources are *Furniture Repair and Refinishing* by Brian Hingley and the video series Repairing Furniture and Refinishing Furniture by Bob Flexner.

Craftsmanship

In order to date your antique and period furniture, there are key things to look for revolving around the way it was made, or its craftsmanship. Also, look for wear or patina to the piece: a build-up of dirt and oils from wear over the years will help you feel confident that it is an older piece. The following are very simple guidelines to use as you start selling on eBay.

- *Dovetails.*   A dovetail joint is the way two pieces of wood are held together. Most likely you have seen this on an edge of a drawer. Some new furniture is also made with dovetails. A general rule is that the fewer the dovetails, the older the piece. In the early eighteenth century, one dovetail may have been used to join the sides of a drawer. After that time, a drawer may have three to five smaller ones, all hand cut. In the Victorian period, the dovetails were machine-cut, more evenly spaced, and greater than five (see Figure 11-2).
- *Wear Marks.*   Run your hand underneath or along the back of a piece of furniture. Very sharp edges can mean a new piece. If a piece has some age to it, it is highly likely that it will have some wear marks. Check the legs on chairs for marks from sliding a chair across the floor. Check crossbars on chairs where feet would rest. On drawers, check for smoothness and marks on the bottom. Smell inside the drawers—if it has a musty smell it has some age. If it smells like fresh wood it is probably new. On tables, check the top area for marks and dings. The legs will probably show some wear from being kicked.
- *Scribe Marks, Signatures, and Manufacturer Marks.*   Look for a pencil, chalk, stamped, or ink inscription on the bottom side of a table or drawer and along the wooden supports under a chair (see Figure 11-3). Look from many different angles. A name of any kind is interesting, although it may not be a famous maker. Stenciled numbers are 1890s to 1940s inventory numbers, and we see these quite a bit.
- *Wormholes.*   These are common in English and Continental furniture. But wormholes are often faked. To tell if they are authentic, stick a tip of a straight pin into the hole. If it goes straight in the

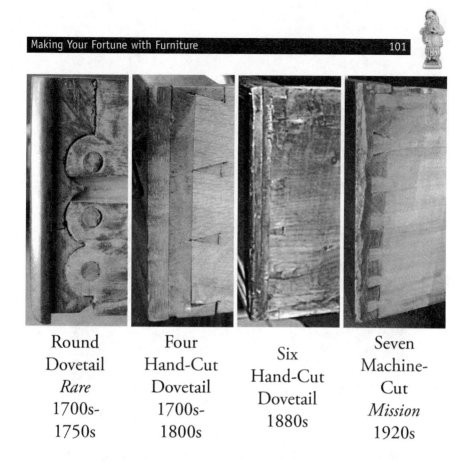

| Round Dovetail *Rare* 1700s-1750s | Four Hand-Cut Dovetail 1700s-1800s | Six Hand-Cut Dovetail 1880s | Seven Machine-Cut *Mission* 1920s |

Figure 11-2 Here is a comparison of dovetails in manufacturing. The round one is oldest; machine cut the newest.

holes are a fake. Worms do not eat in a straight line; they wander back and forth.

- *Shrinkage.* This is to be expected in furniture over 100 years old. Secondary woods to which veneer is glued tend to be soft woods that shrink readily, so veneers will shrink and crack off. Drawer bottoms shrink away from drawer sides. Sometimes sides of chests will buckle and warp.
- *Marriages.* A marriage occurs when a different bottom is place with a different top than originally came together. Or drawers do not match perfectly, or the shelves don't look original or the mirror top does not match the lower bureau. To test for a marriage, check the wood types. Does the grain seem to match? Do the patinas match? Does the construction of the drawers match the construction of the upper drawers? Is the quality the same? Does the brass hardware feel the same, and are the holes consistent?

Figure 11-3   Where to find a signature on a Heywood-Wakefield chair.

With these guidelines, you'll be able to more accurately describe any piece you post on eBay. Remember, too, that the more you sell and the more you study, the closer you will be to becoming an authority.

Dating by Identifying Hardware

Other key ways to date and describe a piece is through the hardware that holds the piece together. Look for these key clues in your search:

- *Pegs.*   Craftsmen made their own pegs and used them to attach joints together. The old wooden pegs are imperfect, unlike new wooden pegs, which we call dowels.
- *Shelving.*   If the shelves in a bookcase or china cabinet rest on pegs inserted into holes in the sides or on supports of any kind, the piece was made after 1820. If the shelving slides along grooves, then it is probably pre-1820.
- *Staples or Plywood.*   Need we say more? If you find any staples or plywood, your piece is modern. This isn't necessarily bad—Eames-era pieces can be considered modern, and a lot of those go for big bucks!

- *Nails.* Original nails on antique furniture should be either crude, handmade, or machine cut. The smooth, standardized nails we are used to seeing today were not made until the 1880s.
- *Screws.* Remove one of the screws in a place that it won't show. If the screw is handmade it will have irregular widths in the spirals and a blunt end. The slot in the head may be off center. This type of screw would be pre-1850. A screw made after 1850 will have a sharp point and evenly spaced spirals.

eBay TIP Keep in mind that as furniture ages sometimes the hardware gets replaced. Lynn has done this with many of her pieces. She has an antique chest of drawers, and each time she moves, she uses a different set of screws to replace the mirror.

- *Hinges.* Seventeenth- and eighteenth-century hinges used a single hole. Craftsman inserted a U-shaped metal wire through two pieces of wood or metal and bent it back flat against the inside of a drawer or door to hold it together. It will leave a single hole and a mark where the pin was bent back. The butterfly hinge was made of iron or brass and consisted of two flat pieces and a middle pin. Nails or screws held each side of the plates in place. These were used from the mid-eighteenth century to the early twentieth-century. Check the hinges for wear and rust.
- *Handles/Hardware.* Is the hardware brass or iron? (Remember, if it is brass a magnet will not stick.) Cast iron was used in earlier medieval times on Gothic-style furniture, up until about 1600. From then on, brass was used quite extensively. Handles/pulls were thinner and hand finished until 1750. After 1750 they were stamped out by machine and were thicker. In the late eighteenth century handles began to also incorporate glass, ivory, and porcelain. Around the turn of the century, copper and leather were sometimes added. Midcentury modern also utilized chrome, aluminum, and plastic or Bakelite.

eBay TIP Original hardware does sometimes get replaced. Often, people will change the hardware to update the look and feel of a piece of furniture. They do this without realizing that they may be affecting its value. Haven't you ever changed the knobs or hardware on your kitchen or bathroom cabinets for a fresh look? To check if your hardware is original, remove a handle or knob and look to see if a pattern of the original hardware is showing and often, the hardware will be marked with a manufacturer's name. Much of the hardware on antique American furniture was imported from England. If the hardware is marked "Made in France" or "Made in England" and you have identified it as original, you will know that the piece is post-1891 (remember the McKinley Tariff Act, mentioned in Chapter 9).

- *Escutcheons.* This is a fancy word for the plate that goes around a keyhole. All but the very simplest furniture had these to protect the wood from a key being inserted. Once again, check around and behind the escutcheon to see if it is original.

eBay TIP Hardware such as hinges, handles/pulls, doorknobs, locks, keys, and escutcheons can sell for a pretty penny all on their own, so don't overlook listing some of these pieces on eBay also. These items are called architectural antiques. A great idea for an add-on sale is to carry replacement new and antique hardware in your eBay Store.

When it comes to accurately determining a piece of furniture's value from its hardware, pay for an appraisal from an authority if you have any doubts!

HOW TO BECOME AN INSIDER

To be able to make the most money selling furniture on eBay, try to learn as much as possible. You can improve your insider knowledge by joining a furniture club in your area or subscribing to furniture-related periodicals. Buy as many books as you can afford and never stop reading about furniture. Some great books are *Field Guide to Antique Furniture* (Mariner Books), and *Antique Trader Furniture Price Guide* (Antique Trader Books). Spend time researching furniture on the Web. Join an online club devoted to your area of study. There are many Web sites devoted to midcentury modern furniture, and you can join for free. Spend some time in the chat rooms. You'll soon see that it's a fascinating area of study.

USING HISTORY TO GET THE MOST MONEY

Once you have determined that your piece is either authentic or a good enough reproduction to sell, it is time to work on getting top dollar for it. This is the fun part. Next, we are going to cover material or wood type, shape and function, and finally, style or period. When it comes to making the most profit on eBay, these are all key aspects to mention in your auction title and description.

Material

Identifying wood is not something that is learned quickly. It will take quite a bit of study on your part. As you learn, remember that you can ask people at antiques stores or shows for examples of each type.

For starters, primary woods are the woods used on the visible portions of a piece of furniture. Secondary woods, which are typically softer and less attractive, are used where they won't be seen, such as the backs of chests and the bottoms of drawers. Poplar and pine are the secondary woods most often used in American furniture. Here is a brief overview of some of the more common woods:

- *Oak.* Oak is a coarse-textured, very hard and durable wood. Most of us know what oak looks like. It was used in the 1600s in the pilgrim style but was eventually replaced with other woods in the early 1700s. It experienced a resurgence in the 1920s with the mission style and is a staple wood for current American furniture.
- *Walnut.* Walnut is a leading furniture wood because it is easily found. It is excellent because it is widely adaptable and has great strength without being too heavy. It cuts well, takes a fine polish, and comes in a great variety of colors and textures. American walnut is typically black and can also be a moderate dark gray brown color. William and Mary and Queen Anne style used walnut until mahogany pushed it out of favor in about 1730. Walnut came back into favor in Victorian furniture, circa 1840 and on.
- *Mahogany.* Mahogany is a reddish brown wood of medium hardness. It has great strength and is among the most beautiful for texture and ease of polishing. It has a variety of grains and figures making beautiful patterns. American mahogany was the first known in the world and was used extensively in the Federal style (1780–1820) often with contrasting inlays and veneers.
- *Cherry.* Cherry is another American wood used in the Queen Anne and Chippendale periods (1725–1780). The wild American cherry has a hard, fine grain and is a lightweight, reddish brown wood. It resists warping and takes a fine polish.
- *Rosewood.* Rosewood is a term for the grouping of several species of tropical woods from India and Brazil, so named for the odor of the newly cut wood rather than its color. It is heavy, dense, a deep red brown color, and richly streaked. It was used quite a bit in nineteenth-century America, in Classical, Empire, and Victorian furniture.
- *Maple.* Maple is a prevalent American wood that comes in both hard and soft varieties. It is typically found in the western hemi-

sphere and can vary in color from a white to a light tan or even a yellowish brown. It is a popular wood these days and was commonly used in simple shaker furniture from 1690 to 1900.

- *Birch.* Birch comes in many varieties and is found in temperate zones. It is white when it is soft, and red, black, and yellow in the hard varieties. It is frequently used for inexpensive furniture and can often be found as a veneer. Birch was also favored by the Shakers, by folk artists, and by creators of midcentury modern furniture.

Shape and Function

Identifying the shape of a piece is an important first step when listing on eBay. When you list a piece of furniture on eBay, you have the opportunity to categorize it by shape. Once you have identified the shape or form, your research becomes that much easier. We will take a look at the forms that furniture takes, organizing our descriptions by room.

THE KITCHEN First we will visit the kitchen—the heart of the American home (see Figure 11-4). A kitchen queen was used before kitchen cupboards

Kitchen Queen   Icebox   Metal Cupboards   Pie Safe

Folk Art Chest   Rustic Farm Table   Stove

Figure 11-4 Kitchen furniture shapes.

were invented to hold dishes and cooking ingredients, and usually it has a lot of cupboards and drawers. The icebox was used to hold ice and keep food clean and cool. The iceboxes were mostly made of oak and would have shelves with a metal or porcelain interior, and were made and used between about 1850 and 1930. The ice man was a familiar sight coming up the street. Another common sight in American kitchens was the pie safe, which was used to keep cooling pies away from animals. A pie safe is a little cupboard with pierced panels to allow for air circulation. These are quite collectible to-day, depending on the quality of the panels and the types of woods. Most kitchens also had a table for gathering around to prepare and finally eat the food. A drop-leaf table was popular for the kitchen because it has leaves that would extend and then fold down and so could be placed in a small space. The large farm table, an example of French country style, makes a great addition to a kitchen.

THE DINING ROOM Next let's look at the dining room. The hutch was a chest or cabinet with doors and usually on legs. It is an early form descending from the Gothic and the precursor of the sideboard. The sideboard, or buffet,

Comb Back Windsor Chair

Dining Set with 4 Chairs

Art Deco Sideboard or Buffet

Barley Twist Credenza

Cupboard

Mission Gate Leg Table

Figure 11-5 Dining room furniture shapes.

was invented for the dining room during the Federal period (1780–1820). It held dishes and food to be served. Another name for a sideboard is the Italian *credenza*. What a modern convenience! The gateleg table originated during the pilgrim period (1630–1690). This type of table has legs that swing out to make a full-sized table. The dining table with a matching set of chairs did not come into being until the late nineteenth century. If you find one that someone claims is 1790s, you will know better!

In the dining room you may also find a cupboard (see Figure 11-5). These were built to proudly display the china and porcelain owned by the homeowner. They were often open on the top so that these precious wares could be seen easily.

The Windsor chair came into American popularity during the Queen Anne period (1725–1750) and is still quite recognizable today. The Windsor chair originated in England in the seventeenth century, and was first made in the Americas in 1720, promptly becoming our most popular furniture form. It was light, strong, comfortable, and handsome. These chairs were originally painted or covered with a heavy varnish to hide the fact that different parts of the chair were made from different types of wood. Many of the originals were painted dark green or black and used in the gardens of wealthier clientele. George Washington had Windsor Chairs on the porch of Mount Vernon!

THE LIVING ROOM   Next we visit the living room, or the parlor as it was previously called (see Figure 11-6). Wing chairs came into being in the Queen Anne period. A wing chair was finally something comfortable to sit in while reading. It had side pieces and was overstuffed. The side pieces looked like wings, thus the name. Also during the Queen Anne period tea tables, tilt-top tables, and pole screens appeared. A tea table meant that you could afford the silver service that belonged on it and it just screamed *nouveau riche*—just kidding, but it *was* a statement about taste. The tilt-top table was very attractive because it would tilt into a flat position a could be stored against the wall. The pole screen was brass and held an adjustable needlepoint screen that would slide up and down to protect the lady of the house from the hot flames of the fireplace. Also during this time frame, the settee arrived, providing a light open seat about twice the size of a chair. The love seat, also called a courting chair, is from this same time period and was a double chair or small sofa. Circa 1800 the rocking chair was invented in America and is fundamentally American, rustic, and inelegant. During the Federal period the china cupboard or cabinet appeared on the scene; this was a glass-front cabinet, or curio cabinet, to hold collections or china. The Federal period also saw the development of the card, side, and sofa tables. During the Victorian time period (1837–1901) the parlor set was very popular. It included an overstuffed settee, a lady's and a gentleman's chair, and a footstool or ottoman. The parlor set may also have included a sofa table with a marble top. A chaise lounge

| Queen Anne Settee or Loveseat | China Cupboard | Victorian Gentleman's Chair | Victorian Lady's Chair |

Victorian Side Table with Marble Top   Art Deco Side Chair   Caned Oak Rocking Chair   Queen Anne Wing Chair

Figure 11-6 Living room furniture shapes.

is a long chair in the form of a sofa with an upholstered back for reclining. The coffee table did not appear until about 1920, so if you see a coffee table that someone claims is from the Federal period, it is not!

THE BEDROOM Let's visit the bedroom (see Figure 11-7). A chest was originally a large box with a hinged lid used to store all a person's belongings, to sit and sleep on, and to carry belongings from place to place. As it evolved it became known as a trunk. This eventually turned into a chest of drawers, which then became a highboy. Highboys came into being during the William and Mary period (1690–1725). A highboy was a set of five or six drawers set on a stand high enough to open without stooping down. It was set on a lowboy, which was a dressing table with drawers. A lowboy typically had six tall legs made with stretchers and balls. During the Federal period the highboy and the lowboy fell out of favor. Their replacements were the smaller chest of drawers and bureaus, also known as a dresser. A vanity, sometimes called a dressing table, is a low piece of furniture with drawers and a mirror attached at the top. It was made for a woman to use when putting on her makeup.

Dresser

Mission Oak Bed

Chest

*Chamber
Box*

*Rustic
Trunk*

*Craftsman
Night Stand*

*Art Deco
Vanity*

*Art Deco
Armoire*

Highboy

Figure 11-7   Bedroom furniture styles.

A commode is a small piece of furniture that has a towel bar along the top, a cupboard below, and a flat top to hold a wash basin or bowl-and-pitcher set. There were also bedroom commodes, or chamber boxes, that served as primitive toilets. Remember, these types of pieces were used before indoor plumbing!

The first bed with a mattress, cloth stuffed with feathers and placed upon a low bench, first appeared in Sweden in the year 943. Most early American beds were wooden and twin or twin half size (Empire). Metal frames with iron or brass headboards came into being in 1850. Beds now come in twin, full/double, queen, or king size. You will not find many true antique king- or queen-size bed frames, because these sizes were not common until the 1940s to 1950s.

A nightstand is a small chest placed next to the bed and they usually came in pairs. The armoire began as a tall cupboard or wardrobe. Originally they were used to store arms and armor, hence the name *armoire*. They are still tall and are used for many purposes: as a wardrobe (before built-in closets were common) and to store linens, dishes, and now, sometimes, televisions.

THE LIBRARY AND FRONT HALL   Finally, let's visit the library and front hall (see Figure 11-8). During the Federal period, the bookcase came into being, and it since has developed many variations (among the rarest are those that are circular and spin around). A secretary was the marriage of a bookcase top and a fold-down desk. The original desk was a writing box, a small,

Rolltop Desk

Game Table
Civil War
Federal Style

Lady's Writing Desk
Queen Anne

Secretary

Handmade
Smoking Stand

Telephone
Table

Figure 11-8   Library and front hall furniture shapes.

portable chest with a sloping lid. As these grew larger they turned into frames with drawers down to the floor. The library table was a large table with drawers in a pedestal form; this was sometimes called a kneehole desk in America. There are many variations on the desk. Rolltop and ladies' writing desks were especially fancy styles popular in Europe. A writing desk or table is a flat-top desk or any table of proper size for writing, usually fitted with drawers or desk compartments.

In the front hall, a hall tree was a common fixture. It is a stand or framework of wood or metal for coats and hats to hang on.

Eras

There are so many different furniture eras that for the purpose of this book we will just discuss American eras of style and period (followed by descriptions of two influential European eras). Most of the early furniture that will be found in the United States was made in the United States. It wasn't until much later that we began importing European furniture and we didn't import that much of it! Many of the American styles and ornamentation do come from and cross over into European styles. Keep in mind that all these styles and eras tend to overlap and that nothing is very clear-cut when you are discussing furniture eras. The years given below are "circa," which means give or take a few years.

When discussing style and period, it's important to understand what these terms mean. *Style* is the way the furniture shows and *period* is the time or era that it was originally made, put into use, and offered for sale. As we already mentioned in Chapter 9, styles will often be made long after the period has ended. Remember, if a piece was made during the original period or era, it is a period piece and therefore quite valuable, depending on its condition! The key American eras we will be discussing are Pilgrim, William and Mary, Queen Anne, Chippendale, Federal, Classical/Empire, Victorian, Shaker/primitive, Mission/Arts and Crafts, Art Deco, and Eames/Midcentury Modern. Note that the last six categories are six of the eight eras that eBay recognizes. This is important to remember when you pick a style in your listing. The other two that eBay recognizes are Gothic and French Country, which we will address at the end of this section.

SHAKER, 1620–1900 Shaker or primitive furniture, with its clean simple lines and unassuming stature, is as American as you can get and is currently very popular. Shaker furniture from this era is made from cheaper woods and handmade on the east coast by a very plain people. The original Shaker furniture was made by members of a religious order founded in the late 1700s. With no ornamentation of any kind, although sometimes plainly painted, this furniture was in keeping with the Shakers' belief in and dedication to putting their "hearts to prayer" and their "hands to work." While most of this furniture was made for their own use, they made chairs to sell to the outside world and produced them in impressive quantity. If any painting was done, the color used was mainly dark red.

There was a lot of primitive furniture, along the lines of the Shaker's work, being handmade in the United States beginning in 1620. Many of these offhand pieces were made by an individual workman with a fancy for furniture for his own home or for friends' homes. This is where the term folk art comes into play. *Folk Art* is a huge category on eBay and may generally be described as pieces that were made for a specific purpose, examples include a table or bed, and then decorated. They were not made to be pieces of art in and of themselves. The furniture was also plain and of sturdy construction and was often painted and brightly decorated with such characteristic motifs as hearts, peacocks, parrots, and geometrical designs borrowed from barn signs.

PILGRIM, 1630–1690   In the 1600s, there wasn't much importing going on. We hadn't all arrived yet! Furniture was bulky and expensive to bring over from Europe, and European pieces tended to shrink and crack in our drier air. This early American furniture was unsophisticated, informal, and straightforward. It was smaller and quieter than its European counterparts, but it did have spontaneity and pride. Pilgrim furniture showed the freedom of the New World. American furniture tended to be more vertical and slender, whereas English furniture tended to be more broad and horizontal. By the 1650s, the pilgrims were making their own furniture. Most was made of oak and was modeled after English styles, specifically Jacobean, Tudor, and Restoration. Bulky, yet simple and strong shapes. Oak chests, cupboards, chests of drawers, dining tables on trestles, and gateleg tables were all popular items. Turnings, shaped on a lathe, were a characteristic decoration.

WILLIAM AND MARY, 1690–1725   This period is named after Queen Mary of England and her husband, William of Orange from Holland. The King's Dutch heritage influence began right away. During this time period, life was becoming easier for the colonists and they could pay attention to the niceties of living. Styles moved away from the heavy and bulky Jacobean style that so influenced early pilgrims and turned to lighter, graceful, and more ornamental pieces. Inlay, painting, and gilding were popular. Walnut came into vogue. Turning was still important.

This period is notable also for the introductions of highboys and lowboys and for the higher bedsteads, some of which reached upward 16 feet toward a lofty ceiling. Gateleg tables were favorites, so much so that they continued to be popular for many years after. The legs of these tables were turned in the shape of inverted cups or in a trumpet shape. Other characteristics were high backs on chairs and the presence of a broken pediment, or hood. On furniture, a pediment is the ornately shaped top at the head of a

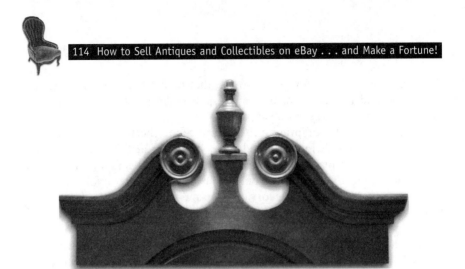

Figure 11-9 William and Mary broken pediment.

cabinet or other tall piece. *Broken pediment* means that the line stops short of the peak, leaving a gap for an ornamental finial (see Figure 11-9).

Much of this style of furniture has been copied through the years, and we often see late pieces of these styles—some from during World War I—so seeing something in the William and Mary style does not mean it is a true period piece, of which few exist.

QUEEN ANNE, 1725–1750 The Queen Anne period reached America after her highness's death. Queen Anne was Mary's sister, and her influence was one of an air of grace and curves. Carving, the cabriole leg, fiddle-shaped backs on chairs, and the scallop shell found favor in this period, and Oriental and classical motifs appeared on certain pieces. The pieces were well made and built to last, and because of this, more true period pieces exist from this time frame. The colonists were feeling flush, and they spent their money on good furniture that was both fashionable and comfortable. Among the new forms were spacious wing chairs, tea tables, tilt-top tables, and pole screens. The most popular wood was walnut, and it was the most suitable material of the day. At this point, there was a lag of 10 to 20 years between development of the newer styles in Europe and their transmission to America (some of this was due to slow communication).

CHIPPENDALE, 1750–1780 In this period, the elements of the Queen Anne style were kept, but you start to see a good deal of rococo ornamentation, with carving as the principal embellishment. American Chippendale furniture of the great centers—Philadelphia, Newport, Boston, and New York—compares favorably with the best efforts of the contemporary English craftsman.

The period is named after Thomas Chippendale, who published *The Book of English Furniture Designs* in 1754, and it had a huge influence on

American styles of this period. Furniture during this time was also showing more Dutch, rather than French, influence. Triumphant fashion statements seen frequently in these pieces are the claw-and-ball foot, the Cupid's-bow top rail, and, again, cabriole legs. Lines were crisp, not flowing, and this new style was more elaborate and luxurious than those that came before it. It was more ornate and had both a Chinese and a Gothic influence.

FEDERAL, 1780–1820 The intensely national atmosphere of the young American Republic in the years immediately following the American Revolution found expression in the Federal style, which is made up of three very well-known styles: Duncan Phyfe, Hepplewhite, and Sheraton. This is the period of classicism and of the eagle, which was carved, painted, or inlaid on furniture made of mahogany, maple, cherry, or satinwood. During this era, the most common hardware used were bail pull handles.

The three subdivisions mentioned earlier overlap a great deal:

- Hepplewhite, 1780–1795
- Sheraton, 1795–1815
- Duncan Phyfe, 1800–1820

Hepplewhite was square and masculine characterized by tapered legs and shield backs. Sheraton was known for its straight lines, rectangular forms, and was more feminine in appearance. During the Duncan Phyfe period, the legs became more tapered, and the furniture became more delicate in appearance, and more adornment, such as brass mounts, inlay, and veneer, were common. Also driving changes to furniture were that rooms started to have more purposes. For example, tables were made to fold against the wall so that the dining room could become the ballroom. There was also a new convenience in the dining room known as the sideboard. The highboy with lowboy and other tall chests were going out of style, and their replacements were more moderately sized: waist-high chests of drawers; bookcases; china cabinets; and card, tea, side, and sofa tables. Duncan Phyfe was an eclectic style.

Very little furniture bearing the name of the great cabinetmakers was actually made by them; their fame was usually based on designs they produced and that were used by others. Even finding a label of a particular cabinetmaker means only that the piece bearing his label came from his shop, not necessarily that it was made by him. The story of Duncan Phyfe, the first American furniture maker to have a style named after him, is somewhat unique. Originally from Albany, New York, he traveled to New York City to open a shop of his own in 1790. He was not an originator of design but incorporated the Adam and Hepplewhite styles, as well as the Sheraton and Directoire into his work. He was an excellent craftsman whose sense of proportion was always good and who possessed the ability to combine the best elements of these styles in a single composition. He became famous for his mastery of the curve, and his tables with lyre bases and chairs with lyre backs were much in demand. He was, in fact, the best and most prolific of the many American cabinetmakers who worked in the style called by his name.

CLASSICAL/EMPIRE, 1815–1850   Classical is named for the Greek and Roman influence and Empire for the French. The work of Duncan Phyfe, who used stenciled and fancy chairs as his signature, embodied the classical style. The chairs of this time featured caned or rushed seats and could include patriotic shapes in the structure, such as an eagle back. Many of the motifs included lyres, cornucopias, and paw feet with hair.

   The Empire era is named after the French Empire. This style marks the first time people saw a French, instead of the English, influence in American furniture. The change began after the War of 1812, when America wanted to get as far away from English influence as possible. This furniture was large and bulky, cubic or rectangular form, and frequently made of mahogany and rosewood veneers. It's common to see a small amount of brass ornamentation, animal feet (in the shape of the Egyptian Griffin), sleigh-shaped beds, Grecian sofas, lion's-head ring pulls, and gilded paint and stenciling. This was indeed a very different style!

VICTORIAN/REVIVALIST, 1837–1901   We discussed the Victorian era in general terms in Chapter 9. Now let's take a look at this era in regard to furniture. This was the time of the Industrial Revolution. Mass production and specialization came into play, and for the first time in history bad craftsmanship on a large scale became profitable, so price became more important than workmanship.

   Victorian style, as mentioned earlier, borrowed from all facets of the past, including Gothic, Renaissance, and rococo influences. It was quite eclectic. Overall, it was a time in America when people were well established and had money. Americans turned to Romanticism, and much of the furniture was designed around just that; intense creativity, nostalgia, and exaggeration played key roles in design.

   Furniture from this time was also patterned somewhat around the French period from Louis XIV to Louis XVI, inasmuch as it was more ornate than the furniture of earlier American cabinetmakers, although never as ornate as true Louis styles. These pieces are large and elaborate, with overstuffed upholstery and rich fabrics. The parlor set came into being during this time, made complete with the addition of an overstuffed easy chair and the footstool or ottoman. The wardrobe and bookcase were well known and common. Mahogany, black walnut, and rosewood were the popular woods of this era, and marble-top tables were very fashionable.

All of a sudden, it was all the rage to decorate your home by room instead of decorating your entire home in one style. You could have a somber English library, a happy French parlor, and a rustic American kitchen.

MISSION/ARTS AND CRAFTS, 1895–1920 During this era, there was a reaction to the mass-produced and overly gaudy pieces of the Victorian era. It manifested itself in the Arts and Crafts movement. Craftsmanship and simplicity were the driving forces, and these artisans looked to the past—even as far back as medieval times—for their inspiration. Oak, once again was king, just like it had been in Jacobean times.

Mission furniture was originally designed by Gustav Stickley, which is still a very recognizable name. This furniture was simple and honest and used construction elements as part of its design. You may see exposed joinery, pegging, and mortise-and-tenon joints. Stickley would have preferred the name *craftsman*, but *mission* seems to be the more common designation. Craftsman, instead, has become a term for a movement in architecture. Craftsman homes—bungalows—can be found in all parts of the country and are very recognizable, very well made, and very much in demand.

Many of Stickley's pieces were marked, so check for signatures. A Stickley corner cabinet recently sold for $390,000 at an estate sale in Zion, Pennsylvania.

ART DECO, 1910–1930 As discussed in Chapter 9, art deco is very streamlined and geometric. Pieces from this era mark the beginning of more sleek styles and laid the foundation for midcentury modern decor.

eBay TIP Sometimes it is hard to distinguish between art deco and midcentury modern. When listing a piece on eBay, consider calling a piece "Art Deco and Eames-Era Midcentury Modern" in the title.

Images used in this era were often repeated and overlapped in all forms, and it was considered an elegant style of cool sophistication. Pieces ranged from luxurious items made from exotic materials like leather to mass-produced chrome pieces. Bakelite, an early form of plastic, was often used for hardware. The end of art deco came with the stock market crash of 1929 and the worldwide depression. It wouldn't be until after World War II that a new style would emerge.

EAMES/MIDCENTURY MODERN, 1945–1969 Steel, plywood, teak, and plastic were the major ingredients in this time period. We were exploring and changing the way we thought about life, and this carried over into our furniture styles. A man had just walked on the moon. Technology was starting to change at the speed of light.

We were also rebelling against years of rigid rules and tradition. We no longer wanted William and Mary or Victorian pieces. We were mod, hip, and "with it" and we wanted our home environment to show it. Who knew that this furniture would someday become so collectible and in demand that it would sell for more money than true antique pieces? It's still easy for many readers to envision this time period, with its mod green shag carpets, sleek lines of teak forming the dining room table and chairs, and white plastic kitchen chairs that you could spin around on for hours at a time.

Welcome to the 1960s! Look for this furniture at yard sales, estate sales, and even in the trash at the side of the road. People still do not understand the value of these "space age" pieces. However, lucky enough for us, eBay does! And they pay quite handsomely. If this era interests you, consider specializing in Eames-era furniture and items. Nothing is hotter, and it will get you closer to making your fortune more quickly than ever!

GOTHIC, 1000–1600 eBay has placed emphasis on this non-American style, so it's worth a few words here.

This furniture was originally made during the Dark Ages and was very crude and homemade. People made items that they required out of the materials at hand, but they had a deep need to make them beautiful. The only stable influence was the church, so most of the expression comes from Rome and Christian Europe. Because of this, you'll frequently see great pointed arches, pillars, and buttresses that are decorated symmetrically. Cast iron was used for hardware and was quite simply fashioned. Tables did not exist, and boards were set on trestles (this, by the way, is where the expression "set the table" comes from). Chests were the most common furniture piece, used to store and move belongings and to sit upon. Beds were simple and covered with textiles for warmth. Most of the furniture was made from unpolished oak.

FRENCH COUNTRY, 1790–1940 *French country* is the other non-American furniture style included among eBay's categories. Paris set the style for ornate furniture in France as early as the seventeenth century, but the craftsmen in the sunny countryside did not follow this lead. Because they were more influenced by cost and practicality than by fashion, they created their own simple look using local materials. The colors are earthy and bright. Natural materials such as carved wood and woven rush seats were used. Armoires, benches, chests, and large farm tables are common pieces from this era. The influence came from regions as diverse as Brittany, Bordeaux, and Provence. By the 1880s, the less formal nature of these country styles became popular with the middle class and can now be found in chateaus as well as on the farm. French country is a very popular way of decorating today because of its rustic, warm, and cozy appeal.

LISTING FURNITURE ON eBAY

With all your furniture knowledge, you are now in great shape to list an item on eBay. The best way to learn how to do this is by example. We're going to walk you through this process with two examples of furniture that Lynn has sold. One piece is an antique cabinet that needed work, which was bought at a garage sale for $20, including delivery (see Figure 11-10). The other is a set of four matching, signed, Heywood-Wakefield dining chairs purchased at a garage sale for $80. Through these examples, you will see the best places to go to get the information you require to make the largest profit on your pieces.

Figure 11-10 The secretary that cost $20 delivered. A real fixer-upper.

eBay asks sellers to list item specifics in the *Furniture* category. As you fill out your listing, you will be asked for:

- *Product or Shape.* This could be a chair, or a dresser, or so forth.
- *Style.* These are the 13 eras we discussed at length earlier in the chapter.
- *Region of Origin.* Is the piece American? English? French?
- *Age.* Use the discussion of eras and dating pieces as a guide: is it pre-1800, 1800–1899, 1900–1950 or post-1950?
- *Authenticity.* eBay asks if the piece is original (meaning period), contemporary reproduction, or unknown.

Step One: Product Identification

Once you have identified the wood, shape, and era of your piece, the first thing you want to do is research the product on eBay. For the antique cabinet, we first took a look at the wood, which was a light blondish red color. We knew it wasn't oak, so our best guess was mahogany or maple. We decided to use both of these in the listing.

Next, the shape needed to be identified. Was it a cupboard, hutch, or desk? This piece had a fold-down desk. A search on eBay showed a very similar piece labeled as a secretary, so we decided to call it a secretary/hutch/desk in the title. The style element that jumped out the most was the William and Mary–style broken pediment at the top of the piece.

eBay TIP When furniture is signed, your research and identification becomes so much easier. For our second example, the set of chairs, Lynn was able to find a Heywood-Wakefield signature on the side of the seat base. Remember that the signatures are not always in obvious places, such as the underside of the piece. Always look in different spots because placement of signatures varies.

To figure the era or date, we took a look at the hardware and craftsmanship. The piece was put together with relatively modern screws, so it was obviously not a period piece circa 1690–1725. The brass hardware was Baroque style with a solid backing that if original would have dated to 1750–1790. It had dovetailed drawers. There were five on each drawer, and they were evenly spaced, indicating a Victorian date or slightly later, so 1890s to 1930s was used in the listing. As you can see, this was a reproduction utilizing many different period styles. Even though it was a reproduction of a period piece, we felt that it was still antique and therefore decided to list it as antique and give a date range.

eBay TIP Giving a range of dates is always a smart thing to do to protect yourself. In our example, the range of dates—from 1890 to 1930—allows buyers to have an indication of the time period the piece is from.

Once you have a name, do some research on the Internet. For our second example, we searched for Heywood-Wakefield on Google and found out that the company originally produced these chairs from 1930 to 1960 in Gardner, Massachusetts. We also learned that the company mostly used solid birch in a champagne or wheat finish and that the company was still producing pieces today (see Figure 11-11).

Next, take a look on eBay, doing both a completed-auction search and current-auction search, by type of furniture and designer name if possible. In our example, we searched for "Heywood-Wakefield chair," instead of "chairs," because we wanted to pull up both "chair" and "chairs." This search showed that similar sets sold for up to $545. There was also a similar set currently listed as a Buy-it-Now for $750. We knew that if we priced ours for less, our set would seem like a bargain and might be bought quickly.

Step Two: Key Words for Titles and Descriptions

Because you only have 55 characters for the title, you have to decide what are the most crucial elements of your piece of furniture. A good way to determine what aspects to play up is to do an eBay search and see which key elements bring the highest prices.

eBay TIP If you have too much information to put into 55 characters, you can add a sub-title for an extra 50 cents. For our second example, the title read "Set 4 Signed Heywood-Wakefield Period Chairs Eames MOD" and the subtitle read "2 Arm 2 Side Chairs Mid Century Danish Modern Wink Eye"! Heywood-Wakefield used catchy names for their furniture styles, so we guessed that this style may have been "wink eye" because the chair back cutout looked like a winking eye. Including information about being signed is very important to show that these are period pieces and not reproductions. Remember that with this newer furniture, era and maker's name are what really sell merchandise!

When we sold our first sample piece, our title was "Antique Secretary Desk Hutch Light Wood As Is." Because it was a combination of so many eras, we didn't list this in the title. It is important to include "as is" if the piece is not in mint condition.

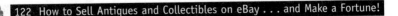

Figure 11-11   Signed set of Heywood-Wakefield chairs purchased for $80 at a garage sale.

eBay TIP   When Lynn was selling the secretary she could also have said the piece was a fixer-upper instead of "as is." Many people who are looking for furniture are looking for a project. Because of this, "Fixer-Upper," "As Is," or "Project" are all smart terms to use in your title.

Other key words to include in your description are the type of wood (such as mahogany or maple), type of construction, and other details (such as the dovetailed drawers or the broken pediment from the William and Mary period in our first example). Remember to carefully list all the damage. You want to be very careful when describing condition. This can make or break your sale. If you misrepresent a piece and don't offer a partial credit, you will most certainly receive a bad feedback rating, which may cause you to lose sales in the future. You will also increase the likelihood of having a piece returned to you, which can be very expensive.

Step Three: Photo Tricks

On the more expensive items, and especially with furniture, consider taking a lot of pictures to show your buyer the piece from every angle and to emphasize key features or any damage to the piece. For our sample secretary, we posted six pictures, showing the drawer construction, the back side, the interior, the piece with the desk dropped down, and some close-ups. On eBay, you can pay extra for a picture pack and you get the supersized photos and the gallery picture. eBay has just started offering larger picture packs as an extra feature. If you use the picture pack and include 7 to 12 pictures, you get all the extra photos, the photos super-sized (larger than the eBay 330 × 440 pixel limit), and the gallery shot for only $1.50. As a point of reference, each additional picture, after the first free one, costs 15 cents each.

eBay TIP Because you can make more money with furniture than in any other antique or collectible category, it is worth it to pay a little extra to list more photos. More photos allow you to show as much of the piece as possible, which can ultimately drive up the price.

Step Four: Pricing Strategies

Pricing furniture is very tricky. For starters, you should take into consideration that your customers may be restricted to people who live in your geographic area because the piece may not be worth enough to pay for expensive shipping. Then again, a rare piece could sell for a high price, regardless of where the customer lives. In general, furniture should be priced at a higher price than smalls. Look at the starting price and the reserve prices of similar pieces as a guide to the current market price.

eBay TIP Get more bids by lowering your starting price. For our secretary example, we had a starting price of $99 and the requirement that it be picked up in Palm Desert, California. Guess what? We had no bidders but a lot of inquiries, mainly from people in the Midwest and on the East Coast who wanted to know how much shipping would cost. The lowest price for shipping was $250 by a trucking company, and this scared away most of the potential bidders who didn't want to pay that much for a $99 piece. We re-listed the secretary the next week with a starting bid of $9.99 and no reserve. Amazingly enough, 275 people looked at this auction when it had the lower starting price (as opposed to 151 at the higher price), 12 people bid, and it ended up selling for $127.50! Not bad on a $20 investment.

One the flip side, sometimes the higher you price an auction from the start, the higher the perceived value will be to your customers. This could help drive up prices so you get more money in your pocket.

The Heywood-Wakefield chairs were listed with a starting price of $149 to show a high perceived value. They ended up selling for $204.52 which is 2.5 times what was paid. This auction had 275 people view it. This is Eames era at its finest. The buyer picked up the chairs in person, making it an even better transaction!

Packing Specifics, If Required

Furniture is a very difficult item to ship. It is best if the pieces can be picked up from your location, and this works very well if you are in a very populated region. If not, check with your local trucking companies, Craters and Freighters, and Greyhound to get prices and specifics. Furniture can either be blanket wrapped, boxed, or crated. Blanket wrapping may be easier for you but not as safe for the piece of furniture. If you box the item, your piece should be blanket wrapped or bubble wrapped first unless it is unlikely to incur any damage from the box. Crated furniture should almost always be blanket wrapped first to protect the furniture's wood from the wood of the crate.

EXPANDING YOUR FURNITURE BUSINESS

Customer Incentives that Work

The best way to be successful at selling furniture on eBay is to go the extra mile. Make it extremely easy for your customer to receive their furniture with little or no hassle on their end and at a low, competitive shipping price. Shop around for the most reasonable shippers. Buy cartons and packing supplies in bulk and specialize only in furniture. If you can ship a large piece of furniture cross-country for $200–$300 you will be out-maneuvering the dealer who is selling a piece of furniture in a one-time transaction and is forced to use Craters and Freighters. Craters and Freighters quoted Lynn $700–$900 to take a large china cabinet cross-country. Do you see how that extra $500 can go right into your pocket? You will make your mark and position yourself as a market leader by being competitive in shipping prices.

Another great idea is to invest in an inexpensive truck or van. If you live in a large metropolitan area, offer in your listing that you will deliver the piece for *free* within a 2-hour radius. Another option is to hire a college student to drive for you and pay his or her way by charging low delivery prices. For example, you could list: "Will deliver within the tri-state area for 50 cents a mile one way." This way, if the buyer lives 300 miles away—about a 10-hour drive round-trip in a truck—you would charge $150, which is enough to pay for gas and pay the driver $10 an hour. Be creative. Think up ways to get your items delivered for less.

Advertising and Promotion

As a furniture vendor on eBay, you will want to do some advertising and promotion. The eBay keyword banner ads are a great idea (see Chapter 8 for more information). Place small classified ads in your local newspaper in the Merchandise for Sale column. Say something along the lines of "Great antique furniture available on eBay under user ID FurnitureFactory. Save on shipping with free local delivery." Hand out your business card to everyone you meet and tell them to check out your auctions.

What If It Doesn't Sell?

If your furniture piece doesn't sell on eBay, you may want to incorporate it into your home. If you don't have room for it in your home you can always consign it at your local consignment stores or sell it at your next garage sale. We have been doing really well with items in our eBay Store. Try listing your furniture pieces for 90 days at a reasonable fixed price. If none of these options appeals to you, consider donating it to charity. Write it off and feel good about it at the same time!

12

Ethnographic and Cultural Categories: From Asia to Classical to African and Beyond

---

The category of ethnographic and cultural items is very broad. It encompasses original classical (Grecian and Roman) antiques as well as antiquities of Japan and China. Finally, it includes items from the South Pacific, Egypt, Europe, South America, North America, and Africa. Another common word for ethnographic items is *artifacts*. Generally speaking, an artifact is a handmade item of some historical or cultural importance; typical artifacts include tools, weapons, and decorative items. This eBay category really covers anything and everything indigenous to the seven continents of the world, which is obviously a vast amount of material. We will break down this section by continent and look closely at the most famous, popular, and collectible items for specific areas, focusing on items that have a proven broad appeal.

WHAT ARE eBAY SHOPPERS LOOKING FOR IN THIS CATEGORY?

For the purposes of this chapter, we will examine six out of the seven continents. We aren't going to discuss Antarctica, because nobody really lives there and, therefore, nothing is coming out of that continent for us to sell! The six continents we will be exploring in this chapter include Africa, Asia, Australia, Europe, North America, and South America (see Figure 12-1).

All types of people are looking to collect quality, handmade items from each continent. Collectors focus on a particular region for a variety of rea-

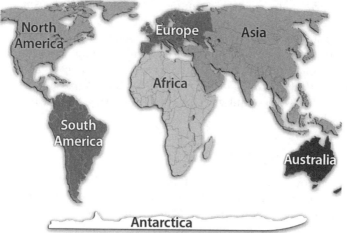

Figure 12-1 The seven continents of the world.

sons. They may have traveled in the area or have family roots there. They may find the aesthetics or the general culture of the given country or region appealing. They may simply consider its artifacts good investments. Because it is not practical to cover every collectible artifact from every country on each continent, we will focus on the more popular and in-demand ethnographic items. Here is a quick, general breakdown of the hottest items, by continent:

- *Africa.* Africa is well known for its trade beads, masks, and tribal items. Egypt, which is on the African continent, is home to mummies, sphinx artifacts, and bronzes.
- *Asia.* Japan and China are home to many wonderful items. Japan is famous for its swords, *netsuke* (miniature sculptures), bonsai horticultural items, Imari porcelain, and Satsuma ceramics and earthenware. China is well known for celadon, jade, ivory, and foo dogs. Both Japan and China are famous for their cloisonné. India is well known for brass and Buddhas.
- *Australia, or Oceania.* Oceania is home to the islands of the South Pacific. The islands of the South Pacific give us Aboriginal art, wooden artifacts, and the boomerang.
- *Europe.* Europe is the original home for classical antiquities from the Greeks and Romans. Figures of Greek mythology were represented in sculptures, vases, and bronze work. The Romans had marble, sculpture, and bronze as well. Russia is famous for icons, Fabergé, hand-painted lacquer boxes, and Russian enamel. Vienna gives us its very collectible miniature bronzes.

- *North America.* This continent brings us Native American collectibles that include both Indian and Eskimo baskets and scrimshaw. Also from the United States, snuff boxes and Hawaiiana are very collectible. Finally, the United States is home to highly sought-after folk art and primitives from the early American home.
- *South America.* For the purposes of this book, South America includes Mexico and gives us colorful pottery, masks, furniture, and silver.

WHAT ARE THE TOP CATEGORIES?

When you are trying to determine top categories for artifacts, the first place to look is at eBay's *Hot Seller* report. A recent report revealed that glasses, cups, plates, and vases from China were very popular Asian antiques. From Japan, boxes were selling extremely well. As for super-hot collectibles, African masks from 1900 on and Hawaiiana photos were winners. The report also indicated that the following were very hot items:

- Bronzes
- *Native American General items*
- Native American items from pre-1940
- Hawaiian apparel, dishes, bowls, and plates
- Chinese bowls, paintings, and scrolls
- Japanese plates

WHERE TO FIND ARTIFACTS

Each and every one of us probably has an item from another culture right in our own home. Lynn's office boasts an ancient African mask above the fireplace and a South Pacific oar standing next to it. The first place to look for ethnographic items is right in your own home. Dig out those boxes you put away after your trip to Tahiti and see what treasures you can uncover.

Next, hit the garage- and yard-sale circuit. If you own items from other cultures, you can assume that other people do too. They turn up in garage sales regularly. We recently found two Mexican carved wooden masks and a scrimshawed cribbage board at a garage sale. Look for any handcrafted items that are unusual and unique (and being sold at a reasonable price).

To find ethnographic bargains on eBay, try typing in misspellings. *Cloisonné* is often misspelled in online auctions. As a test we did a search for "cloisonné," and found 5027 items; typing in the popular misspelling "cloissone" gave us 181 items. Which pieces do you think fetched higher prices? Because fewer potential bidders will view the auctions with misspelled titles, there are bargains to be had with misspellings in every single category. Be creative in your searching.

Ethnographics is also a great place to find items that have been incorrectly or imprecisely labeled, because people are generally less knowledgeable about the artifacts of other cultures than they are about the artifacts of their own regions. Try to describe a piece of cloisonné as if you didn't know the term *cloisonné*. You might mention the piece's enamel, or its wire work. Valuable ethnographic artifacts are sold for pennies on the dollar every day by sellers who don't know what they have. Try to hunt on eBay using general terms to pick up underpriced items. If you become very knowledgeable about Asian antiques, you can also just shop by category. For example, watch the *Antique Asian* category as it closes and pick up things that were identified incorrectly. It happens all the time. Not everyone can be an expert in every category.

Take a Trip!

One of the best places to pick up cultural items is right in that country or cultural area. If you have decided to specialize in items from the South Pacific, head down to Australia and the surrounding islands to learn more and import things back to the States. If you want to become a big seller in Native American items, visit the Southwest region of the United States looking for merchandise. These trips can be fun, profitable learning experiences, which can often be written off for tax purposes.

eBay TIP You may even consider building relationships with people in other countries. Lynn's grandmother worked with someone in Hong Kong as her agent for that country. He would send photos with descriptions, and she would buy based on these. Setting up relationships with agents you trust in other countries can save lots of travel time and money; if you find the right agent, you can also improve your access to really desirable artifacts.

Antiques, consignment, and thrift stores are more great places to hunt for cultural items. Placing wanted-to-buy ads in your local papers and in national publications like the *Antique Trader* can also pay off. Many ethnographic items go unnoticed and undervalued because they are rarely signed. If you do your research and become an expert in any of these areas, you can do quite well.

HOW TO BECOME AN ETHNOGRAPHIC AND CULTURAL INSIDER

Because this is such a broad category and there is such a wide variety of items that could fall into this category, it's important to really know your stuff so that you can make the highest profit on eBay. There are many great places to learn and network in the area of ethnographics. For Asian antiques, try subscribing to *Arts of Asia*, which is the largest circulated publication for Asian items in the world and has been published since 1971 (*www.artsofasianet .com*). Check out the International Netsuke Society if you are interested in *netsuke*. That organization can be found at *www.netsuke.org.* The National Museum of African Art is part of the Smithsonian, and they have a wonderful Web site (*www.nmafa.si.edu*). The Metropolitan Museum of Art has another fantastic Web site with examples and history of Egyptian art (*www .metmuseum.org/explore/newegypt/html/a_index.htm*).

As you can see, the resources for learning in this category are endless. Visit some museums, check out some Web sites, and join some clubs. Do you see how fun all this is? This is why so many people love selling antiques and collectibles!

KEY SELLING POINTS IN THIS CATEGORY

When you post your *Ethnographic and Cultural* items on eBay, there are three main topics that you'll want to address in your description: material, form, and function. If you know the right information about these three areas, you'll have a better chance of making a great sale. Let's examine these key selling points so you'll know how to play them up in your title and description on eBay.

Material

To understand cultural items that come from the far reaches of the world, we must first look at some common materials or processes used to make them. The materials used most commonly throughout the world are ivory, bronze, brass, wood, enamel, jade, and marble. (Note: materials that come from only one continent will be covered in the treatment of the particular continent in the "Form and Function" section that follows.)

The term *artifact* typically refers to an object made thousands of years ago. With that in mind, it becomes obvious that the materials used to make them would be simple. Things found in nature, like ivory, wood, and jade were used earliest. Porcelains and metals came later, and enamel work was used more recently.

IVORY Authentic ivory is derived solely from the tusk of the elephant, though several similar substances have been used in the same way, including the tusks and teeth of walrus, hippopotamuses, and sperm whales. Ivory is a popular substance to work with, because it is hard and thus takes on a high polish. It discolors with time and acquires a pleasing gold tone with occasional dark streaks. For more information about identifying your piece as ivory, please read the "Avoiding Fakes and Frauds" section later in the chapter.

Ivory

This area is complex, and sellers should consult with the <u>U.S. Fish and Wildlife Service</u> and their state wildlife regulatory agency to ensure that the particular item involved may lawfully be sold. Generally, ivory from African elephants may be sold within the United States so long as it was lawfully imported into the United States. Wooly mammoth ivory may be sold inside or outside the United States. Hippo ivory may be sold within the United States, but may not lawfully be imported into the United States, but may only be imported/exported in compliance with <u>CITES</u>.

Figure 12-2   The eBay Help page outlining the rules for selling ivory on eBay.

There is a bill from 1978 that regulates the sale of ivory within the United States. eBay policy states that although the issues surrounding ivory are complex, it is generally legal to sell ivory from the African elephant within the United States as long as it was imported into the States legally (see Figure 12-2). As a side note, be careful when shipping ivory out of the United States. Lynn shipped an ivory bangle bracelet to a repeat customer in Australia. The customer received the box—but it was empty. The customs people in her country had confiscated the bracelet!

e B a y   T I P   Any time you have a question with regard to what is legal to sell on eBay, click on the "Help" button at the top of the page and type in your question. Information about ivory, for example, is spelled out in detail on eBay.

Bronze   Bronze is an alloy of copper (usually about 90 percent) and tin. It may also have some traces of lead or zinc. Since ancient times, it has been the metal most commonly used in cast sculpture because it is strong, durable, and easily workable by a variety of processes. Casting of bronze is time consuming, but when done correctly it yields beautiful, heavy, and permanent sculptures. It is easier to cast than pure copper because it has a lower melting point. The color of bronze varies from a silverish color to a rich coppery red. The surface becomes more beautiful once it acquires a patina. Remember that *patina* refers to the buildup of materials on a surface over time. Bronze is often mistaken for brass. Spend some time looking at examples of both, because if you have a piece of bronze it is typically worth a lot more money than a piece of brass.

Brass Brass is an alloy of copper and zinc (typically 60 percent copper and 40 percent zinc). It has a nice yellow color and is vulnerable to black or green tarnish. Again, a magnet will not stick to real brass. Many bronze guns from the Civil War were mistakenly called brass, but brass is not suitable for artillery.

Wood Wood was used for many artifacts because it was readily available and quite easy to carve into utilitarian items such as bowls and spears. Other woods used from around the world include teak, rosewood, and porcupine (from the coconut tree). For more information on the types of wood, please see Chapter 11.

Enameling The art of applying glasslike glazing fused to a metallic surface is called enameling. It originated in Europe and was introduced to Chinese craftsmen by French missionaries in 1662. The copper surface was first covered with opaque glazing, usually white, then the enamel colors were added, typically in delicate and interesting patterns. Enameling is the basis of Russian enamels, Limoges, and cloisonné.

Jade Jade is a semiprecious gemstone that takes a high polish. It is also a material that is very revered in Chinese culture. It is credited with many mystical powers, such as safeguarding health and assuring happiness. The Chinese consider it their most sacred gift, believing that in giving jade they are giving a part of themselves. From the beginning of China's recorded history, the Chinese attitude toward the stone has remained constant: never worshipped but always revered.

Jade can be two distinct stones: nephrite and jadeite. The color of nephrite varies from white to shades of green, yellow, brown, and black. Jadeite is shiner and can be found in a broader range of colors, from white to green to lavender to red.

Marble Marble is hard metamorphic limestone that is white or variously colored and streaked or mottled. It takes a high polish and is used quite frequently in sculpture and architecture. It is often irregularly colored by impurities. It has a cold feel to it and is quite heavy.

Form and Function

The next two key selling points, form and function, are best described by looking at artifacts from each continent.

Figure 12-3 Circa 1880s Italian millefiori trade beads are extremely popular on eBay.

AFRICA Africa is famous for the trade beads that have been collected for years in this country. Most of the beads were made in Europe and transported to Africa by Arab traders beginning in 1600. Around 1824, the Europeans began trading beads with the natives from their sailing ships. The beads were used as currency to purchase gold, ivory, and slaves. The beads are very intricate, and most came from Venice, although some were made in Bohemia, Holland, Egypt, and Germany. The Venetian enameled beads and millefiori (literally, "1000 flowers"; see Figure 12-3) are some of the more beautiful, and therefore more popular ones. To learn more about any of these items we are discussing, go to eBay and do a completed-auctions search. Go to "Search," then "Advanced," and then check the "Completed Auctions only" box. This will show you the past 2 weeks' worth of sales history. Type in "African trade bead" and start learning!

African masks were, and still are, made of many materials, including leather, metal, fabric, and many types of wood. Most likely, the masks were worn during celebrations, initiations, and other rituals. They can be worn in three positions: vertically covering the face, as a helmet over the entire head, or as a crest resting on the forehead. The African mask is considered one of the finest creations in the art world and is highly sought after. A recent check on eBay revealed 1562 masks listed or sold in the two weeks prior, with the most expensive selling for $3,250 for a single mask. This is a field that can definitely yield profits to those who know what they are doing.

Many other African tribal items are highly sought after as well. Here are just a few key words to search for on eBay and to think about: ceremonial pieces, garments, clubs, weapons, spears, paddles, statues, loincloths, knives, bows, idols, and headdresses.

Egypt has some of the most unusual and sought-after artifacts in the world, and the most popular Egyptian artifact remains the mummy. Mummies are, of course, embalmed and dried-out bodies. Mummification was used by the ancient Egyptians to preserve the outer shell of the body after death. The body was dried, preserved, and wrapped in linen. This was thought to help identify people when they were reincarnated. After going through the mummification process, a mummy was placed in a sarcophagus (usually a stone container that would house a coffin along with the mummy). There aren't many mummies coming up for sale on eBay, but you can cash in on the enduring popular appeal of the mummy by looking for items such as mummy-shaped burial relics or masks, sculptures, and beads that use mummies and sarcophaguses as decoration (see Figure 12-4).

The sphinx is another creature that was used extensively in Egyptian art. It is a figure either made up of two different types of animals or that is half man and half animal. The best known example is the Great Sphinx of

Figure 12-4 This reproduction life-sized sarcophagus is now being used as home decor.

Giza, which has the body of a lion and the head of a king or god. The sphinx is a symbol of royal power, strength, and wisdom. On eBay, in a completed-auction search for a 2-week period, there were 1298 items listed with "sphinx" in the title, and these sculptures came in bronze, silver, and terra-cotta. The most expensive, a bronze sculpture, sold for $1,525.

ASIA   The Chinese have used ivory for centuries because of its natural oil. Ivory holds a special fascination and, when carved by a master, yields incredible detail that cannot be readily obtained from other materials. Ivory artifacts from China take many forms, from the entire elephant tusk to very ornate carved figurines. Ivory should be kept in a cabinet with a dish of water to prevent cracking.

The Japanese used ivory for their *netsuke*, which are miniature sculptures. The Japanese wore straight-cut kimonos that had no pockets; thus, everything they wanted to carry with them, such as a money or a medicine pouch, had to be tied to a cord. These cords were then counterbalanced with *netsuke*. The *netsuke* had two holes to thread a cord through; the cord was held together with an *ojime* bead. The accessory for which the *netsuke* was chosen would hang below the obi belt, and the *netsuke* would show above, preventing the accessory from slipping through the sash. These *netsuke* are highly collectible. In China, too, *netsuke*, though called a toggle there, were used to balance accessories such as pouches. But in China, these toggles typically were carved from jade. These small toggles can be found in many interesting forms—animals, people, and vegetables. Jade was also used for many sculptures, tea sets, and small carvings.

Chinese painted enamels, also called Canton enamelware, were produced mostly for export, because the Chinese thought of enamelware primarily as a foreign art. In spite of its perceived foreignness, this method of painting on copper did become an important cultural craft for the Chinese. Typical motifs used were flowers mingled with birds and butterflies and scenes from Chinese legends and mythology. Pieces range from tea sets to decorative plates.

A more complicated art than painted enameling is cloisonné. To produce cloisonné, a design is outlined by soldering fine wires of metal at right angles to the base plate, which is gold, silver, or copper. In its earliest forms, the wires were always attached to the base plate by soldering, but in late work (and particularly in Japanese cloisonné of the nineteenth century), the wires are secured by temporary adhesives and are finally held in placed by the enamel itself. The wire outlines are then filled in with different-colored enamels made of finely ground glass, which create a picture that is fired onto the metal. The process of making cloisonné is tedious and time consuming. There are 13 steps in the process, including multiple baking, coating, and finishing tasks.

136 How to Sell Antiques and Collectibles on eBay . . . and Make a Fortune!

Chinese

Japanese

Figure 12-5 Here are two Cloisonné pieces. Compare the small Japanese vase to the small Chinese ginger jar to understand the different types of cloisonné.

Cloisonné has been made since the sixth century, but we are interested primarily in that which was made in the last 2 centuries. Chinese cloisonné is rougher and not as delicate as that from Japan. Chinese cloisonné objects are usually patterned across their entire surfaces; Japanese cloisonné tends to employ lots of empty enamel space (see Figure 12-5). Japanese cloisonné is much more finished, shiny, and smooth and tends to use finer wires to separate the enameling. The older Japanese pieces from 1890 to 1920 are incredible and can fetch much higher prices than the Chinese pieces can. It can be hard to date cloisonné without extensive study. Do your research and spend some time on eBay searching by "cloisonné Japanese" and then "cloisonné Chinese," paying careful attention to the photos you see with each listing.

e B a y   T I P   Remember that when you use eBay for research you may be reading a description from a seller who does not have extensive knowledge. Check out the seller's feedback ratings, read their About Me page, and use your best judgment before taking what they say to be accurate.

Cloisonné pieces from either country done with silver instead of copper or brass wires will usually sell for more. To tell if the wires are silver, copper, or gold color, find an area without heavy patina. It is best not to try and clean an older piece of cloisonné and let the new owner decide if they want to leave the original aged finish.

Plique a jour is another form of cloisonné. It does not have a base metal that the wires are attached to, so it is translucent. It resembles stained glass and is beautiful when held up to the light.

Celadon is a popular Chinese ceramic. It is a greenish blue gray glazed ware developed to imitate the color of jade. It is transparent, and the color comes from the reduction of iron oxide in the glaze during a very hot firing. It is a beautiful color that most of us will recognize. Celadon wares have been made in China since the Shang dynasty (about 1700 BC).

The Chinese foo dog shows up in many materials: ivory, jade, wood, bronze, and marble. It is important to familiarize yourself with what a foo dog looks like. The foo dog (or foo lion, as it can be called) is mainly found near temples, gardens, and home entrances, as it is considered a protector and guard against evil spirits. Foo dogs have a fierce appearance and usually come in pairs. One of the pair has its mouth open to suck in all the evil spirits, and the other has its mouth closed so that the evil spirits cannot escape.

Bonsai is the Japanese horticultural art of pruning plants to produce dwarf trees or shrubs. Most bonsai are grown in shallow trays or pots. Japanese bonsai are big business on eBay. They sell in their live state and also in ornamental forms. Ornamental bonsai made from brass, glass beads, bronze, and wood have sold on eBay for a lot of money.

Japanese sword collecting is a fascinating field. It requires extensive study, but since the majority of expensive Japanese items sold on eBay are these swords, it demands a mention. There are three categories of swords: replicas, swords used in martial arts, and the "real thing." Real Japanese swords can vary in price from $100 or less for a damaged sword to six figures for a rare sword in good shape. A great resource for information on Japanese swords is a Web site called Richard Stein's Japanese Sword Guide (*www.home.earthlink.net/~steinrl/nihonto.htm*). Stein's site contains a lot of great links and recommends several books for further study.

Imari is the name given to the world-famous porcelain produced primarily in Arita on the island of Kyushu. The name comes from the Japanese port town from which the porcelain was originally shipped to other parts of the world. Imari is a hard paste porcelain; it comes in many forms (including plates and vases), and the earliest pieces were blue and white. In 1640, the first pieces were fired with red, green, blue, yellow, purple, and eventually some gold. Imari typically has an underglaze of cobalt blue and the other colors are on top. This means that first the blue is applied onto the ceramic, then a glaze, and then the enamel colors are hand-painted on top. Imari is still being made today, and it is an area that requires intensive study if you plan on buying and selling it.

Satsuma was made in the same southern area of Japan as Imari. Satsuma is a ceramic or earthenware overlaid with a glaze that forms hairline cracks. Over the glaze, figures, flowers, and decorations are painted in enamel. The pieces are varied—anything from ginger jars to vases. Mostly done in earth tones, these pieces can be very valuable. They are still being made today, so do your research before purchasing a piece and don't assume that a piece of Satsuma you find is old.

A lot of great brass comes out of both India and China. Chinese brass items will be vases, incense burners with foo dog designs, plates, chargers, and many other forms. India used brass for vases, candle holders, and the like. Much of the Indian brass will be etched with fancy designs and patterns. Most of the brass we see today will be marked with its country of origin (signifying that it was made after 1891). This brass work can still be highly collectible, depending on shape and condition.

The historical Buddha and founder of the religion named after him was born about the sixth century BC as Siddhartha Gautama, a prince in India (now Nepal). *Buddha* means "the one who has awakened." The Buddha form can be found in many mediums and is a great seller on eBay. Look for Buddhas in ivory, jade, marble, bronze, brass, and wood. Buddha is popular in many countries and cultures of the world.

AUSTRALIA AND THE SOUTH PACIFIC   Australia and the islands of the South Pacific may be home to the world's first people. Stone tools found there date back to 12,000 years before humans appeared in Europe. There are many great artifacts that come from this region. These early people are most commonly called Aborigines, meaning "earliest known."

The Aborigines moved their family groups from place to place, depending on the season and availability of food. The need to be mobile meant that these original settlers could only carry possessions that were essential to their way of life. Many of these belongings had to serve more than one purpose. The *coolamon*, a curved wooden dish, is believed to have been used to dig, carry anything from water to infants, and toss seeds. The men would carry spears and other weapons.

All of these early items were made from natural resources. String and hair was often woven into nets, baskets, and mats. Wood and bark was used to make dishes, shields, masks, spears, and boomerangs. Bone was used for spears and needles. Art was a large part of the life of the early Aborigine. Bodies, rocks, and walls were painted. Bark painting is probably the best-known Aboriginal art form. Aboriginal artifacts sell very well on eBay. A recent search for "aborigi" on eBay yielded 1261 items sold and/or listed in a 2-week period. The study of these early people is fascinating, which contributes to the popularity of these goods on eBay.

Wooden artifacts from the South Pacific in later times, 1800s to 1900s,

Figure 12-6 This 3-foot-long bowl is from Utupua in the Solomon Islands.

are usually quite heavy and well made. Often the bowls are shaped in large ovals and look like boats (see Figure 12-6). African and South Pacific wood items can look similar. You may want to list them as either African or South Pacific in your title and ask for help if you aren't sure of your item's country of origin. Look to South Pacific culture for other fun items like the *didgeridoo* (a ceremonial wind instrument) and boomerangs. Do a completed-auction search on eBay using words like *aboriginal, South Pacific, Australian,* and *artifact* to learn more about these fascinating items.

EUROPE   Greek history can be traced back to Stone Age hunters. Greek life was dominated by religion, so many of their antiquities reflect images of their gods. These gods were memorialized in many materials, including marble, bronze, stone, terra-cotta, clay, and pottery. Since bronze is heavy and sturdy and would survive the test of time, it was a favorite of both the Greeks and Romans.

The Romans derived much of their culture and art from the Greeks. The Romans changed much of this culture, however, by adapting it to their own particular views and needs. The Romans were very practical, and much of their energy was devoted to military strategy and technology. Roman items that are still to be found and sold include armor, statuary, and marble sculptures. Keep in mind that the Romans took the 12 primary gods of the Greeks, kept their stories, and just changed their names. A Web site for researching mythology is *www.mistupid.com/mythology*. One nondivine figure that shows up quite a bit in Roman artifacts is the griffin. The griffin is a mythological creature with a lion's body and an eagle's head and wings.

Many great antiques and collectibles come out of Russia and are being bought and sold today. A name that many of you probably recognize is Fabergé. Peter Carl Fabergé was born in 1846 and was very famous for opening a new era in jewelry art. He was a master at working with gold and enamel. The most interesting thing about Fabergé is that he did not actually create any of the famous eggs that bear his name. Michael Perchin and Hen-

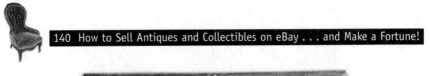

140 How to Sell Antiques and Collectibles on eBay . . . and Make a Fortune!

Figure 12-7 A very beautiful example of a Russian enamel icon made around 1880.

rik Wigstrom from the House of Fabergé were actually responsible for the famous eggs. The signed eggs will either have "MP" for Michael or "HW" for Henrik. Of course, as is the case with most antiques, not all genuine Fabergé eggs were actually signed.

Russian enamels are a variety of cloisonné enamel. To tell the difference between cloisonné and Russian enamel, here's what to look for. Russian enamels are not polished like their Asian counterparts. Also, Russian enamels use twisted (rather than straight) wires to hold the cells of colorful enamel. After the firing, the enamel in a Russian piece lies slightly below this filigree wire so as to show the wire's beauty. The Asian cloisonné enamel will usually go right to the top edge of the straight wire. Many of the beautiful Russian enamels are signed, and these can be very valuable. Russian enamelwork comes in many forms, with some of the most common being boxes, spoons, crosses, and mugs.

Russia is also famous for its icons. In old Russia, life was centered around religion, and icons are a distinctly Russian form of representing saints and religious themes (see Figure 12-7). Most were painted on wood, but others were made from metal or Russian enamel. *Icon* derives from the Greek word for "picture" or "likeness," *eikonoi*. The value of an icon depends on its age, the material it is made from, the quality of its workmanship, and its condition. When the Soviet government introduced antireligious measures, many of the better icon artists were drafted into workshops that produced nonreligious lacquer boxes.

The lacquer box is another very popular Russian craft. Lacquer boxes typically have a black background with colorful detail, and can be beautifully hand-painted with very detailed scenes from Russian life and from famous Russian fairy tales. The signed boxes with the most elaborate detail bring the most money.

Vienna, Austria, is very famous for its bronzes, mostly miniatures, and figural. *Figural* means "in the shape of a figure" (either human, imaginary, or animal), and it's a great word to use in your eBay listings because many people collect—and search for—figural art. Viennese bronzes were very popular in the Victorian era and were often hand painted. They can sell for hundreds of dollars.

From France come Limoges enamels, which are named after a region in central France. As with many of the other European and Asian artifacts we've discussed, Limoges is created by placing an enamel backing on a surface and then hand-painting the top. Limoges enamels are known to be brilliant in color, strong in composition, and beautifully painted. From Limoges come the very popular tiny trinket boxes. A trinket, patch, dresser, or powder box is typically hinged and tiny. There is a category on eBay just for trinket boxes, which can be found by looking in *Collectibles*, then *Decorative Collectibles*, then clicking on "Limoges" and, finally, on "Trinket Boxes." Search on eBay for "Limoge Box" just for fun. For a recent 2-week period, 1679 of these boxes were listed on eBay.

Italian mosaic is art consisting of a design made of small pieces of colored stone or glass. These designs are incredibly intricate and wonderful. Italian mosaic can be found in frames, jewelry, trinket boxes, and other small pieces. And they can fetch big prices on eBay.

NORTH AMERICA   From 1680 to 1820, snuff was the most popular form of tobacco and the social vice most in vogue, not only in North America, but also in Europe and Asia. It was an addiction that transcended all economic classes. With everyone snuffing, the particular snuffbox a person used was an important symbol of social standing. Small hinged or lidded snuff boxes came in any and all materials and shapes. They ranged from the plain to the luxurious and came in metals, porcelain, papier-mâché, wood, and ivory.

There were also snuff bottles that were more common in the Pacific Rim than in North America. These bottles had a little spoon attached to the lid so that the tobacco could be placed in the nose easily. eBay's *Pacific Rim* classification is made up of eleven nations: Japan, South Korea, Indonesia, Singapore, Australia, New Zealand, Malaysia, Thailand, China, Taiwan, and Hong Kong.

The original settlers of North America, the Native Americans, produced many wonderful artifacts. Many of these are still being made today. The term *Native American* is used to refer both to the Indian nations of North America and the Eskimos. Native American artifacts include wonderful leather works, stone tools, fetishes (charms that supposedly have magical powers), blankets, arrowheads, beads, and baskets. All of these items are highly collectible, but baskets are the pinnacle of the Native American items on eBay. Prior to the arrival of the Europeans in America, Indians created basket styles that were unique to their tribes. The basket styles remained constant over time, with little experimentation or variation. The members of each Indian nation used to trade these wonderful items with other native groups.

In the 1890s, it was believed that the Native American culture was destined to disappear. Motivated by this belief, a craze to collect Native American artifacts began. This new fad created opportunities for the weavers who had never before made baskets to sell to nonnatives. The result was a new period of experimentation and creativity. The Eskimos also produce wonderful baskets, hunting tools, and scrimshaw. Scrimshaw is a carving or engraving on ivory, usually made by whalers and sailors from Alaska. This incredible form of art looks almost like a tattoo. Some of the drawings are so fine it is hard to believe that they have been carved into ivory.

These days, anything from Hawaii is also hot, and we aren't just talking about the weather! Collectors especially want anything from 1950s Hawaii. These items are more cultural and kitschy than true artifacts but are collected, just like artifacts, based on the region of the world that they come from. Hawaii collectors are looking for shirts, menus, barware, tikis, sculpture, lamps, hula dolls, nodders, and so forth. You name it, and if it's vintage Hawaii, it will sell on eBay.

An early American farmhouse is another great place to look for cultural items from North America. Most will be found in the kitchen. Primitives (a great word to remember) are objects made—often crudely—for utilitarian purposes. Originally, *primitives* referred to those survival essentials needed by the first American settlers. Now, the definition has been expanded to include objects needed or desired by subsequent generations as well. It also encompasses what is known as country collectibles. Mostly made by carvers and blacksmiths, examples of country collectibles include iron ladles, carved wooden spoons, tin candle molds, and butter churns.

Folk art is another very popular category for early Americana. We touched on this in Chapter 11. Remember that the term *folk art* refers to art that also has a practical function. One popular type of folk art is known as toleware or tole painting. Toleware was originally a French term meaning "sheet iron." The term now refers to hand-painted, decorated metal items, most notably tin. A tole-painted ash bucket would have been made for cleaning out the hearth, not simply for adorning it. New England is the area of the United States best known for toleware. Toleware began its rise in popularity in about 1800, and after 1850 many of the toleware pieces were made using stencils rather than free-form drawings. Geometric designs, scenery, floral, and fruits were all common decorations. Just for fun, take a look on eBay and search for "toleware" or "tole." A search of a 2-week period on eBay turned up 1052 toleware items, and the most expensive was a toleware teapot that sold for for $1,525! Imagine finding one of those at a garage sale!

SOUTH AMERICA AND LATIN AMERICA–MEXICO   The great thing about items from South America and Mexico is that they are often very colorful, lively, and fun. Who wouldn't want a few pieces like these to brighten up their home? Some examples are gourd carving from Peru that dates back thousands of years. The gourds are carved with scenes depicting festivities and daily life. They are beautiful. Guatemala offers us Mayan weaving in wonderful colors. Mexico has pine-needle baskets woven by the Tarahumara Indians. These baskets were originally used to carry water and were made from needles five to six inches long. They have a wonderful smell when wet. Mexico also has wonderful ceramics, the beadwork of Huichol, Milagro crosses, and blanket wares. Spend some time on eBay doing your research. Do a completed-auction search for "Mexic*" or "Latin America" and see what items have sold for the most money. Many of these items were originally made for sale to tourists, so check out your attic!

AVOIDING FAKES AND FRAUDS

Fakes and frauds are a real concern in the area of ethnographics because there is a lot of deliberate fraud being practiced on collectors. Most of the deception is in regard to an item's age. In other words, newer reproductions are often passed off as genuine artifacts. In Bali, Indonesia, wood is often buried for months to make it look ancient. The same is true for wood items from other countries. For someone starting out in antiques and collectibles, the idea of accidentally buying a fraud can be worrisome. Until you have more experience in this area, make sure you trust your seller or limit yourself to small-ticket items.

How can you tell if something is legitimate? Let's examine several techniques. It's easy to tell if brass is really brass. A magnet will not stick to it, and it will have a yellowish color. Identifying the age of brass is trickier. New brass can be aged quickly to make it appear antique. Real bronze will be heavier than brass and should show tiny areas of brass (one of the base metals) on the underside. Unfortunately, the ancient Greek and Roman art market is cursed with a high proportion of fakes. To the inexperienced eye, fakes often look better than real antiquities. Keep in mind that fakes are often perfect, without a hint of repairs, and their colors are often more vivid than the colors on genuine classical artifacts.

Cloisonné is still being made today in the Orient. There is demand for new items but it will never sell for as much money as the old. Look for very fine quality to date the Japanese as antique and the "China" or "Made in China" which would indicate manufacture after 1891, marked on the Chinese goods.

Dating porcelain and sculpture is even trickier. Look for hand-painting versus a stencil or stamped pattern. Hand-painted items, which are much older, will not look perfect. The older pieces may have pitting, which is tiny dark marks made from ash that has fallen into the glaze during firing. There should also be some wear marks on the tops and bottoms of older pieces.

Modern ivory from China is often stained with tea to give it an antique appearance. Bone is often passed off as ivory. Bone is less dense and duller than ivory. There are also plastic imitations of both ivory and bone. Ivory has no smell, and a plastic imitation may smell. If you see a mold mark, it is plastic. The majority of true ivory has cross-hatch marks that you will learn to identify. Telling ivory from other materials takes some experience. If you can, spend some time looking at ivory (and its imitators) at your local antiques shops or shows until you become familiar with what it is supposed to look like.

Many pieces of jadeite are dyed to enhance their color. True jade has a cold feel to it, and if you scratch it with a knife (only try in a hidden place), it will not cut. If cutting does leave a white line, then it is probably soapstone or serpentine.

Be very careful when purchasing and selling ethnographic and cultural items. Know what you are doing, or take care not to pay a whole lot of money. If you are going to spend a lot of money, it would be wise to pay for an expert's opinion. Hire an appraiser!

CONDITION AND REPAIRS

As always, you must be very careful in buying any ethnographic pieces, checking them over very carefully for any defects before purchase. When purchasing ivory, look for cracks that come with age. Jade is also capable of cracking or chipping. Even though cloisonné is a metal product, it is still very fragile. Look for missing enamel and "bruises." A bruise happens when a piece is bumped or dented. Bruises can drastically reduce the value of your piece. Chips and cracks on porcelain pieces must be looked for very carefully. A good way to do this is to slowly run your hands over the entire piece, feeling for defects. With beadwork and basketry, look for missing beads and loose straw.

LISTING YOUR ETHNOGRAPHIC AND CULTURAL ITEMS ON eBAY

Now that we have some background for this fascinating area of antiques and collectibles it is time to actually list an item on eBay. Most of the items in this category are not signed, which makes researching them and listing them quite tricky.

Step One: Product Research and Identification Word Searches

For our example, let's look at a bronze inkwell in the shape of a bird (see Figure 12-8). Most high-quality hand-painted metal animals are bronze. If you are lucky, your bronze pieces will be signed. This piece had a partial signature impressed in the bronze near the bird's tail. The letters "Gesch" were visible, but not the rest.

Research showed us that "Gesch" was part of a German or Austrian word found on most Vienna bronzes. By getting on eBay and searching by "Gesch" we discovered several items with "Geschutzt" in the title. A German-to-English translation Web site showed us that Geschutzt means "registered"— a very important word to find on a true Vienna bronze.

Step Two: Getting Your Title and Description Just Right

As we know, the title is very important. When you list in this category, be sure to work era, shape, material, and an adjective into your title. For our sample, we used "antique" for era, "bird chickadee inkwell" for shape and "Vienna bronze" for material. Then, for added spice, we ended the title with "wonderful!"

Some of the key points covered in the description for our example in-

Figure 12-8   This Vienna bronze bird inkwell sold on eBay for $860.

cluded the fact that the item was originally painted and that some of the paint was remaining. The description also noted that the inkwell was marked near the tail with "Geschutzt," German for "registered" or "copyright," and that the base showed tiny areas of shiny brass, as is typical of bronzes. As we do for most auctions, we also included accurate measurements. We also pointed out any flaws, which is a must if you want to keep a stellar reputation. For this piece, we said it was dirty and needed a cleaning. We also mentioned the cracks in the porcelain inkwell insert.

Step Three: Listing Tips and Tricks

The piece really fit Lynn's criteria for a two-category listing: the two categories are very specific and also have a huge following of collectors. Therefore, we listed it in *Antiques>Decorative Arts>Metalware>Bronze* and in *Collectibles>Pens & Writing Instruments>Inkwells*. There are a lot of bronze collectors, and the same is true of inkwell collectors. Inkwell collectors will pay big bucks for the right piece. Because this piece looks different from every side, we took four pictures showing it from all sides and from the base, and paid 25 cents extra for the gallery picture.

Step Four: Pricing Strategies

As usual, seeing what similar items are selling for will help you to come up with a pricing strategy. We found several animals and birds on eBay that had sold in the $200 range and determined that the inkwell would probably sell for at least $249. Therefore, this item was listed with a starting price of $49 and a hidden reserve of $249. The inkwell ended up selling for $860.

EXPANDING YOUR BUSINESS IN THIS CATEGORY

Now that we are in a category where the items are typically smaller, it is a great time to offer incentives to your customers to encourage them to buy multiple items. This will really help expand your business in this category. Consider having a line in each and every auction description that says "We have a lot of other great similar items up for sale this week. Save on shipping with multiple purchases. Usually the base s/h/i (shipping, handling, insurance cost) for the first item and an additional $1–$2 for each extra item depending upon size." You'll find this strategy really works; you'll be surprised by how many customers will buy more than two items from you at a time!

This is also a great category to do some extra marketing with. For example, let's say that you decide to specialize in Japanese swords. There are many Web sites, magazines, and organizations dedicated to this area. You will have multiple arenas in which to advertise and from which to start compiling customer lists. Then, each time you start an auction with a great item, you can automatically e-mail your customer base. You can even offer your qualified customers an incentive like free shipping or a 30-day money back guarantee with purchase.

Ethnographic and cultural artifacts are some of the most interesting and expensive items that sell on eBay. This is a really fun category to learn more about and there are many clubs and Web sites devoted to these studies. If you like to experience other cultures and explore the world, this is a fantastic area of opportunity. It's also a great category for your travels down the road to an eBay fortune!

13

Pottery

Pottery and Glass is a huge category on eBay, second only to this book's number-one category, *Decorative Collectibles*. Because it's such a big topic, we're going to split it up and discuss pottery in this chapter and glass in Chapter 14.

Pottery is huge business and offers a big dollar volume opportunity. Some of the pottery you will see is not signed, which can make for a marketing and selling challenge. When you are lucky enough to find signed pieces, your job becomes that much easier. Everyone has pottery in their homes, which means you have pottery items you could put up for auction right now—as soon as you learn more about them.

In this chapter, we will look at pottery according to where it was made—either in America or Europe. First, we will touch on the hot California pottery companies and next, on specific American makers, such as Abingdon, Bennington, Fulper, Rookwood, Uhl, Van Briggle, and Weller. Europe doesn't tend to have as many famous factory names as America; instead, it has famous regions. England gives us Staffordshire, France has Faience, and Gouda come from Holland. We will also discuss three important British art potteries: Wedgwood, Moorcroft, and Poole.

We touched briefly on pottery from China and Japan in the last chapter, and in order to give American and European pottery adequate space we have to exclude Asian pottery from our coverage in this chapter. If your hope is to specialize in Asian pottery, we recommend that you invest some time and money in reference books devoted exclusively to Chinese and Japanese pottery.

What Falls into This Category?

Pottery and porcelain are the two primary subcategories of the broader category *Ceramics*. All ceramics are made by firing or baking a nonmetallic material. A ceramic can be identified by examining its body composition, glaze, decoration, shape, era, and maker. *Body composition* simply means the material from which it is made; in other words, is the piece pottery or porcelain? And what type of pottery or porcelain is it? In this chapter, we will focus on pottery. Porcelain (which includes china, bone china, and bisque) will be explored in more detail in Chapter 15. Pottery comes in three basic types: earthenware, stoneware, and ironstone, all of which we will discuss and learn to identify. Then we will consider glazes, as well as some of the more common and popular decorative styles, such as majolica and art pottery. Next, we will figure out what the piece's form tells us about how it was intended to be used: is it a vase, trinket box, salt dip, or something else? Finally, we will discuss important makers like Van Briggle and Rookwood and their wares.

What Are eBay Shoppers Looking For?

When it comes to pottery, anything that was of high quality and good craftsmanship when it was made is highly collectible today. A recent top-category sales report from eBay shows top sales for Dakota, Maling, Uhl, and Poole pottery items. The next most popular categories were British Art, Coors, Folk, Fulper, Gouda, Quimper, Rookwood, and Van Briggle. Art Pottery, Abingdon, Bennington, McCoy, Hull, Roseville, and Staffordshire were also listed as being sought after.

Pottery Is a Great Place for Hidden Treasures

Dealing in pottery affords huge opportunities to find great buys and hidden treasures. One of the best ways to do this is to become an expert in unmarked pottery. If you can find unmarked pieces for a reasonable price and you have the time to research them, you can make a fortune on eBay. Most antiques dealers and eBayers today take the easy route and only buy and sell well-marked pieces. But some of the best items are often unmarked.

What to Look for When You Buy

As pottery is concerned, it is essential that you check for markings when you're shopping at garage sales and thrift stores. The markings will tell you a lot about the piece and will help you sell them successfully on eBay. Keep in mind, though, that the lack of a marking shouldn't necessarily prevent you from making a purchase. As we just mentioned, unmarked pieces can be worth quite a lot.

WHAT ARE THE ESSENTIAL THINGS TO KNOW ABOUT POTTERY?

In order to get the highest prices possible for your pottery pieces, it's important that you know a few key things about this category. The following information will give you a basic knowledge of this category, which will help you sell with success.

Material

One first needs to understand the differences between the two primary types of ceramics: pottery and porcelain. Both pottery and porcelain are made from clay baked in a kiln. The form can be created by hand, thrown on a potter's wheel, or pressed into a metal mold. When pressed into a metal mold, the piece will usually show mold marks on the sides. The difference between pottery and porcelain is all in the combination of clays and minerals they're made of and the temperature at which they are fired.

POTTERY VERSUS PORCELAIN   How can you tell pottery from porcelain? Pottery is usually thicker and heavier than porcelain. It can be multicolored, because of the way it is fired. Pottery is usually used for kitchen and utilitarian wares and may have a glaze or other coating to make it watertight. Porcelain is usually hard and shiny and won't have any pores like pottery does. Porcelain normally has a white base, is semitranslucent, and is fired at very high temperatures (1450°C).

eBay TIP   One simple test for distinguishing pottery from porcelain is to hit the edge of a piece with a pencil. If the piece "sings," it's probably porcelain. The sound you will hear from a piece of pottery will be duller, not as attractive. If you plan to buy and sell ceramics, it's a good idea to practice this pencil test on pieces you know to be pottery and pieces you know to be porcelain. Learn to "hear" the difference.

VARIETIES OF POTTERY: EARTHENWARE, STONEWARE, AND IRONSTONE   Earthenware is the most porous of the three main types of pottery. Most of the clays used to make earthenware can only be fired at a relatively low temperature (800–1100°C). Earthenware must be glazed or it will not hold water. The glazes are usually brightly colored. The base color of the pottery is usually white, tan, or reddish. It is known as a basic, inexpensive pottery. Redware is a form of earthenware and is the crudest type of pottery and has been made for many centuries. It can be thrown on a potter's wheel or formed by hand. It is usually glazed, often in green. Yellowware, which has quite a few collectors, is a more refined earthenware that was made in both England and America.

Any pottery with a yellow base can be called yellowware. These pieces were usually utilitarian and not signed.

Stoneware is a natural blend of clays that is fired at temperatures of 1200–1400°C. It may be unglazed, partially glazed, or multiglazed. It is harder and stronger than earthenware because it is fired at higher temperatures. Most art pottery from the nineteenth and early twentieth centuries is made with a stoneware body.

Ironstone is an overused term that should be used only for earthenware of good quality and better-than-average strength. True ironstone was developed in England and was said to contain powdered iron slag. It is a white earthenware that is tough and thick and used mostly for large dinner services or as commercial tableware.

Types of Glazes: Salt, Tin, Lead, and Luster

After material, the next key thing you should know about pottery is the type of glazes that are used. Using a salt glaze is a very old technique in pottery manufacture. When the kiln reached the right temperature, salt was thrown into the firebox. The salt vaporized and formed a mottled glaze similar in texture to an orange peel. Salt glaze can be semimatte, half-glossy, or hard and glassy. A salt glaze is typically used on stoneware.

If an earthenware piece was glazed with a white coating, it contains tin in the glaze. Some examples of tin glazes are majolica and faience (which we will discuss in "Decorative Styles" in this chapter). Tin glazed ware tends to chip easily.

Lead glaze was also commonly used on an earthenware base. A lead glaze covers earthenware and makes slipware. A lead glaze may be transparent, or it may be artificially colored.

A lusterware glaze is produced when metallic oxides are added to the glaze. Pink lusterware is very collectible and is identified by a shiny metallic pink colored glaze. Copper and silver luster are also popular.

There are many other types of glazes that we don't have room to discuss. Just remember that mixing glazes is an art, and obviously has a big impact on the way the piece turns out overall. Potters glazing their wares are much like painters mixing the paints on their palettes to create wonderful colors and finishes. Pieces with unique glazes will fetch a higher price than pieces with more common finishes.

Decorative Styles

The style of a piece is also crucial. eBay shoppers frequently look for a particular style when they do a search. For that reason, make sure you know as much as possible about the various styles available. Below are some of the most popular ones selling on eBay today.

MAJOLICA   Majolica is usually associated with Italy, but majolica pieces were also made in England, France, Germany, and the United States. The name came into use in about 1850 and (as you might expect) much majolica has a typically Victorian feel. It has a somewhat runny glaze and it is mixed with colors applied with a brush or by dipping. The most popular colors for majolica were blue, green, yellow, orange, and purple. For the most part, majolica patterns are loaded with personality and jump out at you in three dimensions. You can find cauliflower, fruit, vegetables, leaves, berries, corn, birds, shells, coral, seaweed, bamboo stalks, baskets, and people as the decorative motifs. The brightly colored pieces are often whimsical. The older pieces were press molded and are typically heavy and rough. The base of a majolica piece should have the same glaze as the rest of the piece.

THE 3 SS: SLIPWARE, SPATTERWARE, AND SPONGEWARE   Slipware is so called because it is decorated by trailing or pouring slip, which is white liquid clay, over the surface. Decorations of animals, flowers, and patterns were frequently painted on with the slip. Pottery of this kind was also decorated with designs scratched through the glaze. It was the main decorative technique of the seventeenth and mid-eighteenth century. It was used a lot in Egyptian pottery and North American Indian wares, as well as on Staffordshire pottery.

Spatterware, made in the nineteenth century, is another type of decoration. It is an earthenware that gets spattered with colored slip, usually around the border. The brightly colored paint or slip (clay) was dabbed onto the piece to achieve a spattered effect. It was mainly made in England and exported to the United States. Typical patterns are very American: schoolhouses, eagles, and floral designs.

Spongeware was also made in the last part of the nineteenth century. It was crudely decorated by dabbing color onto the drying earthenware with a sponge. Spongeware usually has a splotched design done in simple patterns or at random. It was then covered with clear glaze and fired. Spongeware is generally utilitarian and quite collectible, particularly the blue-on-white pieces. A recent 2-week search period on eBay showed that 700 pieces of spongeware had been listed. The most expensive were two figural pieces (a pig and horse) that sold for $1,300 as a set. Spongeware is still being produced today. Watch out for reproductions.

FLOW BLUE   Flow blue is a stoneware first made in Staffordshire in 1825 that was usually decorated with oriental patterns. It is highly collectible (see Figure 13-1). The flowing color is produced by vapors that cause the color to spread and blur. Some say that flow blue started out as a mistake. Flow brown and flow purple were also made. Some well-known manufacturers, include Adams, Wedgwood, Ridgway, Alcock, and T. Walker.

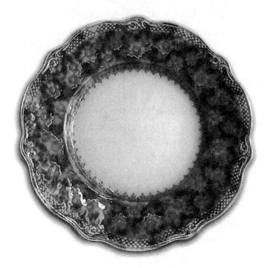

Figure 13-1 This extremely collectible flow blue plate sold for $75 on eBay.

CREAMWARE AND JASPERWARE Creamware is a pottery that could pass for porcelain. The most successful maker was Wedgwood, who sold 900 pieces to Queen Charlotte of England for her palace. After that sale, creamware was also known as Queensware. It was tough, inexpensive, and beautiful and was sold throughout the nineteenth century.

Jasperware is another of Wedgwood's famous inventions. It is a stoneware body, either white or colored, noted for its fine, soft finish. It is unglazed and is most famous in Wedgwood's powder blue and white pieces. The decoration on jasperware was typically classical, with Roman and Greek figures as raised embellishments.

ART POTTERY Art pottery in America was mainly created in art nouveau and mission styles. Americans were inspired by all the wonderful European and Asian ceramics at the international exposition in Philadelphia in 1876. China and pottery painting became an accepted career for women, and there were many potteries founded by and worked by women. The end of the nineteenth century also saw an increased interest in home decorating, and art pottery helped fill the demand for attractive home furnishings. Art pottery was mostly made between 1860 and 1920, although some experts claim the time period was much shorter (1900–1915).

Art pottery was artist made and hand decorated. Art pottery is mostly decorated in earth tones and has a carefully applied glaze and often beautiful, hand-painted flowers or other decorations. A good piece will have an even base, a nice shape, and a maker's mark. Most came from a mold. When look-ing at a mold piece from a production line, keep in mind that the first pieces out of the mold will be the sharpest in detail. As the mold gets worn, there will be a loss in detail. Some of the most famous of the American art potters were Rookwood, Weller, and Van Briggle.

UTILITARIAN   Utilitarian or folk ceramics are earthenwares and stonewares made by regional potters for their own or local use. These pieces were made to be used as jugs, crocks, spittoons, and other storage vessels. Mostly done in redware, yellowware (the earliest), or gray-bodied stoneware decorated with cobalt blue, these were produced in the eighteenth, nineteenth and early twentieth centuries. They came in three shapes—oval or pear, ball, and straight sided. When you come across these crocks and jugs, look for birds and landscapes instead of the flowers that are more common. Pieces with less-common decorations bring in higher prices.

SHAPE AND FUNCTION

Another key part of selling pottery on eBay is knowing how to evaluate the shape and function of various pieces. This idea is applicable to all pottery, porcelain, and glassware, with the exception of some dinnerware and stem-ware, which will be addressed in Chapter 15. Use the shapes shown in Figure 13-2 to help identify your piece, and use that shape name to search on eBay—and, of course, when you are listing your own items on eBay.

Listing by Eras and Style

The best art pottery was made from the 1890s to the 1920s, so it would be classified as late Victorian, art nouveau, mission, and art deco. For more de-tails on these eras, please refer back to Chapter 9. Most American and Euro-pean Arts and Crafts potters of the late nineteenth century worked in pottery rather than porcelain. Most pieces were handmade and used the natural ele-ments that this era was most famous for. We are seeing some Eames-era pot-tery that is also fetching big bucks. Read about Poole pottery in the "European Pottery" section of this chapter for more on midcentury modern.

Listing by Famous Makers

If you are lucky enough to have a marked piece, you will need to determine what type of marking it is. There are three kinds of marks on pottery and porcelain: factory, workman, and pattern. You will seldom find the date. Marks are most commonly placed under the glaze, using a stamp, hand-painting, or transfer. Sometimes they are placed on the lower back of an ob-ject. They can also be painted over the glaze.

The factory mark (like "Wedgwood") is usually placed in a prominent

Apothecary Jar	Bud Vase	Coffeepot	Compote	Cordial or Shot Glass

Crock	Cruet	Egg Cup	Ewer	Figurine

Flower Frog with Vase	Flower Pot or Planter	Napkin Ring	Paintbrush Holder	Paperweight

Patch Box - Hinged	Perfume	Pickle Jar	Pinch Jug	Pitcher

Porringer	Powder Jar	Rose Bowl	Sake Cup	Salt Dip - Open

Snuff Bottle	Stamp Box	Teapot	Toothpick Holder	Trinket Box - Hinged, Limoges

Figure 13-2 These are a few common shapes of pottery, porcelain, and glassware.

position and is sometimes accompanied by the mark of the decorator or factory artist. It is wonderful to have this extra artist mark. The pattern mark is usually a number and was used to good advantage while the factories were still in existence and buyers were reordering by pattern number. These numbers do not mean much to us today. It's easy to mistake these printed or impressed numbers for dates, but remember, pottery is rarely marked with a date.

CALIFORNIA POTTERY   Let's take a look at some famous American potteries. California pottery was not created by a single manufacturer, but instead consists of the output of hundreds of commercial plants. It was such a huge movement in the pottery world that California pottery has its own category on eBay. These wares were mostly made between 1900 and 1955 and ran the gamut from mission style to midcentury modern. California is often on the cutting edge of culture, and in the 1930s it sparked a solid-color revolution that changed the way we look at pottery. Some recognizable California pottery makers include Bauer, Pacific, Catalina, Gladding McBean, Sascha Brastoff, and Vernon. A great reference for those interested in California pottery is *The Collector's Encyclopedia of California Pottery* by Jack Chipman.

ABINGDON   Abingdon gets its name from Abingdon, Illinois, where the pottery is located. It is a hot seller on eBay, so it appears that many people are collecting this type of pottery; in fact, the smaller American pottery houses (including Abingdon, all of the California potteries, and Uhl) are becoming highly collectible. Abingdon only produced art pottery from 1934 to 1950; after 1950, they went back to producing the plumbing fixtures that had been their bread and butter before the art pottery craze hit. They began producing the art pottery to stay in business after the Depression. Their art pottery had a white body that was decorated with many lovely glaze colors. Abingdon pottery has a very art deco and midcentury modern look and feel (see Figure 13-3). Abingdon made novelties, cookie jars, vases, and some dinnerware. During the short 16-year time span they were in the art pottery business, they produced 6 million pieces in 1000 styles and 149 colors.

BENNINGTON   Bennington pottery has become a generic term for the mottled brownware produced in Bennington, Vermont, where two very important potteries were located. They were the United States Pottery Company (1847–1858), known for its Rockingham glaze, and the Norton Pottery (1785–1894). The Rockingham glaze is a shiny, glossy brownish color that you may recognize. Many people emulated the Rockingham glazing technique, and reproductions are common. The Rockingham pieces typically are not signed. Shapes included many figural pieces (lions, deer, cows, fish, and dogs) as well as pie plates, mugs, jugs, and flasks. The Norton Pottery began

Figure 13-3   Remember to show labels and signatures in your photos when possible. This pair of Abingdon pottery cobalt blue vases is shown with its original paper labels.

in 1785 and made utilitarian earthenware and stoneware. It was brilliantly decorated with flowers, birds, and animals. There is a wonderful museum in Bennington that traces the heritage of pottery from this area. A great peek into early Americana and the Victorian era can be found at their Web site: *www.benningtonmuseum.org*.

FULPER   Fulper began manufacturing utilitarian wares, including drainpipes and tile, in 1814 in Flemington, New Jersey. In 1909, Fulper entered the art pottery field. Fulper's glazes are what really set them apart. Vasekraft was the name of their first art pottery line, and some pieces are signed with this paper mark. A paper mark was used when the maker didn't want to impress or stamp their name into the base or side of the piece. It was added almost as an afterthought and was easily removed. Fulper's shapes were unadorned and simple—almost sleek—but it was their exotic color combinations and fantastic thick, drippy glazes that really put their name on the map. They had flair and imagination, and the pieces are truly works of art.

A fire in 1929 resulted in an operations takeover and the end of the Fulper art pottery era. Fulper pieces can sell for big bucks on eBay. Most are signed. Look for a vertical mark that says Fulper, a horizontal mark that says

Rafco, Prang, or Flemington, and paper labels that say Vasekraft. The bigger pieces are worth more. A Fulper lamp, made with a pottery shade and base, just sold on eBay for $8,900. This is obviously hot, so look for Fulper when you are out and about!

ROOKWOOD Rookwood established in 1880, was the first art pottery company in the United States. While the founder, Mrs. Longworth Nichols Storer (Maria), began experimenting with china painting with overglaze colors in 1874, it was not until 1880 that her wealthy and generous father set up a pottery for her in an old schoolhouse in Cincinnati, Ohio. Mrs. Nichols named the plant Rookwood for her father's country estate in Walnut Hills and because it contained the word "wood" and had the same number of letters as the famous name "Wedgwood."

The Rookwood pottery operated at a very low profit in order to give its artists (over a hundred and mainly women) the maximum opportunity to create unusual pieces. Many pieces were artist painted and the artist would sign or initial the piece. Characteristics of this pottery are soft coloring and mellow tones, simple and classical forms, and a good deal of naturalistic decoration. A variety of glazes and some biscuit finish (matte finish) was produced.

Rookwood's designs are incredible. Many experts consider them to be the pinnacle of American art pottery, and their pieces typically fetch the most money of all the art pottery on eBay. The pieces included lovely decorated

Rookwood
Signature
from 1899

Figure 13-4 Rookwood Pottery pieces and a sample signature—look for similar pieces with the same signature.

vases, tiles, plaques, book ends, and lamps. Rookwood had thousands of glaze formulas and kept evolving in both designs and finishes. Initially, all pieces were made by hand. Later, around 1900, Rookwood added production pieces that featured molded decoration and no freehand decoration. The stock market crash of 1929 hurt the company, and it never recovered, finally closing in 1967.

Almost all Rookwood is signed—which means great opportunities for sellers! Signatures on Rookwood contain a lot of information and follow a standard pattern. There are four marks on the base of most pieces. The first mark is the symbol for date. From 1880 to 1886 the mark is a block mark. From 1886 on, the mark is a reversed R and P monogram, with a flame point added above it for each year thereafter until 1900. After 1900, a Roman numeral at the bottom indicated the year. The second mark is the private mark of the decorator, usually his or her initials. The third mark is an initial to identify the clay: *C* represented cream-colored clay, *R* is red, *W* is white, *S* is sage green, *Y* is yellow, *G* signifies ginger-colored, and *O* means olive. Finally, the fourth mark is a letter from *A* to *F* that indicates size. What a great company it was to give us so much history in its signatures!

Rare pieces of Rookwood can sell in the tens of thousands of dollars. Most Rookwood from early in the company's history can sell for close to $1,000. Get very familiar with the starburst signature and watch for it! Lynn just searched eBay, and the most expensive piece to sell in the 2-week period prior to this writing was a hand-painted ewer with flying geese that sold for $5,119. Another reason to love Rookwood is that the signature does not say Rookwood. Most people are not in the know and will not realize that the starburst symbol on their piece of pottery indicates that it is a signed piece of amazing, highly collectible pottery (see Figure 13-4). It is still possible to pick up Rookwood for a song.

ROSEVILLE Roseville is a pottery in Roseville, Ohio. George F. Young invested in this pottery in 1890 and decided to compete with the art line made by Weller by designing a similar ware he called Rozane. Rozane is an underglazed pottery made from local clays and cast in molds. It was tinted by spraying and blending the colors. The decorations were painted with slip colors on the damp clay and, when dry, given the first firing. Then the glaze was applied and the piece was fired a second time. Their mark is a circle enclosing a rose and the name Rozane Ware.

In 1917, a fire destroyed the original plant, and in 1918 George's son, Russell, took over as general manager. He changed the trademark to "Roseville, U.S.A." in raised letters. The plant closed in 1954. Keep in mind that early wares were made and decorated by hand. Later works were molded and painted on assembly lines. Still, any authentic Roseville in good condition, with a desirable pattern and the right color, is highly collectible.

UHL　Uhl pottery is less well known than some of the others we've already discussed, but it does have a growing following and currently shows up on eBay's *Hot* list. Uhl is a very interesting American company founded in 1849 in Evansville, Indiana, though it eventually resettled in Huntingburg, Indiana, in order to take advantage of its more suitable clay. Uhl pottery is known for its utilitarian acorn stoneware jugs and crocks as well as dinnerware and miniatures. Pieces are signed with either an acorn logo and "Uhl pottery" or a circular ink stamp with "Uhl" and "Huntington, Indiana." Jane Uhl, sister of the owner, Louis, made the rarest pieces of Uhl pottery. Her handmade pieces can sell in the thousands of dollars. They are marked with four different hand-lettered variations: "JANE VHL," "J:VHL," "VHL," and "Uhl." These marks, which use Roman *U*s and *V*s, set her items apart from routine production. Watch for these valuable pieces, which were no longer produced after the company closed in 1944.

VAN BRIGGLE　Artus Van Briggle was enchanted with the dull, or dead, glaze found on a Chinese Ming dynasty vase at the Louve Museum in Paris. He experimented with glazes until 1896, when he rediscovered the formula for and secret of creating the dead glaze. Van Briggle was employed at the Rookwood Pottery, and his glaze was acclaimed at the Paris Exposition in 1900 as being the finest on exhibition. Van Briggle created glazes ranging from a completely dead finish to a dull gloss with slight texture and quality rarely found except in older Chinese wares. His dream of owning his own pottery came true in 1901, when he built a plant in Colorado Springs. He used native Colorado clay and original designs. No paints were used, the colors being achieved only in the glaze itself.

His natural forms typified the art nouveau movement. His wife, Anne, was also an artist, and they combined the *A*s of their first names to form a trademark, a double *A* enclosed in a square. Prior to 1920, this was used along with a year mark in Roman numerals and a shape number. After 1920, the pottery was marked with the Van Briggle name and the Colorado Springs origin, with no dating. Van Briggle passed away in 1904 from tuberculosis, but his wife continued the work, and the factory is still in existence. Pieces made prior to his death are the most valuable. New pieces have different glazes than the old, so do your research before investing. A great reference is *The Collector's Encyclopedia of Van Briggle Art Pottery: An Indentification & Value Guide* by Richard Sasicki and Josie Fania.

WELLER　Finally, we come to the last of our American potteries: Weller. Samuel A. Weller was a country potter who began making milk crocks and red earthenware pots in his hometown in Ohio in 1872. He started out with a one-man one kiln shop in a log cabin, but by 1893 he had 60 employees and a pottery factory in Zanesville, Ohio. He produced art pottery that was similar to Rookwood, and it was named and signed Louwelsa, after his daughter Louise and himself ("Lou" for Louise, "wel" for the first part of his last name and "sa" for his first two initials). This line was made in at least 500 shapes and sizes including vases, jardinieres (planters), and clocks. It was produced from 1895 until 1924 and is the most popular of the Weller lines.

Another popular Weller line was Dickensware, and there were two varieties put into production around the turn of the twentieth century. The first was an underglaze slip on a dark background featuring scenes from literary works by Dickens. The second variety was a caramel shading to turquoise matte background with great decorations as varied as Native Americans, golfers, monks, and scenes from Dickens novels.

The sgraffito technique used for these designs involved scratching a pattern into the piece's soft clay with a large needle. Color was then added with a brush, and the pieces were covered with a semimatte glaze. In 1901, Weller brought Jacques Sicard over from France to work with him. They created a wonderful metallic luster glaze on an iridescent dark green, purple, or brown background. These pieces are usually signed on the side or near the bottom with "Sicard" or "Weller Sicardo." This line was only made between 1901 and 1907 and is supposedly the most expensive of any pottery coming out of Zanesville, Ohio (see Figure 13-5). Many wonderful Weller lines were made over the years, and one of the best known is the company's standard matte-green art pottery. From 1895 until 1915, Weller was marked with "Weller" im-

Figure 13-5 A rare Weller Sicardo art glass vase made sometime between 1901 and 1907.

pressed on the bottom and the name of the pattern curved above it. After 1915, the name of the pattern or line was dropped and only the name Weller remained. Samuel died in 1925, and at the time of his death the three factories employed 600 workers! The Depression brought about a slow decline in sales and forced the closure of two of the three plants. In 1948, the last remaining factory was closed.

European Pottery

Europe gives us Staffordshire from England, Faience from Quimper, France, and Gouda from Holland. In addition, there are several famous makers whose items are consistently popular, Wedgwood, Moorcroft, and Poole, and we will discuss them in turn.

STAFFORDSHIRE   Staffordshire is a county in England, and in the early eighteenth century many potteries sprang up there. Staffordshire has become a generic term for the type of ceramicware typical of that region; typically white with some hand-painted decoration. Figurines and groups were made in great numbers. Trinket boxes were a favorite form, and dogs were one of the favorite subjects. Often, pieces were made in pairs and were mirror images of one another. The wares were cheaply made and were marketed to the lower and middle classes to adorn their mantles and china cabinets. Many Staffordshire companies signed their wares, although there are too many companies to mention.

QUIMPER AND FAIENCE   Quimper and faience are terms for French-made earthenware pottery that has highly colorful tin glazing and usually lovely hand-painted scenes. Many factories in Quimper, France, made this pottery beginning in the 1600s. Some of their patterns feature peasant figures in bright traditional costumes, birds, roosters (the symbol of France), and botanical scenes. It really is a type of French folk art. One company in particular, Quimper Faience, began making ceramics in 1690, and they are still in business today.

GOUDA   Another type of pottery named for the region it comes from is Gouda. Gouda was the main center of the pottery industry in Holland, beginning in the eighteenth century. The Dutch Gouda style that most people attribute to this region was first manufactured in 1885 and lasted until about 1915. Goudaware is highly decorated and colorful. It looks almost like a raised enamel mosaicware done in three dimensions. Most of the pottery was finished in a matte glaze, but glossy pieces can be found and they fetch higher prices.

Goudaware is very art nouveau in form, with stylized flowers, birds, and geometrics as the main patterns. Watch for the Gouda name, which is usually part of the signature from many of the various manufacturers. Pieces in this style can sell in the thousands of dollars. Do some research on eBay so you can recognize these pieces at garage sales at a bargain price.

WEDGWOOD Josiah Wedgwood of Burslem, England, founded Wedgwood in 1759. He was a marketing and creative genius who would invite famous artists to help design his lines. He was famous for his jasperware and Queensware, which we already touched on in the "Decorative Styles" section of this chapter. Three-color jasperware is very rare; most pieces were just two colors. In the twentieth century, several lusterware lines were added (butterfly, dragon, and fairyland). These are very sought after. Although Josiah passed away in 1795, the company is still in business today, and most people know what Wedgwood looks like.

 eBay TIP Be very careful when listing Wedgwood on eBay: buyers and sellers alike frequently misspell it "Wedgewood," and including both spellings in a listing title (or searching for both spellings) can pay off.

Because of its popularity and distinctive look, Wedgwood has been plagued by more than its share of imitators. In order to distinguish true Wedgwood from its copiers, remember that true Wedgwood was never signed "Wedgwood & Co." but simply marked with an impressed "Wedgwood." After 1891 (when the McKinley Tariff act was passed), "England" was added to the Wedgwood mark. The "Wedgwood England" period continued until 1908, when the company began marking their wares with the phrase "Wedgwood Made in England." Most Wedgwood after 1860 was also signed with a three-letter dating code. The first letter represents the month of manufacture, the second identifies the potter who made the shape, and the last letter signifies the year it was made. After 1929, the year mark was replaced by the last digits of the year. In other words, if the piece is marked "40," it was made in 1940. Check out *www.thepotteries.org/mark/w/wedgwood-date.html* if you need more help with dating Wedgwood pieces.

MOORCROFT Moorcroft was founded in 1897 in England as a studio within a larger company, Macintyre Potteries. The designer was 24-year-old William Moorcroft, who soon began to sign or initial each piece of pottery he produced. This did little for the Macintyre company's business, and in 1912 William Moorcroft went out on his own. He was making art pottery that ri-

164 How to Sell Antiques and Collectibles on eBay . . . and Make a Fortune!

Figure 13-6 This small Moorcroft Pomegranate pitcher sold for $1092 on eBay.

valed that of the American manufacturers. He began making his popular "Pomegranate" ware around 1914 (see Figure 13-6). Queen Mary collected his pottery, and in 1928 he was named Potter to the Queen.

During the 1920s and 1930s he began experimenting with red glazes, also known as "Flambe." These were made through a very difficult procedure. He passed away in 1945, and control of the company went to his son, Walter. The company is still in business in Stoke-on-Trent, England, and their pottery is fabulous. Check out their Web site at *www.moorcroft.com*. Most pieces are signed with an imprinted "Moorcroft" or a script "William Moorcroft."

POOLE Jesse Carter founded Poole Pottery in 1873. He bought a run-down pottery studio in the town of Poole, Dorset, and the pottery remains in the same location today. Jesse was a smart man and saw that there was a large deposit of clay close by and a wonderful harbor out of which to export his goods and bring fuel in. Jesse retired in 1901, and other members of his family continued to run the pottery. In 1921, the company was set up as Carter, Stabler and Adams (CSA). "Carter" stood for Cyril Carter (Jesse's Grandson), "Stabler" stood for Harold Stabler (a designer and silversmith), and "Adams" signified John Adams (a designer and potter). John Adams's wife, Truda, was also a big influence over the work that followed in the next few years.

eBay TIP Poole pottery produced in the 1920s and 1930s, not yet even true antiques, is some of the most desirable. Its rise in importance is akin to what has happened in recent years to 1950s and 1960s collectibles. In fact, a search on eBay recently revealed that some of the most expensive Poole items are chargers (large plates) from the 1960s, with several selling for over $700!

In 1958, the company appointed Robert Jefferson as its designer, and he developed a whole new range of studioware. It was soon to become known as the Delphis line. Poole's Delphis designs of the 1960s and 1970s were a departure from anything they had ever done before. The painters were given free reign, and their abstract patterns were trendy and perfect for the era. In 1964, CSA once again reverted to the name Poole Pottery Limited. The early pieces of Poole were marked with an impressed "Poole England." Later pieces have a dolphin and "Poole England" in ink. Poole is a great name to look for in your hunt!

AVOIDING FAKES AND FRAUDS IN THE POTTERY SUBCATEGORIES

Keep in mind that a valuable piece of pottery is worth trying to reproduce. There are a lot of reproductions coming out of Asia. The Roseville "repros" are so good, even having the raised signature mark, that they may even be using some of the original molds. The best way to defend yourself against reproductions is simply by studying the lines and pieces that interest you. Learn more about this category with books, by joining Web-based clubs, and by going to antiques shows and asking to see examples of both antiques and reproductions. Always keep learning, as every year there can be new kinks in the marketplace.

As a general tip, however, older pieces of pottery should have some wear marks on the base of the piece. These wear marks can include small scratches or dirt. If the base of your piece is shiny, bright, and clean, it may not be very old. In the beginning, you may want to buy only from reputable dealers who will provide you with authentication for your purchases.

CHECKING FOR CONDITION AND REPAIRS IN POTTERY

Condition is king in this category. Always take the time to check your piece very carefully for chips, cracks, crazing, discoloration, scratches, repairs, missing glaze, and missing pieces. Note all of these things in your listing. If a piece is perfect it is a good idea to spell that out in your eBay listing by saying "no chips, no cracks, no crazing, and no repairs."

A chip can range from a tiny pinpoint, called a fleabite, to a flake to a really large missing piece. It is always good to measure the chips when you prepare your listing, saying something like "2–3 small chips, with the largest being ¼ by ½ inch." Sometimes, from a chip, a crack will grow. Always look very carefully around the edges of a chip to check for cracks. If your piece does have a true crack (as opposed to crazing), you will be able to feel the crack from both the front and back of the piece with your fingernail. If your piece has crazing, this must also be mentioned.

eBay TIP Crazing is tiny lines, sometimes called spiderwebbing, that appear on pottery and porcelain. Crazing occurs if there is a difference in the amount of shrinking of the clay versus the glaze. These lines usually appear after firing but can also appear years later. They can also occur as a response to the environment. Once again, if your fingernail catches top and bottom, it is a crack and not the less problematic crazing.

Discoloration occurs when a piece has not aged well; certain areas will have turned darker, usually a brownish color. Age spots can also be seen on some older pieces. Be sure to note all of this in your description for your listing, but don't be entirely discouraged if your piece is discolored—that's often evidence of its age and authenticity.

Scratches can be found on glass and porcelain. Repairs of scratches can be tricky to spot; in fact, any flaw can be hard to spot, especially if it's been hidden or repaired very well. A great idea is to take a black light and shine it all around your piece. If there have been any repairs to the piece, the black light will highlight the glue and the area repaired. On a piece of pottery there can be spots of missing glaze where the glaze didn't take due to moisture or oil. Make sure to note these and describe them fully in your listing. Finally, always look for missing pieces. Missing lids and fingers and toes of figurines are quite common.

Keep in mind that there are flaws that may have occurred during the making of the piece. Some of these include bubbles that have popped, chips under the glaze, and dirt or ash that was trapped under the glaze. If you can ascertain that the damage was done in the making, your piece will be more valuable than if the damage was done after it left the factory. A bubble that may have popped during firing will show as a small concave hole. Sometimes a piece will be made with a small chip but the factory will decide to release it as it is anyway. If the chip has been covered with the glaze or paint, then it was done in the making. Many of the old factories had ash and soot flying around when they made their items. You will sometimes see these bumps or small dirty specks on a piece of pottery. They were done in the making and will help to date your piece as being an early item.

LISTING POTTERY ON eBAY

For our sample pottery listing, we will use the white pottery dog (see Figure 13.7) that Lynn found at a garage sale for 50 cents. The dog was white and Lynn recognized it was Staffordshire pottery. After you have spent some time around different types of pottery, you will be able to readily identify the different types as well. Staffordshire is one of the easier ones to spot because a lot of Staffordshire is marked. The dog's base was marked "L & Sons Limited Made in England." It is always a good nice confirmation for a piece you suspect is Staffordshire to be marked "England," since that is where all Staffordshire comes from!

Step One: Start with Your Research

For our first step, we went on eBay under the Advanced Search page (which you all know how to find by now) to hunt for completed auctions containing "L* Sons." The search returned an auction listing for a piece by "Lancaster & Sons Ltd." We then used Google to do some further research on this firm. Within seconds, we learned that Lancaster & Sons Ltd. made Staffordshire in Stoke-on-Trent, England, for only 44 years, between 1900 and 1944. Having a fairly narrow production date range is very useful information to put in listings. Further research revealed that Staffordshire companies in general made a lot of spaniel dogs in pairs to be displayed on fireplace hearths. That was enough information to write a good listing.

Step Two: Key Words for Pottery

We knew it was important to get the type of dog, name of the company, type of pottery, and the era produced into the listing so we chose the title: "Lancaster & Sons Staffordshire Spaniel Dog Antique NICE."

eBay TIP Whenever you have a piece that features an animal (be it a cat, dog, or bird), do your research and find out the type. Dogs are a huge business on eBay, but most dog owners and collectors are very specific about their type of dog. They only want to collect their particular breed (whether it is a bulldog, boxer, or spaniel). If you can figure out the name of the breed featured on your piece, make sure you use that in the title as well as the word *Dog*.

In the description of this Staffordshire spaniel, we were careful to tell exactly how the piece was signed (with "L & Sons Ltd. Made in England"). Here's a test. What does the Made in England tell us? Right! It was made after 1891! But we had already figured that out another way. The description

Figure 13-7 This Staffordshire dog was found at a garage sale for 50 cents and sold on eBay for $37.67! That's a great return on investment!

then explained what the "L" stands for and the years of operation of the firm. It also provided the colors of the dog, noted the damage, and remarked on the parts that were hand-painted. The final listing read:

> This darling dog is off-white Staffordshire with yellow and black handpainted details. He has overall crazing (quite normal and typical) and there is a flake chip on the backside near the base that measures 3/8 by 3/8". There is also a tiny speck of black paint missing. These dogs were used in Victorian times and later, on either side of a fireplace and were usually made in a left and right facing pair. This auction is for only one dog. This dog probably dates to the 1910's to 1920's. Cute!

Note the words used—*darling* and *cute*—to make the dog sound very desirable. Again, if you don't think your piece is fantastic, neither will your buyers. If you're enthusiastic, you improve the chances that they will be too. Spend the extra time and words to convince your buyers to buy. It is your only chance to persuade them.

Step Three: Using Other Listing Techniques

Since we didn't think we'd make too much on this piece, we chose to use only one photo. We listed the spaniel in the category *Staffordshire* (#458). Because we knew it wasn't worth over $100, we didn't double-list the piece in the *Dog: Spaniel* category. If this dog would have come with his mirror-image pair, they would have been worth $100 and Lynn would have put them in both categories because both categories are very specific. Because this piece only cost 50 cents, we knew we'd be happy getting $9.99 for it; therefore we started the auction bidding at $9.99 with no hidden reserve. The auction ended with 5 bids, and the piece sold for $37.67! Not too shabby.

Pottery is a very fun category to buy and sell. It can be found at many garage sales, in every antique store, in most thrift stores, and even in your home. Take your time and turn over every piece you see. Don't be discouraged if it is not signed. If the piece looks like it was expensive and seems unique, do some research. You can make your fortune using your investigation skills in this category. You may decide that you want to specialize by country or region or maker. Spend the time and money to become knowledgeable about your area and it will pay off when you sell a piece for big bucks!

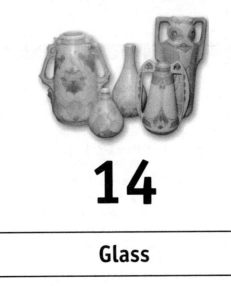

14

Glass

As we mentioned in Chapter 13, the second biggest eBay category that we will be covering in this book is *Pottery and Glass*. We covered pottery in the last chapter; this chapter will focus on the second half of this popular category: glass.

Exploring the Glass Category

This chapter will cover all types of collectible glass, excluding glass dinnerware, serveware, and stemware, which are covered in Chapter 15. In order to make this chapter more manageable, we will also discuss Early American Pressed Glass (EAPG) and Depression glass in Chapter 15. Most of our time will be spent looking at art glass, as it is by far the most valuable and collectible type of glass on the market.

Because the majority of glass is not marked, the first step in identifying glass is ascertaining the manufacturing technique. Was the glass cut, pressed, or blown? Does it have a rough or polished pontil? The next step is to analyze the decorations. It is etched, acid cameo cut, or does it have applied rigoree? In the "Identifying a Piece by Decorations and Types" section of this chapter, we will also analyze the glass by color and finish, looking at glassware like cranberry and amberina. The third step in the identification process is to examine the shape, and the fourth is to date the piece by era. Some sample shapes of glass and pottery were illustrated in Chapter 13; eras were covered in Chapter 9. Please refer back to those chapters. The final step in identifying glass is (if possible) to identify the maker; as examples, we will take a look at art glass from such famous and identifiable makers as Galle, Blenko, and Tiffany.

What are eBay Shoppers Looking For?

There are many types of glass that are consistently hot on eBay. We will start our survey of glass by looking at glassware by American makers such as Blenko, Fenton, Steuben, and Tiffany. We will then investigate various European glassware companies, beginning with French art glass from Galle, Lalique, and Daum Nancy, then move on to Waterford from Ireland. We will also examine glass by region, focusing on glassware from Bohemia, Scandinavia, and Italy. This is such a huge area of opportunity that we suggest you invest time and money in some good reference books if you intend to do much business in glassware.

When it comes to finding out what eBay buyers want, we looked once again at a report on eBay's top-selling categories. On the day we looked, we found French and Scandinavian art glass to be the hottest categories. The Scandinavian art glass is most likely Eames-era mod and retro, which is further proof that items from the 1950s are really selling. In the *Hot* category for glass we found Bohemian/Czechoslovakian and North American art glass, as well as anything from the 1940s, 1950s, and 1960s. Other well-known glassware that eBay names as their best in the collector's showcase (a rotating advertisement that sometimes shows up on the front page) were Steuben, Italian art glass, and Waterford.

LEARNING ABOUT GLASS TO IMPROVE YOUR BUYING STRATEGIES

Finding Your Fortune in Unmarked Glass

One of the best ways to make your fortune on eBay is to become an expert in unmarked glass. If you are able to find good unmarked pieces for reasonable prices, take your time and research them. You can do really well. For example, Lynn bought a vase for $4 at a thrift store. She saw an etched mark on the base, but it was extremely difficult to read. She took it home and started to do some research. With a lot of effort, she was able to make out the words "Venin," "Italia," and what looked like "TXX" on the base, but that was all. Lynn searched for completed auctions containing the words "Venin" and "Italia" on eBay. Up came an auction for a vase from a very famous Italian glass company called "Venini," and she determined it to be the company that made her piece. Lynn included all the information about Venini that she could find in her listing. She also included the last part of the signature, "TXX." A nice eBayer immediately e-mailed Lynn to let her know that it wasn't "TXX," but "TW" for Tapio Wirkkala, a very famous artist. With all that information, Lynn was able sell her $4 vase for $365! Remember, you make your money by researching and correctly identifying your piece (see Figure 14-1).

Figure 14-1 The signature on an art glass vase that sold on eBay for $365.

Key Resources on Glass

The *Glass* category is constantly changing and you need to be continually learning more. Some great resources are *Maine Digest*, the *Antique Trader*, and any of the Web sites listed in this chapter.

POPULAR SUBCATEGORIES OF GLASS

Glass is just as fascinating as pottery. Glass has been around forever (well, at least since the Bronze age—about 3000 BC). Collecting glass can become addictive! Be careful. You don't want to lose all your eBay profits to a new collection.

Glass is basically created from silica (made from flint, quartz, and sand) that is heated with an alkaline such as flux or potash (derived from the burnt ash of wood and plants). Silica is most commonly made from pure white sand that has been mined, washed and cleaned, and transported very carefully. The purity of this sand is directly related to the quality of the final glass product. The silica-alkaline mixture must be heated above its melting point (2400–2700°F), which produces a fused melt that, when cooled rapidly, becomes a rigid substance.

The addition of certain chemicals produces colors. Ruby glass is made by adding metallic selenium and sulphide of cadmium to the glass batch. Ruby glass can also be made with gold or copper. Chrome oxide or salts will make green glass. Copper and cobalt oxides will produce blue, and the list goes on. Mixing the chemical additives will produce a fascinating variety of tints.

The addition of metals during the production process results in the heavier, famously brilliant glass known as crystal. The production of crystal can be traced back to an Englishman named George Ravenscroft, who discovered that substituting oxide of lead for soda in the production process resulted in a heavy glass with diamond-like brilliance. This glass was called flint. It was the precursor to lead crystal. Any fine crystal will most likely have lead in its makeup.

Looking at a Piece's Material and Craftsmanship

There are three basic ways to make glass. It can be completely mouth blown (called free-blown), blown into a mold (blown-molded), or pressed into a mold (mold-pressed).

FREE-BLOWN Free-blowing glass is a difficult art and can take years of study. The techniques of a glass worker (or, flint) are often handed down from generation to generation. It can take up to 10 years of training to be ready to blow glass. Blowing glass is the oldest method of forming pieces. The hot molten glass is gathered on the end of a long pipe, called a blowpipe. The gob of molten glass is blown by means of the mouth and lungs into a hollow body. It is worked into a basic shape and then place onto a pontil rod for further shaping. If a handle is to be applied, the handle gatherer will bring a gob of glass to the finisher who sticks it on the body of the pitcher, pulls it out like taffy, cuts off the desired length, attaches it to the piece, and shapes it while the glass is still pliable and hot.

This is really an amazing craft, especially considering that during its entire production the glass article has to be kept at a working temperature of 1000°F to keep it from cracking due to premature cooling. When the glass piece is finished, it is broken off of the rod, which leaves a rough scar called a pontil mark on the base. The pontil can then be polished to a lovely smooth texture or left rough. When you see a pontil you can be assured that the piece was blown.

Certain companies, like Tiffany, polish their pontils, and certain companies do not. Blenko rarely signed their pieces (they used only paper labels), but they did not polish their pontils, and this can help to identify their glass.

BLOWN-MOLDED Another way to manufacture glass is to blow the glass into a mold. Glass produced in this manner is called blown-molded glass. A hot glob of glass is placed into a mold with the blowpipe and then blown into until it fills the mold. When the glass has cooled the item is removed from the mold and then finished. The outside of the glass will have the mold pattern, and the inside will follow the reverse of the pattern.

MOLD-PRESSED   The third way to create glass is to press it by hand, rather than by blowing, into a mold. This method, called mold pressing, was invented in the United States in 1820. To make a piece of mold-pressed glass, you place a hot glob of glass into a metal mold and then it press it all the way into the mold with a metal plunger, or follower, to form the inside shape. Mold-pressed pieces are different from the other two types because both the inside and outside surfaces are formed and shaped by a mold.

The inside of mold-pressed glass is perfectly smooth, as distinguished from blown-molded glass. Pressed glass will also have thicker walls, and you will be able to identify the mold marks or lines on its outer side. We will discuss pressed glass (both clear and colored) and Depression glass in Chapter 15. Colored pressed glass includes, custard, milk, carnival, and vaseline. Some makers include Heisey and Imperial.

Identifying a Piece by Decorations and Types

In this section we will go through decorative techniques, as well as styles and types of glass that are made by more than one company. We will focus on glass that is free-blown or blown-molded.

CUT GLASS   Cut glass is decorated by a moving wheel and is always cut and finished by hand. The glass to be cut is either free-blown or blown-molded. Cutting wheels are made of iron or stone, and finishing wheels are made of cork, wood, felt, or leather. In rough cutting, a small stream of sand and water falls onto the wheel while it is in motion. It is the sand between the wheel and the glass not the wheel itself, that cuts the groove. When this heavy work is done there are many steps to finishing it. Cutting glass is very expensive and labor-intensive work. Cut glass is distinguished by the geometrical lines of its patterns that form prisms and facets of four, six, and eight sides.

There are three general periods of American cut glass: the early American period (1771–1830), the middle period (1830–1880), and the brilliant period (1880-1905). Cut glass of the brilliant period was made in quantity and was a very popular wedding gift in the day (see Figure 14-2). Some glass after 1900 was signed, so look very carefully in the bottoms of bowls for acid-etched signatures from firms such as Hawkes. Cut glass was frequently used by its owners, as opposed to being strictly decorative, and as a consequence many of the pieces will have chips on the points. Be very careful when you look these pieces over. Pieces vary in value and importance according to the

Figure 14-2 This is an example of a cut glass bowl from the American brilliant period.

purity of materials used, the skill of the manufacturer, and the artistry and talent of the cutter. The pontil mark, if there is one, will be polished or hidden by a cut pattern.

CASED AND CARVED CAMEO GLASS   Cased glass is produced when layers of different colors of glass are placed on top of one another. This type of glassware can also be called overlay glass. These pieces were sold in many forms, but cased-glass tumblers were particularly popular. When these pieces were carved, they were known as cameo art glass. Making cameo art glass is a very difficult and costly process, but the results are incredible. As many as five layers of glass are used to develop the design. Hand carving can be supplemented by the use of a copper engraving wheel, and acid may have been used to cut away the layers more quickly. The value can be gauged by the ratio of actual hand carving to acid-etched work; the more hand carving, the more valuable. Please refer back to Figure 9-6 for an art nouveau carved cameo glass perfume.

A different and easier way to achieve a somewhat similar result was to coat clear glass with a colored glass and then cut through to show the transparent glass beneath. This glass-making method was very popular in Czechoslovakia.

ENGRAVED GLASS   Engraving is used on free-blown glass and entails the cutting of the glass surface with stone wheels. Very fine detail can also be made using diamond-pointed wheels. Engraving is used mostly on thinner pieces of glass, such as stemware. To check to see if a piece of glass has been engraved, examine the cuts that form the design. They will have curved edges.

ACID ETCHING The technique of acid etching almost resembles engraving. The entire glass blank is covered in wax or resin, and the design is etched through the coating with a sharp tool. The piece is then exposed to hydrofluoric acid, which eats away the exposed area, leaving a design. In contrast to the curved edges of an engraved design, the cuts in acid-etched glassware will have straight edges.

APPLIED DECORATIONS: HAND PAINTING, GOLD LEAF, AND RIGAREE Glassmakers looked for ways to set themselves apart with their wares. Spirals, ruffles, beading, and other patterns of hot glass were applied for decoration before the piece cooled. Hot-glass decorations are called "applied rigaree," and "rigaree" is a great key word to use when listing glass on eBay.

Hand-painting was also used to fancy or "doll up" a piece. Sometimes the decor was very heavy, much like an enameling. These hand-painted pieces are lovely and very Victorian in look and feel.

Gold leaf was sometimes added to the mix and could be applied very thinly or quite heavily. This gold leafing does wear with age, so be sure to note the condition in your description.

ART GLASS *Art glass* is the term used to describe the experimental glass made in Europe and America beginning in 1870. The new styles established by makers of art glass included innovative surface textures, shaded colors, and casing. Some examples are the iridescent Tiffany surfaces, the carving of Webb cameo glass, and the aurene of Steuben. Art glass was developed as popular taste was turning away from factory-made objects and embracing handmade art pieces that came right from the artists' studios.

Although this period is called the art nouveau era of glass and lasted until just 1900, it was also taking place during the Arts and Crafts era. Keep in mind that lots of wonderful pieces were made in the 1950s and later, and that there is still great art glass being made today.

IRIDESCENT GLASS AND FAVRILLE Louis Comfort Tiffany was best known for his wonderful iridescent hand-blown glassware. He developed his own formulas of vaporized metals and continued to experiment with them, with delightful results. Tiffany was a creative genius and was greatly influenced by the glass he saw in Europe, most notably pieces by Galle and Loetz. His white and red iridescent pieces are impossible to find. Most pieces are in the gold colors, but his blue is famous. Steuben came out with aurene iridescent art glass to rival Tiffany and remained Tiffany's primary competition for many years.

CRANBERRY GLASS Cranberry glass, as it is known today, is not a specific type of glass but a specific color of glass. As you might suspect, it derives its name from the cranberry. The mix for cranberry glass contains gold, and the color is developed by reheating the glass. It can be either free-blown or blown-molded. It is still being made today, so don't assume that a cranberry glass piece is older. Cranberry glass was at its most popular in the United States right after the Civil War, and this is when the largest quantities were manufactured. Many companies, such as Fenton, still make it, and it is a very popular item on eBay.

MARY GREGORY   Contrary to popular myth, Mary Gregory was a real person. She was born in Providence, Rhode Island, at an unknown date, and she died in Sandwich, Massachusetts, in 1908. She worked for the Boston and Sandwich Glass factory. Mary was a spinster who loved children and specialized in painting or enameling pictures of children on glassware. She worked during the 1870s and 1880s, and her style is now so well known that the glass-painting and enameling technique she used has come to be named for her, despite the fact that it was originally developed in Bohemia (see Figure 14-3).

Obviously, the majority of what we know today as Mary Gregory glassware was not painted by Mary herself. It may include many different colors of glass, with cranberry being the most popular. Mary Gregory work is still being done today, and a lot is currently coming out of Czechoslovakia. The older pieces are lighter and finer in detail. The newer pieces may show mold marks.

Figure 14-3 This is an atypical antique Mary Gregory type vase, decorated with an angel (instead of children) on cobalt blue glass.

AMBERINA   Amberina was patented on July 24, 1883, and was one of the earliest types of art glass. Typical amberina pieces shade from an amber at the base to a rich red color. The glass comes out of the blow-mold an amber color (a sprinkle of gold is used in the mixture) and is then put back into the glory holes, which are the openings in the furnace that are used in glass blowing. The extra heat, usually at the top part of the object, causes it to strike, or turn red. The color at the top of a piece of amberina should be a deep wine red. If the base of the object, instead of the top, is put back into the glory hole the piece will shade from a deep red at the base to amber at the top and is called reverse amberina.

Several companies made this glass, including the New England Glass Company, Mt. Washington Glass Company, and even Baccarat. It is still being made today, so keep that in mind as you try to date your amberina piece. The newer pieces tend to be thicker and of brassy, brighter yellows and reddish oranges.

SATIN GLASS AND MOTHER OF PEARL   Satin glass is glassware with a velvety matte finish, which is created through a bath in acid. It has been made since 1857 in England and since about 1880 in America. Mother of pearl is a type of satin glass. Mother of pearl is blown-molded so that an intaglio design (a type of cutting or engraving that leaves a slightly depressed design) is left on the surface of the glass. Then the first layer is sealed with a second layer, trapping air. Some of the more common patterns for this intaglio design are the diamond quilted, raindrop, and herringbone. Mother of pearl is usually done in pastels that include a soft blue, pink, and yellow.

Reproductions have been rampant in this style since the 1960s so be very careful. The newer pieces are heavier and their colors not as true. Another thing to watch for is a powdery substance either inside or out. It is the residue from the process of the acid dip that gives the satin finish, and although it can be washed off, it often isn't on newer pieces.

BURMESE   Burmese is a beautiful velvety satin glass that shades from a light yellow to a rosy salmon pink. The pink color comes from the addition of gold salts. It was patented in 1885 by Mt. Washington Glass Company and was then licensed to Thomas Webb of England. Webb often added more gold to his glass, which gave it more of a fuchsia color. Early pieces were always hand blown and usually have a polished pontil. Watch out for reproductions that someone is trying to pass off as period pieces. Burmese glass is still being made today, and Fenton quite often comes out with a Burmese line, usually with hand-painted decoration.

WAVE CREST   Wave Crest is a type of art glass that was made by C. F. Monroe of Meriden, Connecticut. It has a satiny and occasionally shiny finish. It resembles porcelain because of the opaque quality of the glass, the finish, and eBay - wavecrest, Glass, Decorative Arts, and Antiques Decorative Arts items at low prices

http://search-completed.ebay.com/wavecrest_W0QQcoactionZcompareQQcoentrypage

home | pay | register | sign in | services | site map | help

Browse | **Search** | **Sell** | **My eBay** | **Community**   Powered By IBM

find items | **find members** | **favorite searches**

Home > All Categories > **Search Results for 'wavecrest'**

| All Items | Auctions | Buy It Now |

wavecrest   All Categories   (Search) Refine Search

☐ Search title **and** description

Matching Categories

Pottery & Glass (85)
- Glass (82)
- Pottery & China (5)
Antiques (23)
- Decorative Arts (23)
- Antiquities (Classical, Amer.) (1)
Live Auctions (10)
- Antiques & Decorative Arts (10)
Collectibles (5)
Business & Industrial (1)
Consumer Electronics (1)
Home & Garden (1)
Sporting Goods (1)

Search Options

Show only:
☐ Items listed with PayPal
☐ Buy It Now items
☐ Gift items
☑ Completed listings
☐ Items priced
☐ ___ to ___
☐ Items listed as lots

115 items found for **wavecrest**
☑ Show only: Completed listings   · Add to Favorites

List View | Picture Gallery   Sort by: Price: highest first   Customize Display

Item Title	Price ▾	Bids	End Date
VERY RARE WAVECREST CLOCK BOX	$4,049.00	26	Jun-11 16:53
Beautiful Perfect Wavecrest Antique Dresser Box !!!!!	$2,000.00	-	Jun-17 08:29
RARE HUGE WAVECREST 12" SIGNED VASE W/ GILT MOUNTS	$2,000.00	-	Jun-10 19:03
Wavecrest Wave Crest RING BOX	$966.52	9	Jun-13 09:43
Wavecrest Wave Crest Art Glass Ormulu Vase Lamp	$910.00	6	Jun-13 20:12
19c WAVE CREST WAVECREST VANITY JEWEL BOX ORIG LINING	$910.00	-	Jun-17 20:26

Figure 14-4 A Wave Crest trinket box recently sold on eBay for $4,049! Note how several sellers put both spellings in their listing to attract as many buyers as possible.

the decoration. Production of this beautiful ware began in 1892, when the patent was acquired. The glass ranges in color from white to creamy tints to pinks and pale blues. It was made to sell in jewelry stores, so you may see jewel boxes, playing-card cases, vases, and lamps. Most pieces were hand-painted with thick enameling, and quite a few have attached brass handles, feet, and rims. It was marketed and signed as Wave Crest, and there were several other marks used: "Wave Crest," "C.F.M. Co.," and "Nakara and Kelvin" (which are cousins to Wave Crest). The glass is quite distinctive, and so far we have not seen any reproductions. It's also quite valuable. The most expensive Wave Crest item sold during a recent eBay auction was an incredible trinket box with a clock in the lid that went for $4,049 (see Figure 14-4).

eBay TIP "Wave Crest" is properly spelled as two words, but a recent search for "Wave Crest" on eBay returned only 101 items, while searching for "Wavecrest" for the same 2-week period brought up 115 items. To be safe, spell it both ways in your title.

Identifying Famous American Glassware Makers

BLENKO   The Blenko Glass Company was founded in 1893 by William Blenko in Kokomo, Indiana. The company floundered until 1921, when, at the age of 67, Blenko moved the company to Milton, West Virginia, and started over. The factory really took off when his son, William H. Blenko Sr., joined him in 1923. Blenko's son had energy to spare and a keen sense of marketing. All Blenko glass is hand blown and made in small batches; it is not uncommon for pieces to have small air bubbles, lines, or individual marks left by the craftsman. These are not flaws. Blenko pieces are unique and can be inspiring. Pieces of Blenko from the 1940s on are quite collectible, as are many Eames-era items. In 1947, Blenko turned to designer-driven product. It is still paying off for the company today. Blenko pieces were only signed for a very small period, between 1958 and 1961. All other Blenko came with a paper label and a rough pontil. Blenko began sand blasting a signature in 2001. Hopefully they will continue to sign their wonderful pieces! Check out the Blenko Museum of Seattle at *www.Blenkomuseum.com*. These glass pieces are amazing.

FENTON   Fenton art glass is the largest manufacturer of handmade colored glass in the United States. Founded in 1906 by the brothers Fenton, the factory eventually ended up in Williamstown, West Virginia. Fenton is well known for its many colors of glass. It has also stayed ahead of the curve by continually changing its production to meet current tastes and shifts in the marketplace (making it difficult to talk about a "typical" Fenton piece). Various paper labels have been used since the 1920s. They did not start stamping the Fenton logo into the glass until 1970. Fenton art glass is very collectible. See their Web site at *www.fentonartglass.com*.

STEUBEN   Almost synonymous with the name Steuben is Frederick Carder, a multitalented genius. Carder Steuben glass was made by the Steuben Glass Works in Corning, New York (which is in Steuben County), while the company was under Frederick's direction from 1903 until 1932. Since 1932, the Steuben Company has concentrated on crystal. Their most famous ware is the gold aurene line, which was introduced in 1904, and the blue aurene, which followed in 1905. Aurene is classified as a surface technique, and these iridescent objects shimmer with their metallic glazes. Some pieces had paper labels, some were acid stamped with "Steuben" and a fleur-de-lis, and some were not signed.

TIFFANY   Charles Tiffany founded Tiffany & Co. (then Tiffany & Young) in 1837 in New York City. His son, Louis Comfort Tiffany (commonly known as LCT), founded Tiffany Studios in 1900, and it remained open until 1930.

Louis Comfort Tiffany enjoyed making household wares such as stamp boxes with metal components. He was also very famous for his wonderful art glass, lamps, jewelry, and enamels. Louis's work exemplified the art nouveau style of design, but he was also a fan of the Arts and Crafts movement and endorsed their goal of making art more readily available. Most genuine Tiffany pieces were signed, but beware of recent imitations and fake signatures. The signatures on authentic pieces were as follows: "LCT," "Louis C. Tiffany," "L.C. Tiffany-Favrille," and "Louis C. Tiffany Inc., Favrille," and often each piece had a dating number. Again, watch out for fake signatures which imitate the actual original signatures, so be very careful.

Today, any piece of signed true Tiffany is treasured and commands a high price. At the time it was made it was expensive and considered high quality. In a recent search on eBay for auctions over a 2-week period, 28,990 Tiffany items were listed and or sold. Although this figure includes Tiffany & Co. items in addition to Tiffany Studios art glass, it still indicates how large the Tiffany market is. The most expensive Tiffany Studios item sold during the period we were looking at was a $50,000 poppy table lamp made by Louis Comfort Tiffany in his famous stained glass style.

Identifying Famous European Glassware Makers

Of the many types of glass from Europe, we will look at French art glass from Galle, Lalique, and Daum Nancy, and Waterford from Ireland. We will also explore the topic by region, focusing on glassware from Bohemia, Scandinavia, and Italy.

GALLE   Emil Galle was most famous for his carved cameo glass. He began working in Nancy, France, in 1874, and most of his wares were very art nouveau and (fortunately for us) signed. Galle's work, which includes pottery and figurines as well as furniture, is characterized by designs featuring natural images. His fabulous cameo glass is being reproduced today with the raised signatures of "Galle" and, sometimes, an additional "TIP." TIP lets us know that it is an eastern European reproduction. There are also pieces coming out of Taiwan. However, people trying to pass these new pieces off as true Galle are grinding off the TIP. Be very careful with this classification, and only buy from very reputable dealers. Lynn's grandmother bought a Galle cameo glass vase for $100 in 1960 from Lillian Nassau in New York (see Figure 14-5). Lillian's shop was famous for carrying high quality art glass, and it is still in business today.

DAUM NANCY   Daum Nancy was founded by the Daum brothers in Nancy, France, in the late 1800s. They used various techniques to produce their wonderful cameo glass, including acid cutting, wheel engraving, and hand work.

Figure 14-5   Authentic, signed Galle carved cameo vase in deep cranberry, purchased from Lillian Nassau in New York.

The scenes they depicted were beautiful, mostly landscapes and natural images all characteristic of the art nouveau style. Most of their pieces are signed with "Daum, Nancy" and the double-barred cross of Lorraine.

LALIQUE   Renee Lalique was another artistic genius. He was a jeweler who, at age 47, began experimenting in glass. He created perfume bottles for Coty, Guerlain, and many others. These perfume bottles are quite collectible and have sold for tens of thousands of dollars. His work was very art nouveau in style, and his jewelry in particular is amazing. Renee brought art into everyday life by mass-producing stemware, tableware, inkwells, clocks, and vases. He even made amazing glass hood ornaments for automobiles! Most Lalique pieces are marked. Look for "R. Lalique" for pre–World War II pieces. The signature can be found in many different variations. The company was taken over by Renee's son, Marc, and Marc's pieces (from 1948 on) are usually signed "Lalique France." If you see a piece marked "Lalique h France" it is the work of Renee's granddaughter, Marie-Claude.

The Lalique company is still in business. Watch out for faked signatures—they do exist. Don't assume that the signed Lalique vase you find at a flea market is genuine—but don't automatically assume it isn't, either. There is obviously some risk involved in buying unauthenticated antiques and collectibles, but balancing that risk is the possibility of making a tidy profit. As a rule of thumb for any enterprise involving risk, don't spend more than you are willing to lose. If you never want to risk making a bad investment, buy from reputable sources.

WATERFORD The original Waterford company produced amazing crystal cut glass from 1700 until 1851, when the business closed its doors. Another Waterford company was started in 1947 near the original glasshouse, and it is still in business and making wonderful art glass today. Check out their Web site at *www.waterford.com*. Waterford is a very popular wedding gift, and many of us have some pieces in our homes. Most pieces are marked by label or an acid etched signature.

BOHEMIAN GLASS The area now encompassed by modern-day Czechoslovakia has long been home to a thriving glass business. The artisans in the area historically known as Bohemia have been relying on the region's superior natural resources to make glass since the mid-fourteenth century. Their vases, perfume bottles, and other glass pieces are highly collectible and beautiful. The types of glass they produce include cased and ruffled glass with applied rigaree and silver and gold-leaf overlay. In addition, much of the Mary Gregory style comes from Bohemia. Bohemian glass pieces have many different marks. Some will be marked "Bohemian" and some will say "Made in Czechoslovakia" and some won't be marked at all.

SCANDINAVIAN Art glass from Scandinavia is very much in demand these days and is frequently listed on eBay's *Hot* list. One of the reasons for its popularity is that companies from this region were very invested in the modern-art movement of the Eames era, midcentury modern. Their pieces exemplify this time period, and that is what is hot right now. Look for art glass from Kosta Boda, Sweden's oldest glassmaker, which was founded in 1742. Kosta Boda is the glassmaker to his Majesty the King of Sweden. Look, too, for Orrefors, also from Sweden and in business since 1898. From Denmark comes Holmegaard, its oldest glassworks. All of these manufacturers and several others (including Bing & Grondahl, George Jensen, and Royal Copenhagen, which we will discuss in Chapter 16), are today owned by Royal Scandinavia, a company headquartered in Denmark. Royal Scandinavia calls itself an "art industry group" and clearly has a lot of influence in the world of art glass.

ITALIAN The Romans began spreading their glass and glassmaking skills throughout Europe about 2000 years ago, making bottles, vases, and hollow vessels for their empire. Since the nation of Italy was formed, it, too, has always been known for its glass, especially that coming out of Venice and Murano. We have already mentioned the famous Venini glass Company. Italy brought us the millefiori (1000 flowers) and latticino (fine ribbon work) techniques and popularized the production of paperweights from art glass. Paperweights, or weights, as they are known, were used to hold papers on a desk and look beautiful.

Look for famous Italian glass designers such as Dino Rosin, Carlo Scarpa, and Paolo Venini himself. Once again, the 1950s to 1970s Eames-era contemporary-glass movement means big bucks. A search on eBay for all auctions containing "ital* glass" in the title for a 2-week period returned 3352 items.

WATCHING FOR FAKES AND FRAUDS

Remember that a valuable piece of art glass is worth trying to reproduce, and forging a signature on an unsigned piece is one method of defrauding a potential buyer that you'll want to be particularly wary of. Join clubs and visit antiques shops to compare antique versus reproduction examples. Keep on top of your studies, because every year there can be new reproductions in the marketplace.

Pressed and molded glass are sometimes mistaken for the more valuable cut glass; in fact, many of these pieces were intentionally made to deceive. With a little practice, they are easy to spot because the pressed pieces are less brilliant, duller-edged, more rounded in pattern, and less sparkly.

eBay TIP If you're in doubt about a cut glass piece, run your fingertips over its edges; if they feel very sharp, the piece is authentic cut glass. Practice doing this with examples of cut and pressed glass at an antiques show.

It is very difficult to determine the age of a piece of glass; for example, new glass that has a slightly worn base can look old. You will get better at determining age by style and form as you practice. Art glass is tricky. Because of the high prices being commanded by Tiffany and Galle, there are always reproductions coming onto the market. The Tiffany signature on authentic pieces is scratched into the base of the piece, and people have been known to add signatures to unsigned pieces. Be very careful! In the beginning, you may want to buy only from reputable dealers who will provide authentication.

Many newer glass companies have bought old molds from their original makers. Heisey is one of the companies that sold their molds. Reproduction glassware is in general heavier, not as fine, and greasier than the antique. Identifying glassware is a learned art, but it can really pay off if you master it.

CONDITION AND REPAIRS

Condition is very important in the glass category (as with most antiques and collectibles categories!). Remember to check your piece very thoroughly for chips, cracks, crazing, discoloration, grinding, scratches, bubbles, repairs, and missing pieces. Once again, note all of this in your eBay auction description. Now let's discuss the defects that apply to glass that were not covered in the pottery chapter.

Discoloration in glassware can be caused by many different things. The most common cause of discoloration occurs in vases in which water has sat for years; this will cause filmy water marks.

Grinding or ground glassware happens when a piece gets a chip or multiple chips and the owner has the bright idea to get it ground down. You can tell that a piece has been ground if it is shorter than other matching pieces and if the edge is still somewhat rough. Be careful though, because many older pieces have edges that are rough because they were never ground down in the first place after coming out of the mold. Always run your hand completely over the piece of glass or pottery that you are listing and note any roughness. It will protect you from returns.

Bubbles can be found in a lot of glassware. Bubbles are obviously created in the making and are usually caused by carelessness. If your piece has bubbles, just make sure that you note that in the description. Some glassmakers, such as St. Clair and Blenko, use controlled bubbles as part of the decoration.

Scratches are frequently found on glass and can reduce the value of a piece. Repairs to glass can be hard to catch if they were done very carefully. Check your glassware for repairs in the same way you would check pottery: shine a black light over your piece so as to highlight the glue and the area repaired. Missing lids and stoppers are quite common with glassware, so watch for this when you purchase pieces for your inventory.

Again, some things that look like damage may have been done in the making. For additional information, refer back to the "Checking for Condition and Repairs in Pottery" section in Chapter 13.

LISTING GLASS ON eBAY

Step One: Doing Product Research and Identifying Key Words

For our sample glass listing on eBay, we'll look at a glass pickle jar that Lynn recently sold (see Figure 14-6). Pickle jars (or pickle castors, as they were also called) were used in Victorian times on the sideboard or table to hold—you guessed it—pickles. Pickle jars typically are glass and stand in a silver-plated metal frame. They even have their own very special utensil, called a pickle tong, to be used to reach in and remove the pickles.

According to a completed-auction search on eBay, 113 pickle jars were listed and/or sold in a 2-week period. The most expensive one sold for $215.50 for just the cranberry glass insert, with no frame and no tongs. These pieces used to sell in the $500 to $1,000 range, but prices have come down in recent years due to increased supply on eBay and demand switching to the more recent glass of the Eames era. Blenko and other 1950s glassmakers are seeing their pieces selling in that range now.

From our experience, we recognized the piece as a pickle jar. So the next

Figure 14-6 This Victorian pickle jar was originally bought in England for $20 by Lynn's Grandmother in 1960.

thing we needed to do was identify the type of glass insert it contained. It was a light pink color, not dark red, so we could tell that it was, in fact, cranberry glass and not ruby glass, which is a deep red. Cranberry is typically older and more valuable than ruby glass.

The hand-painted flowers on the jar, done in a heavy enamel, pointed to the Victorian era. Once the piece was identified, it was time to develop a listing strategy.

Step Two: Creating a Winning Title and Description

Based on what we know people use in searches on eBay, we wanted to include the type of piece, the era, and the type of glass in our listing title. We decided on "Cranberry Pickle Jar Castor Enamel Victorian!" Every single one of those words was a key word that is used a lot in searches.

eBay TIP Don't waste space in your title, and remember to use every single character available to you.

Our description was quite detailed and included the jar's dimensions and condition. We made special note of the figural bird as the finial on the lid. The silver-plated frame was in good condition but we covered our bases by saying it might need resilvering—always protect yourself this way if it's practical. There were some markings on the metal frame (no manufacturer, but the number 641), and this was also included in the item description. The description also emphasized the piece's heavily enameled florals and the very Victorian dogwood design. The description ended with the sentence "A lovely piece from Lynn's grandmother's personal collection." Provenance helps to sell!

Step Three: Listing Strategies for Glass

We knew not to put an important piece like this on eBay during the slow summer months. Instead, we chose to put it up for auction in February, when business is traditionally better. Lynn keeps a list of good customers who like to buy specific items, so she e-mailed them to let them know that the pickle jar was going up for sale.

eBay TIP   It's always a good idea to e-mail your repeat customers when a special item comes up for auction, if you can manage it. Not every good customer is checking eBay auctions or specifically your auctions on a weekly basis. Give yourself the edge and put the word out.

Step Four: Pricing Strategies

After doing some research, we decided that this piece was valuable and that it shouldn't sell for less than $300. Therefore, we decided to use a hidden reserve of $300 but started the bidding at $49.99. The pickle jar got 12 bids and sold for $300 to a very good customer from Florida who was on the targeted mailing list. See, the e-mail marketing campaign worked!

* * *

Glass is an amazing category to sell on eBay. There are millions of glass lovers. As the years pass, antique glass pieces become harder to find as more are adopted into private collections and other pieces break. There will always be high demand for good-quality antique and vintage glass, but don't overlook newer glass from makers such as Blenko and the Scandinavian companies we discussed. This newer glass can be just as, if not more, valuable than the antique. Glass is not typically signed, and if you play your cards right, by studying and doing your research, you can be well on your way to finding your eBay fortune!

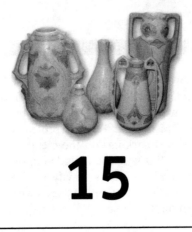

15

Tabletop: Dinnerware, Stemware, and Flatware

Tabletop encompasses anything that you would currently use on your dining room table and anything that may have been used on the table in years gone by. For the purposes of this book, we will break this category down into dinnerware, stemware (which will include serveware), and flatware. Unfortunately, we won't have room in this book to discuss holloware (also spelled *hollowware*), which refers to silver serving pieces. However, we feel confident that with all you have learned through this book you will be able to apply many of the same principles and will know how to do the necessary research you need to do to succeed in holloware.

The materials used for dinnerware, stemware/serveware, and flatware are many and varied. There is porcelain, pottery, china, pressed glass, crystal, sterling silver, silver plate, and stainless. We learned about pottery in Chapter 13 and glass and crystal in Chapter 14. In this chapter we will concentrate on porcelain, Early American Pattern Glass (EAPG), Elegant Glass, Depression Glass (DG), and three types of metals, since they are the primary materials from which tableware was and is made.

After discussing materials we will show how to identify the shape and, most importantly, the pattern of your tableware to help you sell your items for top dollar on eBay.

What Are People on eBay Looking For?

Tabletop items were made by thousands of different companies. Turning tabletop items into a good business really comes down to finding the quality companies and going after their top-selling patterns. The tableware items that sell the best on eBay are those with patterns that people are trying to replace. For example, say someone's wedding china, which they received 30 years ago, was Lenox Rose and someone just broke a plate. That person would want to replace it, and their first stop might be eBay.

Another source of demand for tabletop items is people who only have four place settings of their silverware pattern but would like to expand it to eight place settings. Again, they may check eBay. A third group of tabletop buyers is people with related collections (toothpick holders, for example). What people are looking for in this area are the patterns that they already have in their homes or the items that they are already collecting. Again, keep in mind that in *Tabletop*, as in most other categories, Eames-era 1950s mid-century modern is selling extremely well!

eBay TIP One of the most popular color combination for dinnerware is blue and white. You should be looking for patterns with these two colors.

What's Hot among Tabletop Items on eBay

To learn what is hot on eBay in the *Tabletop* category, we went to the eBay *Hot Seller* list. There are so many manufacturers listed in this category that it is almost overwhelming. Listed under *Super Hot* were:

- Cardew
- Carlton Ware
- Castleton
- James Kent
- KPM
- Paragon
- Steubenville
- Sylva C

Under the next category, *Very Hot*, names listed included:

- Aynsley
- Bing & Grondahl
- Crown Devon
- Dresden
- Frankoma
- Hadley
- LuRay

- Royal Copenhagen
- Royal Copley
- Royal Doulton
- Royal Dux
- Sascha Brastoff

Do you see what we mean about the number of manufacturers? In addition, other reliably hot sellers are Chintz, Haviland, Lenox, and Nippon.

In the *Hot* category for glassware, we found elegant, opalescent, 1940s, 1950s, 1960s, and vaseline. Opalescent and vaseline can be types of Early American Pattern Glass, and the 1940s, 1950s, and 1960s includes some rereleased depression glassware.

In *Hot* we also find "Silver plate other" and "Sterling holloware." "Silver plate other" is a good choice for most silver plate flatware listings. As you can see, the *Tabletop* category provides you with a wide range of options and more opportunities for selling.

BUYING STRATEGIES FOR TABLETOP

Tabletop is an easy category to buy for because these items are everywhere. You can even start in your own kitchen cupboards. You probably have china, crystal, and flatware that you haven't used for years. Now is the time to sell it.

Without fail, most every garage sale has dinnerware, stemware, or flatware for sale. You just need to become very knowledgeable about what is moving and what isn't. The aesthetics of an item—whether it is "pretty" or not—matter far less in tabletop than in almost all other categories. No matter how lovely a dinnerware pattern is, it will not sell if there is not already a demand for it. Some beautiful dinnerware patterns by Sango and Mikasa don't sell well regardless of how lovely they are. Some brands that tend to sell the best are Lenox, Heath, Wedgwood, and patterns created by famous designers. Overall, the English makers and midcentury modern seems to be where the dinnerware market is the hottest. When it comes to buying for your inventory, the best advice is to not pay too much for any set. Try not to pay more than 50 cents for each piece. A typical five-piece place setting includes a cup, saucer, dinner plate, salad plate, and bread-and-butter plate. If it is a set of twelve place settings or 60 pieces, try not to pay more than $30. If you have Internet access and the pattern looks desirable, go to $1 a piece. Buy dinnerware, stemware, and flatware by the set.

 eBay TIP Buying fewer than three to five pieces of a common pattern will not work. People shopping on eBay are looking for multiple pieces in their pattern and want to save on shipping. When you break out a larger set into multiple auctions with four dinner plates, two cups and saucers, or similar groupings, you make more money and give your buyers the options they are looking for.

Great Sourcing Options

Auctions, thrift stores, and garage, charity, and yard sales are the best places to pick up dinnerware, flatware, and stemware for a bargain. Live auctions typically sell box lots of china, and you can do really well selling it. Another great source for tabletop is eBay. Do your research and know what patterns are in demand. When a full service of that dinnerware, flatware, or stemware comes up for auction (especially in the summer) buy it for a good price and then break it out to sell individually. Search for sets by your location and save money on shipping by driving and picking up the set. Also search by manufacturer and pick up patterns that have not been identified by the seller or have been identified incorrectly. You can make a really good return doing this.

How to Become an Expert on Tabletop

Buy as many reference books as you can afford if you are going to be dealing in older flatware, DG, and EAPG. Join the online clubs listed in this chapter and attend the conventions. Another great resource are the national associations for different areas of study, most of which hold conventions yearly. If you attend the convention for your area of expertise it will give you the opportunity to mingle with other dealers, and of course it lets you do some serious buying from other dealers while traveling. If you're interested in immersing yourself in a particular type of collectibles dealing, watch your local paper or look through antiques journals to see what conventions might be held in your area.

COMMON TABLETOP MATERIALS

In order to be able to write the best titles and descriptions for your items, it's key that you know what materials your items are made out of. The following section discusses the most common materials used for tabletop.

The Popular Materials

PORCELAIN   The Chinese were creating porcelain over 1,000 years ago. Yet the formula remained their well-guarded secret for many years. The Europeans were dying to figure out the mystery of porcelain so that they could use it to decorate their homes without spending a lot of money importing it from

Asia. Europeans had already figured out soft-paste porcelain, but what they really desired was the hard-paste porcelain of the Orient. The Europeans had even built special pieces of furniture, called cupboards, to proudly display their porcelain wares. Augustus the Strong of Saxony, in modern-day Germany, heard of an alchemist who claimed he could figure out the secret. Legend has it that he held this alchemist, Bottger, captive until he discovered the recipe!

What Bottger revealed is that hard-paste porcelain is created by mixing china clay (*kaolin*) with china stone (*petuntse*). The less desirable soft paste was a mixture of clays and glass that produced off-white pieces with small black specks and other imperfections. Armed with this knowledge, in 1710, King Augustus opened the Meissen factory near Dresden. Because the porcelain formula had originally been discovered for the king, the German court tried to keep it a secret by threatening anyone who revealed it with death. By 1760, however, it had spread all over Europe due to employees leaving Meissen and taking the formula with them.

The body of porcelain is referred to as paste, and it is often covered with a transparent glaze that protects and can also decorate it. Porcelain does not, however, need a glaze in order to hold liquid. True porcelain will not craze and has a white body all the way through. It can look almost translucent when held up to the light. As discussed in Chapter 13, porcelain will make a ringing sound when tapped with a pencil (as long as it doesn't have any chips or cracks). Porcelain is lightweight, hard, and strong; when it *does* break, it will chip and shatter like glass.

China is the generic term for porcelain from China, so today we often refer to our porcelain as china. Bone china is made when bone ash is added to the china clay and china-stone mix. This formula is the standard for England, and you will often see British tableware marked "English Bone China."

EARLY AMERICAN PATTERN GLASS   According to Elaine Henderson of *www.PatternGlass.com*, Early American Pattern Glass, pressed in America from circa 1850 until circa 1910, is very often misidentified on eBay. In fact, roughly 25 percent of auction pieces called EAPG are newer glass. Notes to sellers: 1. the number of mold marks has no connection to the age of glass and 2. if your piece is *not* very old heavy leaded glass and it does *not* glow yellow green under a black light in a darkened room, it is *not* EAPG.

EAPG, also known as old pressed glass or simply pattern glass, is clear or colored (amber, blue, apple and emerald green, and amethyst, but never light lavender) and it came in matched sets of dishes. These sets included such forms as creamers and sugars, butter dishes, goblets, spooners, plates, pitchers, and fruit bowls—some patterns have as many as 80 forms! Early American Pattern Glass was also used for souvenir items, especially from world's fairs, and will quite often have ruby-colored staining and personal or location engravings.

Early American Pattern Glass is frequently referred to as EAPG on eBay, and any Early American Pattern Glass auction titles you write should reflect that fact. Hundreds of different companies produced thousands of EAPG patterns.

eBay TIP   One of the best reference books about EAPG is Kyle Husfloen's *Collector's Guide to American Pressed Glass, 1825–1915*, and the best book for identifying EAPG patterns is Mollie Helen McCain's *Field Book to Pattern Glass*. There is also a free Pattern Glass school on the Internet at *www.patternglass.com*. It's fantastic!

With EAPG, the name of the manufacturer is typically not as important as it is in other areas of collectibles, such as pottery or art glass. This is in part because most collectors seek pieces of their pattern, and many popular patterns (such as "Feather") have been made by more than one factory. Other collectors focus on kinds of glass (such as milk glass) or a particular form (such as toothpick holders); few collect the work of one particular factory; the merchandise of Riverside Glass Works and the Northwood companies being notable exceptions.

Let's discuss the types of glass used. We already understand clear pressed glass, but let's take a look at some of the types of glass used to make colored EAPG—flint, flashed, stained, opalescent, custard, milk, vaseline, and carnival. We won't be able to go into much detail for each type, but at least you will know the basics of what is out there and you'll learn some key words so that you can do more research on the Internet and on eBay.

Flint is clear, rarely colored, glass made with lead, and it was pressed in both England and America from circa 1820s to 1860s. In 1864, a glass formula using soda lime instead of the more expensive lead was invented, ushering in the era of soda lime or soda glass or simply nonflint EAPG. This bright glass could be pressed into ornate designs, and colored pressed glass became popular in the 1880s.

Some EAPG is true colored glass (with coloring minerals included in the glass formula) and some is what is known as flashed or stained. Flashed glass is made by quickly dipping a clear body into the colored glass mixture to add a thin layer of color. Stained is the least expensive method of coloring glass, and is made using a staining material that is painted on and then fired for permanence. Stained pieces can lose their color when scratched or through years of use. Watch these carefully for condition; most collectors want only unscratched ruby staining, so you want pieces that still have most of their color and no obvious deterioration. Ruby-decorated EAPG glass was stained because of the expense of using real gold to attain the ruby color. There is no actual ruby-colored EAPG glass.

Opalescent glass was first made in England in 1870 and became popular in the United States around 1900. The name comes from the milky white opalescent trim that follows the line of the pattern, typically on the edges. It is made by reheating parts of the piece where the opalescent decoration is desired, just as the piece is starting to cool.

Custard glass is a creamy ivory glass first produced in, you guessed it, England. Harry Northwood founded his Northwood glass company in 1898 in Indiana with the formula that he brought with him from overseas. Northwood became very successful with this type of glass, and a few of his pieces are signed with an *N* in a diamond. Harry's company closed in 1923. Fenton and Heisey also made custard glass. Some pieces rival art glass and have handmade decorations in gold leaf. Custard is generally expensive EAPG, but it is extremely devalued if damaged or if the paint or gold decoration is worn.

Milk glass came into being because Europeans loved the china/porcelain from the Orient and they were trying to reproduce it. This opaque glass was originally called opalware. It was used to make some popular EAPG patterns and was later called milk glass because of its milky appearance. Pieces made between 1830 and 1870 with "fiery" opalescent edges are particularly sought after. Milk glass is still being made today, and many new companies have purchased the older molds. Some popular collectibles are the covered animal dishes, such as nesting hens, sleeping foxes, and rabbits. Because the difference between the very expensive original-issue covered dishes and new reproductions is sometimes very difficult to detect, great care should be used in purchasing from sellers who are not specialists or who will not give an absolute money-back guarantee as to age.

One of the most interesting and popular kinds of EAPG is vaseline glass. Invented by Josef Reidel in 1830 in Bohemia, it was originally called uranium glass. First manufactured in America around 1840, the name was changed from uranium to canary after the color of the bird. It was then renamed vaseline by dealers around the turn of the century who thought that it resembled petroleum jelly. True vaseline glass should be greenish yellow in natural light and glow brilliantly under a black light. The fluorescence comes from the uranium added to the glass to create the color. A great vaseline glass Web site (and vaseline glass club to join) can be found at *www.vaselineglass.org*.

CARNIVAL GLASS Carnival doesn't really fit in with the Early American Pattern Glass section and it doesn't really fit in with elegant glass. Therefore, it is it's own special section. It is pressed glass that has been coated with sodium and fired to create iridescence. It was never an upper-end product and was made in great quantity from 1905 to 1929. Carnival glass was so named be-

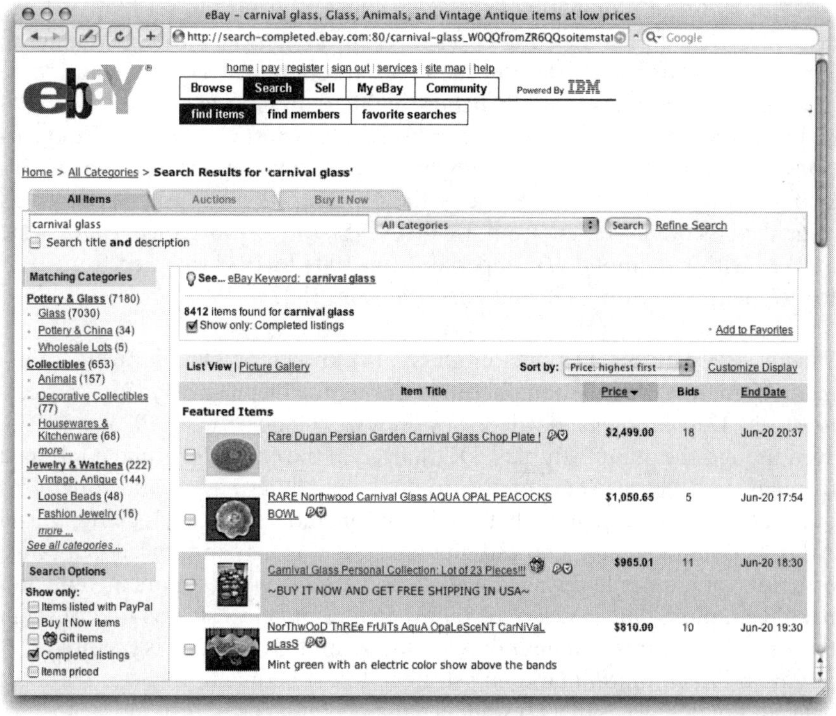

Figure 15-1 A recent search on eBay for carnival glass brought up 8412 items.

cause it was supposedly given away as a premium at carnivals and fairs. It was known as the poor man's Tiffany and today is highly collectible. There are more than a thousand patterns. It comes in mostly the same serving pieces that EAPG does, but not the same stemware. Drinking vessels were shaped as tumblers. Popular colors were marigold, green, blue, and amethyst. Fenton, Northwood, Imperial, and Westmoreland are just some of the many manufacturers. There was a resurgence of carnival in the 1970s, and it is still being made today. Be very wary of reproductions. A quick check of eBay for completed auctions for the past two weeks showed 8258 carnival items being sold or listed! The most expensive was $2,499 for a Dugan Persian Lavender Colored Chop Plate (see Figure 15-1). Because they can go for a high price, you'll definitely want to find these at garage sales and, more importantly, you'll want to be able to identify carnival glass and the patterns correctly! Carnival is listed two ways on eBay, pre-1940 or post-1940, and then by maker.

ELEGANT GLASS   In between EAPG and Depression glass, we find elegant glass. A good reference for this category is *Elegant Glassware of the Depres-*

sion Era by Gene Florence, who actually coined the term to set it apart from both Depression glass and EAPG. There is an *Elegant Glass* category on eBay. This type of glass was made after the 1890s, through the Depression and some into the late 1950s; it is typically better-quality than pressed and blown EAPG or Depression glass. The elegant glass houses used patterns, etchings, and cuttings to enhance the glass. It usually has ground bottoms and some hand finishing and was fire polished. Some of the American companies that made this elegant glass were Heisey, from 1896 to 1957 (after 1901, their wares were marked with a diamond *H*); Imperial, from 1904 to 1984 (marked from 1951 to 1973 with an *I* over a *G*), and Fostoria, from 1887 to 1986.

DEPRESSION GLASS   Depression glass, also known as DG, is pressed glass made by many different manufacturers during the Depression years. True collectors of Depression glass will only want wares made between 1923 and 1939, even though the manufacture of DG started in the early 1920s and continued through the 1980s as some of the original companies have reissued patterns over the years. Companies that made DG include Anchor Hocking, Hazel Atlas, Federal, Jeanette, and Indiana Glass. It was mass produced in a range of colors, and most DG was tableware and kitchenware. Colors include amber, green, pink, blue, black, red, yellow, white, and clear. It was sold through five-and-dime stores and mail-order catalogs and given away as premiums. A premium is a common marketing strategy to get people to buy certain products, and many pieces of DG were given away with cereal or flour, in grocery stores, and at gas stations. Many people thought it would never be worth anything, and many pieces over the years were thrown away. Funny thing, this glass has become extremely collectible! Collectors tend to collect by pattern or color. One thing that we hear frequently about this glass is that it was a bright spot in a very dark moment in U.S. history.

Companies are reproducing some of the more expensive and rare patterns, so make sure you do your research. The best books on this subject have been written by Gene Florence. When you're starting out, buy from a knowledgeable and honest dealer. Ask the dealer to help you understand the patterns, prices, and reproductions.

SILVER METALS   The more recent flatware (1850s and forward) that you will be finding during your treasure hunting will typically be made from three different combinations of metals: sterling, silver plate, and stainless steel.

- *Sterling.*   Silver is a precious metal. It is valued only third, behind platinum and gold. Metal is valued in the following order (highest to lowest): platinum, gold, silver, bronze, brass, copper, pewter, and iron. Because silver is a valuable commodity, pieces were often melted to put food on the table during tough economic times; this

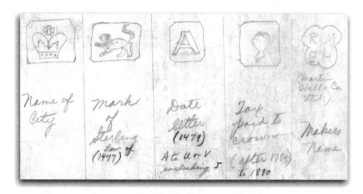

Figure 15-2 These are an antique dealer's sketches of sample hallmarks and the years associated with them.

means that very old pieces are quite rare. *Sterling* is a standard of silver fineness that means 92.5 percent pure silver and 7.5 percent mixed with copper to increase durability. The English set this standard by an ordinance in 1300. We have probably all heard of English hallmarks and that the sterling standard was another way that the government controlled the silver market. In 1477, a law was passed in London requiring the stamping of the leopard's head or crowned leopard's head on every piece of silver of the accepted standard. In 1479, the use of the date letter was used, and finally the maker's mark. The leopard's head was replaced in 1544 by the lion *passant* (a walking lion) (see Figure 15-2).

From 1697 to 1720, the standard for sterling was raised to 95 percent pure silver, and pieces meeting this new standard were stamped "Britannia." Hallmarked pieces will be punched with three to five marks—usually the sterling mark, the maker's mark, the year of manufacture, and possibly a duty mark and the town hallmark. You might find .925 marked on European flatware, although in Europe the standard for sterling ranges from .800/.825 to .925.

e B a y   T I P   Sterling, especially hallmarked sterling, is a fascinating study. While we don't have the space in this book to discuss hallmarks at length, we do recommend *English Silver Hallmarks* by Judith Banister.

There wasn't any such regulation of sterling production in the United States. Most makers marked their silver with their names or initials and maybe an eagle's head. By 1850, American silversmiths were using their first initial and full last name and also adding a second punch to indicate the silver standard. *C* stood for coin (a little less than .925), *D* for dollar and *S* for standard (both meaning sterling). Occasionally they would mark a piece "sterling," but it wasn't until 1907 that this acquired a legal definition in the United States and therefore came into wide use among silversmiths.

This information will be helpful for you when you try to date your silver pieces. If you have a newer-looking piece of Reed and Barton and you see some convincing hallmarks but no "sterling," you can be assured that it is not sterling. A great reference book is *Kovels' American Silver Marks: 1650 to the Present* by Ralph and Terry Kovel.

- *Silver plate.* Silver plate is created when a base metal, usually nickel silver, is coated with a layer of pure silver by electroplating; it is sometimes marked "silver plate" and sometimes marked "EPNS" (electro-plated nickel silver). Unfortunately, if you find silverplated spoons marked with "EPNS," what you have isn't worth what it would be had they been sterling. The majority of flatware from the 1860s on was silver plated, because sterling was expensive.

- *Stainless Steel.* Stainless steel is made of base metal that has been coated with any of a number of finishes to resist stain or corrosion. It is smooth, hard, warp- and scratch-resistant, nonporous, and very durable. Chrome and nickel are primarily what is added to steel alloys to form an invisible film that protects the surface. Stainless steel has been used frequently in flatware from the 1950s on.

IDENTIFYING TABLETOP BY SHAPE AND PATTERN

Now that we have learned about a lot of the important materials, it is critical to identify the shape and pattern of your particular piece as well. An amazing Web site to help with both shape and pattern is *www.replacements.com*. We will discuss material, shape, and pattern as they relate to each of our three tabletop areas: dinnerware, stemware, and flatware.

Dinnerware

Dinnerware is what you would use to set your table for a meal. It consists of the plates, bowls, and teacups that would be part of an individual's place setting. Dinnerware would also include the serving pieces—platters, butter dish, vegetable bowl, and the like if they are part of a matched set that complements the individual's place setting.

MATERIALS Let's recap all the materials out of which dinnerware can be formed, starting from what is considered the highest quality when manufactured and typically most expensive and working our way down:

- Porcelain
- China
- Bone china
- EAPG
- Depression glass
- Pottery
- Stoneware
- Ironstone
- Earthenware
- Plastic

Did we just say plastic? You bet we did; there is dinnerware made from Melmac (a type of plastic) and just plain old plastic, and believe it or not there is demand for these pieces. Lynn recently sold an eight-piece set of Heller White Melmac dinnerware designed by Massimo Vignelli on eBay for $92.96 (see Figure 15-3).

Remember, this ranking of materials provided is just a general guideline. An unusual and perfect piece of ironstone may well be worth more than a common piece of bone china; a spectacular piece of Depression glass may sell for more than a similar piece of porcelain. Supply, demand, condition, and many other factors all figure into an article's market value.

Most dinnerware will have a mark identifying its material; if not, you can generally guess without too much difficulty. If the piece is china, porcelain,

Figure 15-3 Plastic can be a hot seller on eBay. This Heller White Plastic Melmac designer set sold for $92.96.

stoneware, ironstone, or bone china, it will usually be marked as such. It is, of course, easy enough to tell that something is glass or plastic.

SHAPE The most common shapes—or pieces—that you will run across are cups and saucers, dinner plates (usually 9 to 11 inches), salad plates (6 to 8 inches), and bread-and-butter plates (5 to 7 inches). Bread-and-butter plates also work nicely for dessert, which is something you could mention in your listing. Then there are the bowls: soup (7 to 10 inches), cereal (5 to 7 inches), and a fruit or dessert bowl (4 to 6 inches).

Be ready to identify the most common serving pieces, including sugar and creamer, butter dish, salt and pepper shakers, gravy boat, oval or round vegetable bowl, covered vegetable bowl, oval platter, round platter (also known as a chop plate), coffee pot (taller), tea pot (shorter), and relish server.

eBay TIP Check out the replacements site at *www.replacements .com/piecetype/china_piece.htm* and you will find about 40 different china shapes drawn out and explained. All those that we mention can be seen there. It is a great resource!

In Lynn's experience of selling tons of dinnerware on eBay, she has found that cups and saucers do not sell very well, plates and bowls do sell well, and the serving pieces do the very best.

MANUFACTURER'S PATTERN Identifying the dinnerware pattern is probably the most important part of the equation for making your fortune with dinnerware. We'll start our discussion with china (by which we mean anything that is not glass) and then move on to glass.

China dinnerware is almost always marked with the name of its manufacturer. It may not have the pattern name, but these dinnerware makers were proud of their goods and used a back stamp. The back stamp will have the company name and will usually indicate whether the piece is china, porcelain, bone china, ironstone, or something else. Sometimes only the dinner plates are marked. Often, there wasn't room to mark the teacup and saucer. Always check the larger pieces first for maker and pattern.

Lenox, Noritake, and other fine makers almost always list the pattern and style number, which makes your job a whole lot easier. Unfortunately, the majority of the dinnerware you'll encounter will not have the pattern name. You can research it in two ways: on eBay and on the Replacements Web site (mentioned earlier in this chapter).

Since researching patterns can be difficult, let's look at a recent search Lynn did for a 1970s Corelle dish set by Corning that Lynn bought at a garage sale for $3. It was a floral pattern. Once on eBay, Lynn went to the Ad-

Figure 15-4   By doing some research on eBay, this plate was identified as 1970s Corelle dinnerware in the pattern "Wildflower". The 16 pieces sold for $64.97.

vanced Search page, checked the "Completed Auctions only" option and typed in some key words such as *floral* and *Corelle*. When all the search returns came up, Lynn scrolled through the gallery pictures looking for something that resembled her purchase. She also tried searching in current auctions by title and description. When she again typed in *floral* and *Corelle*, an auction with the flower pattern came up and Lynn was able to find a matching pattern with the name "Wildflower." By naming the pattern, she was able to sell 16 pieces of this vintage Corelle in four auctions for $64.97. The research does pay off!

eBay TIP   Keep in mind that you cannot search *completed* auctions by title and description. Instead, you can only search by title. To do research when you need both the title and description you will need to search *current* auctions.

To learn about patterns on the Replacements Web site, first search by manufacturer. Many times, hundreds of patterns will be brought up. A tried-and-true approach is to first go through and click on names that sound like they would fit. If you have a regal looking pattern, don't bother clicking on "Dainty Daisy." If you make your way through all the likely sounding patterns with no match, you may have to go back through and try some of the longshots, and because of this possibility, you may want to start the whole process by printing out a page with all the pattern names so that as you go you can mark off the ones you've looked at.

It can take hours to find the correct pattern; therefore, don't spend too much time searching unless it will be worth it in your bottom line. If you just can't identify the pattern no matter how much time you spend, you can always put a "HELP!" or a "Pattern?" in your auction title and use the description to ask eBayers to e-mail you the pattern name. This works more times than you'd expect! After you have the correct pattern name, be sure to revise or add information to your listings to included the name.

Glass dinnerware is extremely tricky to identify. You won't usually find a maker's mark or a pattern name on Depression glass. So how can you figure out what you have? One great resource is the very informative Web site at *www.ndga.net* run by the National Depression Glass Association. If Depression glass tickles your fancy, you should definitely join their association. This very thorough resource lists 92 different patterns that were made by the seven major manufacturers. There are many pictures to help you identify the pattern and maker you have. Another Web site with photos to help identify Depression glass is *www.budmar.com/depad.htm*. If you still can't find your pattern, invest in a Gene Florence reference book or use the "HELP!" or "Pattern?" trick in the title.

Glass Stemware/Serveware

Stemware and Serveware that are made from glass will be discussed in this section. Stemware includes the glass goblets, tumblers, and wine glasses used to complete an individual's table setting. Stemware is used to serve beverages. They usually do not match your dinner set. Serveware would include such glass pieces as sauce dishes, celery vases, and pitchers.

MATERIALS   Let's recap the materials from which stemware can be made. Stemware is almost exclusively glass, but there are different types of processes used to make the glass. Stemware is often made in cut glass or lead crystal and it can be hand blown, blown into a mold, or pressed into a mold by hand or machine. The serving pieces we will be discussing in this section will also be exclusively glass.

We will focus on pressed glass in this chapter. EAPG and Depression glass are pressed with no extra hand finishing and elegant glass is pressed or blown but then gets that extra hand touch to create a much finer piece of glass.

SHAPE   The simplest place setting for stemware is a water goblet and a red and a white wineglass.

With EAPG, however, you may run across an egg cup, tumbler, footed tumbler, bar tumbler, cordial, wine, champagne, mug, and goblet. In Depression glass, the drinking glasses are even more varied and may include juice, iced tea, sherbet, champagne, cordial, and water glasses.

In serving and decorative pieces, you may find a footed bowl, pitcher, sugar, creamer, celery vase, spoon holder (also known as a spooner), cracker bowl, decanter, nappy, platter, pickle dish, footed salt dip, jam jar, sauce dish, footed sauce dish, butter dish, cake stand, calling-card tray, castor bottle set, and a compote. Please refer to the Replacements Web site for many of these shapes (*www.replacements.com/piecetype/crystal_piece.htm*).

MANUFACTURER'S PATTERN   Identifying patterns in Early American Pattern Glass is as tough as it is with Depression glass. A good resource is Ruth Webb Lee's *Handbook of Early American Pressed Glass Patterns*. Lee first published this book in 1931, and it set the standard for the pattern names, which is why EAPG patterns are often referred to as Lee patterns. A very friendly and fantastic EAPG Web site is *www.PatternGlass.com*. If you are going to specialize in pattern glass, we highly recommend joining the Early American Pattern Glass Society at *www.eapgs.org*. Again, if you can't figure out the pattern name on your own, you can always ask for help in your auction title.

Flatware

Flatware is the third part of the table setting. You already have your dinnerware, stemware, and serving pieces, and now you need utensils to complete the picture. These are the utensils necessary to eat and serve the food: forks, knives, spoons, and serving pieces.

SHAPE   The shapes for flatware are unbelievable; it is truly a study unto itself. In Victorian times, there was a specific utensil for anything imaginable, such as a bone holder, bonbon spoon, and a sardine fork. It is mind blowing. Once again, a great resource for all the unique flatware shapes is the the Replacements Web site at *www.replacements.com/piecetype/flat_piece.htm*.

For the purposes of selling flatware on eBay, you will mostly run across teaspoons, tablespoons (also called place spoons), soup spoons, dinner knives, salad forks, and dinner forks. According to the Replacements Web site, a typical five-place setting would include a teaspoon, salad fork, dinner fork, dinner knife, and butter spreader.

MANUFACTURER'S PATTERN   Identifying flatware patterns is quite difficult. Luckily with flatware, there will almost always be some markings. You will usually find the maker's name and type of material, which should send you in the right direction as you try to identify your piece. If the company that made your piece is still in business, check out their Web site. Just as you learned to do with dinnerware and stemware, spend some time on the Replacements site and on eBay to find the pattern name of your piece.

FAMOUS MAKERS OF TABLEWARE

As we mentioned earlier, the makers aren't really as important with tableware as the patterns are. In other words, people are more interested in the specific pattern they collect than in who made it, although many patterns were chosen based on someone's feelings about the manufacturer. Since maker is not an important issue, we feel confident that you are ready to start doing your own research by maker and patterns. Here are some names to get you started. In dinnerware, refer back to the *Hot* list from eBay but be sure to check out Lu-Ray, Chintz, and James Kent. In glass, look up the "Cherry Blossom" and "Manhattan Depression" patterns. Also the "Daisy," "Button," and "Croesus" patterns in EAPG. Don't forget to check out stemware and serveware from the Eames era. Orrefors, Kosta Boda, and Dansk are super hot right now. Finally, in flatware, look up Wm Rogers, Gorham, Wallace, and Reed & Barton. As you can see, the opportunities for you to sell tableware on eBay are abundant.

FAKES AND FRAUDS

As with any category, there are reproductions out there, and they can be found most notably in the Depression glass, EAPG, and sterling flatware areas. If someone is going to take the time to remake a piece, it has to be financially worth it to the reproducer. Do your research and make all your more expensive purchases through reputable dealers. Remember that newer glass is typically heavier than its older counterparts and may have a greasy feel.

CONDITION AND REPAIRS

Because EAPG is so old and has a lot of angles, buyers should watch very carefully for chips and bubbles in the making. Also, cracks can be hard to spot because of the busy patterns. A way to spot cracks is to hold the piece up in the sunlight and turn it to inspect all sides.

eBay TIP   Never buy EAPG that has turned purple. EAPG that has been turned purple by the sun or any other way is ruined as an antique, and the process is irreversible. Some is advertised on eBay to be "sun purple," but it has been turned by unscrupulous sellers who prey on unsuspecting buyers.

An additional flaw to watch for with dinnerware is utensil marks. These occur on plates when a utensil (usually a knife) makes marks. Often, a plate must be viewed in a very strong light from the side in order for these marks to be visible. Always mention such flaws in your listing. Noting that a plate has "slight utensil marks" or "slight wear" will rarely lose you a bidder and may prevent returns after a sale.

When it comes to flatware, there are a few potential flaws to look for. With sterling, which is a soft metal, watch for dents and bumps. It's a good strategy not to polish your silver before selling it. You might say in your listing that you are letting the new buyer decide how and if they want to polish their pieces. With silver plate, you must note missing plating or scratches made from an overzealous polisher. With all flatware, take note of wear scratches, pitting, and any ends that may have been chewed up by a garbage disposal. These marks will be rough cuts at the ends of spoons, forks, and knives. It happens a lot. Also, flatware can get bent out of shape. Be sure to note this in your listings, but, if possible, you may say something like "it looks like it could easily be bent back."

Another thing to look for is monogrammed initials. Flatware without monograms typically sells for more. Just make sure you mention these defects in your description.

For more information on the overall condition of glass and pottery, refer to Chapters 13 and 14.

LISTING TABLETOP ITEMS ON eBAY

The item that we'll use for our example of how to sell tabletop items on eBay is a set of Gorham Stegor Stainless flatware. Lynn bought it at a garage sale for $5 as an afterthought, and it ended up selling for an amazing amount of money (see Figure 15-5).

Step One: Identifying What You Have

The first step in our research was to carefully examine the pieces. The pieces were all marked "Stegor Stainless" and only the iced-tea spoons said "Gorham." (All of this information was naturally included in the descriptions on eBay.) Next, we looked at the Replacements Web site, searching for "Gorham stainless." After looking through the different patterns, we finally found the pattern name "Pace." Because the pattern name is key, we were happy to have one for our listing.

Step Two: Creating a Strong Title and Description

Since we only had twenty pieces and they only cost $5, we didn't expect the pieces to sell for much. In the title, we used the manufacturer's name (Gorham

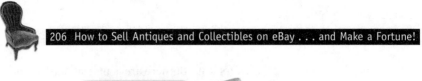

Figure 15-5   A 19-piece set of this Gorham Stegor Stainless cost $5
at a garage sale and sold on eBay for $244.80.

Stegor), the material (stainless), the shape (four iced-tea spoons, six dinner
knives, etc.), the pattern ("Pace"), and, finally, the era (Eames).

Several people e-mailed questions about the knives, which seemed
strange. Everyone wanted to know if one side of the blade was serrated,
which they were. Because of these questions, we decided to do further research on the Replacements site and learned that this serrated edge is known
as a "modern" blade. We also learned that it is one of the most popular styles
and used most often in stainless-steel flatware.

> **eBay TIP**   If the majority of the set is in perfect condition
> with only one or two chipped or very damaged pieces, either donate
> them to charity or throw them away. Listing all perfect items is the
> way to go with dinnerware and cheaper stemware.

Step Three: Listing Strategies

It's not generally a good idea to sell tabletop items individually, unless you
have serving pieces and rare pieces of Depression glass, elegant glass, and

EAPG. It's also generally not a a good idea to sell full sets. Instead, it's a great strategy to break your auctions down into lots of two to four pieces. Let's say you have six bowls, all the same. Make it easy on yourself and do three auctions with two bowls each. You will be able to just click "Sell a similar item" and upload the second and third auctions very quickly—which is another reason to like selling tabletop items.

eBay TIP Here's a great time-saver: put all your information about the pattern, condition, and manufacturer into your first auction, then all you have to change as you continually sell a similar pattern is the number of pieces you're selling and the shape. It makes the listing process go very smoothly.

We decided to use the strategy of lising the twenty pieces of stainless flatware in eight auctions: six dinner knives, a serving spoon and fork, one serving spoon, two teaspoons, two dinner forks, two salad forks, four iced-tea spoons, and a gravy ladle. We used only one photo for each auction, and over the top of each picture we showed the signature.

Step Four: Determining the Price

Because we didn't think these pieces were valuable, we started each of the eight auctions at $9.99. Our strategy worked. One listing, the six dinner knives, ended up selling for $92.00! The twenty pieces sold for a total of $244.80—a great return for a $5 investment. If you play your cards right, you can make a fortune with tableware!

SPECIFIC INSTRUCTIONS FOR SHIPPING TABLETOP ITEMS

Tabletop merchandise requires a lot of extra direction in packing. If you sell a lot of dinnerware, stemware, or flatware, you may have buyers who purchase items from at least two of your auctions (if not 10 or more). Packing many breakables into the smallest box possible in order to save on shipping can be tricky. One approach is to pick up divided boxes (usually used for liquor) that grocery stores and liquor stores give away for free. These are very handy because you can wrap the stemware or dinnerware in tissue individually and then place one to four pieces in each section for extra protection. For example, if you sold four dinner plates, four salad plates, four cereal bowls, and four cups and saucers, you could take four dinner plates and wrap them with tissue or bubble wrap. Then you could cut out two of the dividers and stand them up. Then do the same thing with the salad plates. Then wrap the bowls and wiggle them into position. Finally, stack the cups and saucers similarly. Once you have them all tightly secured in the divided box, place the divided box in a

Figure 15-6 This illustration shows how you can pack a dinnerware set into a divided box first and then into a larger box.

slightly larger box (about two extra inches on each side) and fill the gap around it with packing peanuts (see Figure 15-6).

FINAL THOUGHTS: WHAT TO DO IF YOUR TABLETOP ITEM DOESN'T SELL ON eBAY

Dinnerware, stemware, and flatware may take more than one week to sell on eBay. You may have patterns that aren't being searched for on a regular basis. Put pieces that don't sell into your eBay Store at a fair price (i.e., a price that will move the goods but still make you a profit). The fixed-price format of the store is great and allows you the extra time to wait for a buyer who will pay a slightly higher price. Try pricing the pieces from $4.99 to $24.99, giving more value to the hard-to-find serving pieces. By listing them in your eBay Store for 30, 60, 90, or 120 days, you get the exposure the items require to sell, and you pay a lower listing fee to eBay than with the auction format. You can't lose!

16

Decorative Collectibles

Decorative Collectibles is a huge dollar volume opportunity on eBay. And it's also a lot of fun! This is a popular category for selling for many reasons. First of all, most decorative collectibles are signed, which makes identifying pieces super easy. Second, collectors go nuts for these items, and the bidding can get really out of control. That means money in our pockets! Finally, a decorative collectible can be anything imaginable that someone would collect. Just for fun, start asking your friends and family what things they collect. You'll be surprised to hear what a wide variety of answers you get.

Here are just a few samples of the types of items that many people collect:

- Restaurant menus
- Blenko glass
- Oaxcan hand-painted animals
- Brass
- Milagro crosses
- Bird figurines
- Shells and rocks
- Boyds bears
- Gold coins
- Ice buckets
- Dralle perfumes
- A wee bit o' pottery
- Ceramic animals
- Baseballs
- Winnie the Pooh items
- Magazine articles about actors

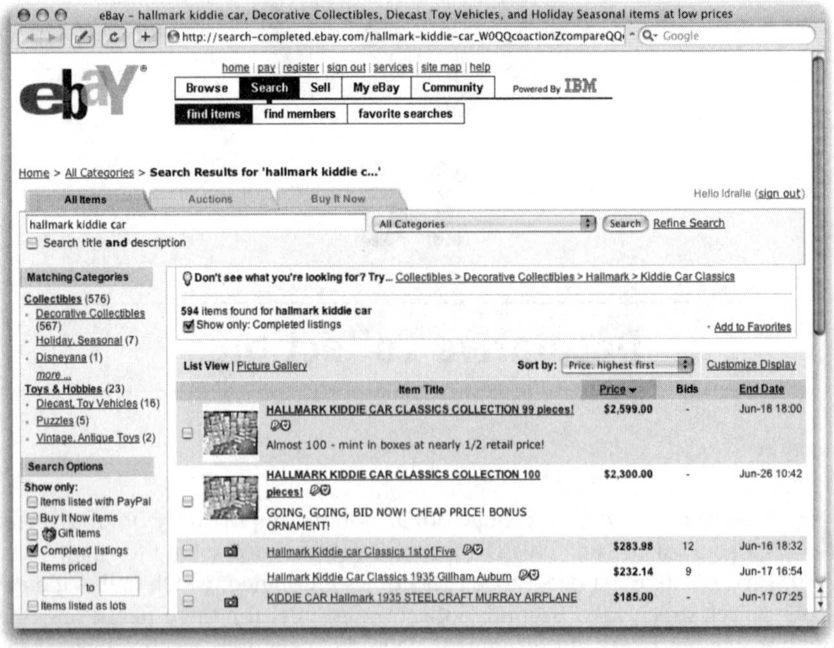

Figure 16-1 This eBay screenshot shows the popular Hallmark Kiddie Classics

- spoons
- Melmac bowls
- types of hot sauce

Isn't it fascinating? Collecting gives people something fun to look for when they're shopping or on vacation. For the purposes of this book, we will just focus on Decorative Collectibles (DC). DC's are any thing that can be used or displayed in your home. From the list above, most of the items could definitely be used or displayed. You can frame menus and have shelves of ice buckets or Boyds bears.

What Are the Hottest Collectibles?

To find the current most popular brands and manufacturers, we looked once again at our favorite eBay resource: the *Hot Seller* report. Recently, we have seen in the *Super Hot* category items made by Enesco, Fitz & Floyd, the Franklin Mint, Mary Engelbreit, and Thomas Kinkade. In the *Very Hot* category we found Hallmark, Harmony Kingdom, HOMCO, Longaberger, Norman Rockwell, Roman, and Wedgwood. And in *Hot* we found Charming Tails, Danbury Mint, Dept. 56, Goebel Hummel, Lladro, Royal Doulton, and Willitts.

To find out more about any of these companies, a vast amount of information is available online. Search for these names in an eBay completed-auction search or by doing a Google search. Watch for these brand names when you are shopping for stock.

eBay TIP   Keep in mind that just because a manufacturer is listed on eBay as hot does *not* mean everything they make is. For example, Hallmark's Kiddie Car Classics (see Figure 16-1) are super hot but their Lou Gehrig Ornaments are not. The most expensive Kiddie Car Classic sold for $283.98 and the most expensive Lou Ornament for only $1.99. Focus on what products are selling for the most money!

If you look through the same eBay report for top categories, instead of manufacturers, you'll find a lot of different areas of opportunity. A main category that is huge is *Animals*. Super-hot animals include these dog categories: *Airedale*, *Borzoi*, *Boxer*, three types of spaniels, *Collie*, *Sheepdog*, and *Yorkshire Terrier*. There are also super-hot categories for *Domestic Cats*, *Dolphins*, *Frogs*, *Insects*, and *Wolves*. *Animation Art*, *Japanese Anime*, and *Dragon Statues* are also listed. eBay has other categories, such as *Breweriana*, which includes lighters, pins, and playing cards, and *Disneyana*, which includes the very popular animation cels and plates.

BUYING STRATEGIES FOR COLLECTIBLES

Buy in quantity! This is the best advice that we can give. When you stumble on a garage sale or store closing that has tons of collectibles, get out your checkbook! Make them an offer they can not refuse. Ask the sellers how much they want for you to take everything away. More often than not they are thrilled with the prospect of only having to deal with one person. The beauty of buying in bulk is that if you have multiples of certain items, they are very easy to list. Once you have done the work to list the first item, all you have to do is re-list it every week until your stock is depleted. It is a time-saver!

Another buying strategy is to look on eBay for collectibles being sold in huge groups or by the lot. Do your research and see if you can break up the lot and sell the pieces individually. You'll find that this is a great way to make money. Also, look for items off season. Buy Christmas ornaments in the summer and Easter items in the winter.

Key Sources for Collectibles

Some of the best sources for collectibles are gift stores that sell these items. For example, many retail locations don't turn their stock as quickly as they would like. Sitting on their shelves could be very valuable, discontinued brand names from companies like Enesco and Dept. 56. Sometimes top name manufacturers will not let stores lower the price on their collectible items. Because of this, they may have slow turning and old inventory from makers like Christopher Radko, Dept. 56, and Fitz & Floyd. Find some stores like this in your own community and make a deal with them to take their slow turning stock at a very discounted price on a regular basis. They will be freeing up space so that they can bring in new fresh merchandise, and you may find a gold mine. If they don't want to work with large quantities like this, watch for when they have sales and do your research, and you can find great things.

How to Become a Collectibles Expert

There are so many collectors' clubs it is mind boggling. We talked earlier in the book about a collectors club for Chatty Cathy dolls. Whatever you decide to specialize in, join a club. These clubs are a wonderful source of information, and often the members find out about early releases, special discounts, and breaking news before the rest of us. For Goebel Hummel collectors there is the "Dorothy Dous" Collector's Club at *www.Hummels.com*. They offer a 5 percent discount to members, and many other great benefits.

UNDERSTANDING THE CATEGORIES IN DECORATIVE COLLECTIBLES

Before we jump into the fascinating history of collectibles, we must clarify a few terms. Keep in mind that the abbreviations to the right of each term are used extensively on eBay in both titles and descriptions.

- *Limited Edition (LE). Limited edition* means that only a certain number were made before the molds were broken, and it guarantees that no more will be made to hurt the value of those pieces in the marketplace. Some collector's plates release in huge numbers— 20,000 or more for plates by Franklin Mint. Some, on the other hand, have very small runs, like 250 for a Jean Paul Loupe French Enamel plate. The backs of most plates will say how many were made (see Figure 16-2). Some companies, however, like Bing & Grondahl and Royal Copenhagen, have never released their numbers. All they will tell us is that production is based on orders from their distributors and sales shops. We do know that around the World War II years—from 1937 to 1945—not very many plates were made, and these years sell for high prices. The 1943 Royal Copenhagen can sell for over $1,000.
- *First Edition (FE). A first edition will usually be marked as such

Norman Rockwell
"A Scout is Loyal"
Boy Scouts of America Calendar — 1932
taken from the series
"Scouting through the eyes of Norman Rockwell"

GORHAM
EST 1831
FINE CHINA
U.S.A

This Original Rockwell Has Been
Reproduced by Special Permission of
The Boy Scouts of America

Limited in Edition

4617
18500

Figure 16-2 This is a back of a Gorham Norman Rockwell plate showing information on how many were made: 18,500 in this case.

with "FE" or "1st edition" on the back of the piece. This means that it is the first in that series. For example, the Goebel Hummel 1971 Angel plate is an FE, the first in that series that was ended in 1995.

- *First Quality/Seconds (1st/2nd).* Most collectible companies release both first-quality and second-quality goods. A first-quality good means that it passes a rigorous inspection before being shipped to the stores. If it has minor problems, like a spot of missing glaze, a smudge in the painting, or ground marks, it may be considered a second by the quality controller. It will then be placed to the side and marked with that company's second mark. Second marks vary by factory. Some use black dots, mark it "second," or use some type of slash mark through the signature.
- *Certificate of Authenticity (COA).* A certificate of authenticity comes with most collectibles made in the last 30 years. It is a paper document that is included in the original box stating that it is an authentic product. These documents may have the number of the item on them. As an example, with a Veneto Flair plate from Italy you will get a certificate with the plate number hand written on it (for instance #567/2000), which would indicate that your plate was the 567th one made out of 2000 total. Some people try and collect all

their plates with very low numbers. This means that they were some of the first off the line.

- *Mint in Box (MIB).* This means that the item you are selling still has its original box, and probably the paperwork, and everything about it is perfect. A great selling feature that will surely earn you more money!

*　*　*

Now that we know the basic terms, let's cover some of the most popular brands and other categories of collectibles.

The Originals: Royal Copenhagen, Bing & Grondahl

The idea of creating items to be collected was a brilliant one. Two of the originals were Royal Copenhagen and Bing & Grondahl. In a way, these companies created their own demand. Ty Warner and his Beanie Babies really took this to a new level in the 1990s, and we will discuss that success later in this chapter.

Bing & Grondahl was first into the collector's-plate business with their first edition 1895 "Behind the Frozen Window" plate (see Figure 16-3). It is beautiful, and in her career as an antiques and collectibles dealer Lynn has sold only two of these plates, and each sold for over $5,000.

The Christmas plate actually has a legend. The wealthy people of Europe had a Christmas custom of giving each of their servants a platter piled high with candy, cookies, and fruit. The food was the important part, so the

Figure 16-3 This first-edition Bing & Grondahl Christmas plate from 1895 is extremely rare and always sells for a high price to collectors.

wealthy did not put much thought into what the platter was made of. It is thought that the first platters were made of wood. The servants, who were very poor, began hanging these platters on their walls for decoration and began referring to them as Christmas plates. The servants began comparing platters, and a rivalry for the most beautiful Christmas plate had begun. The rich began spending more time on the plates and less on the food that adorned them. Eventually, they began dating each platter so that they could see what year it was received. This was the beginning of the custom of collecting Christmas plates. In 1895, Harald Bing, the head of Bing & Grondahl, came up with an idea of issuing an annual Christmas plate. It was the first time in history that something like this was going to be produced commercially! He had little idea of the huge trend he created when he began selling plates. The plate was made and sold just before Christmas in 1895 and said "Jule Aften 1895" on it. This means Christmas Eve 1895. The plates are blue and white and about 7 inches in diameter. Each year, after Christmas, the molds are destroyed to prevent any future reproductions and to enhance the value to collectors. It took Royal Copenhagen, a rival of Bing & Grondahl, 13 years to join the Christmas-plate business. Their first plate was made in 1908 and was originally a smaller size than Bing & Grondahl's—only 6 inches. This first plate was called "Madonna and Child." Lynn has sold about eight of these plates in her antiques career; each sold for more than $3,000. After three years of making 6-inch plates, Royal Copenhagen changed to the 7-inch size in 1911.

Both are excellent Danish companies, and they still make the beautiful blue-and-white, all hand-painted Christmas plates. The current value of each year differs based on supply and demand. Some of the Royal Copenhagen plates from the 1990s sell in the high $300s. Bing & Grondahl claims that they never issued seconds, although some plates Lynn has seen certainly should have been marked and sold as seconds. Royal Copenhagen does issue their seconds, and they are marked with a slash mark through the wavy line signature on the back side. The slash is hard to see, as it is made in the porcelain— you almost have to feel it with your fingernail.

1930s Royal Doulton and Goebel Hummel

In the 1930s, Royal Doulton and Goebel Hummel got into the collectibles business with figurines and jugs. Royal Doulton did a line of Toby jugs (in the shape of a seated man) and character jugs with just the heads. These are a lot of fun and very collectible. A great Web site for seeing some of the fantastic Royal Doulton items is *www.pascoeandcompany.com*. They specialize in the secondary market (resale) of Doulton items. Another great Web site to help you date Doulton items based on their signature is *www.chinafinders .com .audating_ lambeth.asp*.

Goebel entered the marked in 1935 with their Hummel figurines. These figurines were all designed from paintings by Sister Berta Hummel. She was called Sister M. Innocentia and was a Franciscan nun. Most of us know what a Hummel figurine looks like. A real Hummel will be signed "WG" for West Germany, a bee in a "V" mark, or "W. Goebel." Check out the collector's Web site, *www.hummels.com*, which we mentioned earlier, for a great list of the marks. There were many copies made over the years. If you find a figurine that says "Japan" on it, it is definitely a fake Hummel. The Hummels are not selling for as much as they did in the heyday of the 1970s. However, if you can pick them up for a good price, go for it. We find that most sell in the $50 to $100 range. A lot of these older Hummels get all-over crazing that collectors do not like. If it does have crazing, buy it accordingly.

The 1970s and Collector's Plates

In the late 1960s, it seemed as if every company that was in the porcelain or pottery business tried to get a piece of the annual-Christmas-plate business. Many people had disposable income and were looking for hobbies. Collecting plates became the hobby of the 1970s. Companies like Frankoma, Stumar, Metlox, Hummel, Schmid, the Bradford Exchange, and even Wedgwood joined in. In addition to the Christmas plates, all of a sudden there were Mother's Day plates, Easter plates, Father's Day plates, commemorative bells, and Easter eggs. All of these were issued annually. It was a huge business opportunity, and many antiques and collectibles dealers made a lot of money.

When the marketplace saw what was happening, companies like the Franklin Mint came out will all sorts of collectibles. Trains, coins, figurines, and animal series. It was crazy! Many people looked at these items as an investment and put huge amounts of money into their collections. Unfortunately, the bottom of the collectible plate market fell out in the 1980s. There was just too much product and no more demand. The companies were to blame, because they had glutted the market. For example, the 1971 Goebel Hummel FE angel plate used to sell for over $1,000. We have seen some shocked investors when they find that this plate only goes for between $100 to $200 now on eBay.

eBay TIP Two companies made plates with Sister Berta Hummel's designs. The Goebel Hummel plates are more valuable and are done in bas relief. The Schmid Berta Hummel line is flat, and these plates are only worth in the $10-and-under range. Research both brands on eBay so that you are familiar with the difference when you are out shopping.

Some of the other collectibles from this time period sell for next to nothing, and some still have a demand. The Bing & Grondahl and Royal Copenhagen items are the still the very best, and we believe that they will always be a good investment, based on their many years of history. Lladro, Swarovski, and other high-end figurines companies are also still very good investments because a lot of time and effort was put into making these more expensive goods. They have a built-in value. In general, you must be very careful when dealing in these collector plates and other items. Know what you are doing so that you do not overpay.

eBay TIP   When building your inventory for your eBay business, skip any Bing & Grondahl or Royal Copenhagen plates from the late 1960s to late 1970s. Most of these are worth in the $10 range because of the oversaturation of the market during those years.

1990s Ty Beanie Babies

When Ty Warner entered the market with his Beanie Babies in 1993, who knew what a collecting craze he had begun. We had never seen such a phenomenon. Collectors of these plush toys ranged in age from 1 to 100. Men, women, and children were waiting in lines in terrible weather to get the new introductions. It was a marketing strategy created by a genius. The company would officially retire these Beanies at random, creating pandemonium and false values. At one point, the very rare Royal Blue Peanut (an elephant) sold in the $5000 range. Once again, people were betting their retirement money on a collectible with a falsely inflated value. There was no intrinsic value to these goods. They did not take hours of painstaking labor to make, there were no handmade details, and they were mass produced. The market had to crash. And crash it did. A few years ago, prices for the Royal Blue Peanut dropped to $100 and $200. But a recent search on eBay showed one in perfect condition currently selling for $599. The market appears to be gaining a little momentum.

eBay TIP   Every collectible item is cyclical. In 10 to 20 years, Beanie Babies will be in demand again. Why? Because the kids who couldn't afford them in the 1990s will be in their 30s and 40s with money to spend, and they will want to purchase their childhoods. Don't throw those Beanies away yet. Hold on to them for a little bit longer.

TODAY: OUR CHILDHOODS AND KITCHEN KITSCH

1950s to 1980s collectibles are very much in demand these days. People who grew up in these decades are trying to purchase their childhoods now that they are older and have disposable income. They want the items that remind them of those glorious days when they had nothing to do but have fun. This memorabilia makes for great collections: old baseball gloves, tennis rackets, fishing items, the yellow smiley face, pet rocks, mood rings, the Partridge Family, hearts and rainbows, lunch boxes, and the list goes on. Anything that you see at a sale that makes you say, "Do you remember these? We had so much fun," buy it!

   Kitchen Kitsch is another great subcategory. The kitchen is one of those rooms that lends itself to shelves full of collectibles. Colorful items are very much in demand. Mary Engelbreit was on eBay's *Super Hot* list, and her very bright, colorful, and cheery items are definitely geared toward the kitchen.

   Listed recently on eBay's *Very Hot* category under *Kitchenware* was bakeware, canisters, cookie jars, and graniteware. Graniteware was made from a variety of metals and then was coated with enamel. The pattern of the enamel was swirled or mottled and made to look like granite. It was mass produced, so the pieces in good condition and rare colors (cobalt blue, green, and red) are the most valuable. Most of what you will find will be gray. In the *Hot* category, we found pie birds, salt-and-pepper shakers, tea kettles, and timers. Vintage toasters, blenders, teapots, cups and saucers, tins, and mixing bowls are some more of the items that people are buying to decorate their kitchens. Longaberger baskets are another highly collected item. These are all signed and dated. You have got to love it when a company takes the time to sign their goods! Since most decorative collectibles are signed, the next step in selling on eBay will be to identify the material that the item was made from.

Material

At this point in the book we have already discussed most of the materials that these collectibles will be made from. Most are porcelain, pottery, crystal, bronze, pewter, fabric, or resin. You may see a few materials on this list we haven't discussed yet: pewter, fabric, and resin.

PEWTER   Pewter is so marked if it contains at least 90 percent tin. It is a somewhat dull looking silver-colored alloy made of tin, lead, and copper. Pewter has been used over the years for anything from eating utensils to candlesticks. Pewter, as far as its value is concerned, is at the bottom of the list below copper and only above lead. It was known as the "poor man's silver." Early American pewter with marks from the maker, and art pewter from Europe, can be valuable.

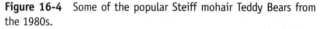

Figure 16-4   Some of the popular Steiff mohair Teddy Bears from
the 1980s.

In more recent times, many collectible companies used pewter for their
figures and statues. Schmid made music boxes with ceramic bases and pewter
figures. The Franklin Mint uses a lot of pewter in anything from Star Trek
collectibles to miniature motorcycles. The most expensive Franklin Mint
pewter piece that sold recently on eBay was a 1963 replica Corvette Sting Ray
for $510! (See, someone is buying his or her childhood.)

FABRIC   Fabric is what those popular Beanie Babies were made from. They
were made from a plush polyester fiber with PVC pellets for the inside. Boyds
bears are another popular stuffed-animal collectible. One of the oldest and
most famous of all stuffed animal makers is Steiff. Margarete Steiff's nephew
designed and created the world's first Teddy Bear in 1902. From Germany,
these animals are incredible, and this company has been in business since
1880 (see Figure 16-4). Steiff animals are either plush or pure mohair. The
mohair pieces sell for the most money. Steiff animals (from 1904 on) originally came with a brass button in their ear. Look for this tiny round mark
(much like an earring) when you are out treasure hunting. A recent search on
eBay for Steiff items found 5033 listings; the most expensive was $10,500 for
an early Teddy Bear. To learn more about this company, check out their Web
site: *www.steiffusa.com.* Don't overlook collectibles made from fabric. You
just never know!

RESIN   Resin is a synthetic material that is much like a hard plastic. Miniatures and figurines are often made from resin, and these tend to have sharp detail but are somewhat brittle. Be very careful when handling these resin figurines, because they will break and chip. Many model horses (check out Sarah Rose) are made from Resin and can sell in the $1,000s.

HOW AND WHY PEOPLE COLLECT

It is very interesting to figure out why and how people collect. We have covered many of the important whys, such as buying our childhoods or maybe just buying things that we couldn't afford when we were kids. There is also the decorating aspect of collecting. It often looks better to have a shelf full of toothpick holders than a hodge-podge display. People also collect as an investment. They would rather have fun buying things that please them, picking up bargains here and there, than just putting their money into the stock market. There is also the adrenaline rush of finding that one illusive piece that keeps people in the collectibles hunt. In the next sections, we'll explore *how* people collect.

Animal, Vegetable, Mineral

People often collect by type. Lynn's sister collects anything with an animal on it, specifically dogs. She has dog figurines, pictures, and trinkets all over her house. People also collect by type of food. Some people collect pears. Lynn had one eBayer who bought a pear paperweight, and when she saw the buyer's last name it all made sense. His name was Paul Partridge. Get it? "Partridge in a Pear Tree."

By Pattern

In Chapter 15 we really explored the idea of collecting tabletop items by a specific pattern. People do look for their certain pattern in many different areas including Depression glass, elegant glass, and Early American Pattern Glass. Some other types of patterns could be art glass with the herringbone pattern or anything of the Mary Gregory type.

By Material

Often collectors will collect by material. There are brass collectors, pewter collectors, and basket collectors. As you can see, this category of collecting is very broad based. Some people will narrow these collections down to, say, brass candlesticks or pewter porringers. A recent article in the *Antique Trader* featured a woman who collects vintage linens, especially souvenir tablecloths from each state.

By Color

Lynn's grandmother collected by color. She loved pink, cranberry glass. She filled her entire kitchen window with cranberry. Her advice was to enjoy your collections. Use them or admire them on a daily basis. It didn't make sense to have them packed away somewhere for no one to enjoy. Other popular color collections are cobalt blue or vaseline glass.

By Maker or Brand

This is a big category for collectors. Many people collect Disney items. In the *Disney* category, very hot items include clocks, radios, figurines, housewares, limited editions, lunchboxes, and snowdomes. Dept. 56 Snowbabies are a big business. People may collect Thomas Kincaide prints or lighthouses. Enesco, Precious Moments, and My Blushing Bunnies are huge. Get on eBay and spend some time in the collectibles categories and learn what is hot.

AVOIDING FAKES AND FRAUDS

There aren't a lot of fakes or frauds in the *Decorative Collectibles* category except for with Beanie Babies. The fakes in this area have run rampant because, as we mentioned earlier, there really is not much workmanship to these items. Also, the factories that originally made them in Asia often produced complete runs of fakes. If you think you have a rare Beanie Baby, it is worth it to get it authenticated before selling it.

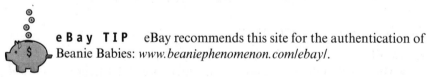

eBay TIP eBay recommends this site for the authentication of Beanie Babies: *www.beaniephenomenon.com/ebay/.*

LISTING COLLECTIBLES ON eBAY

We are going to take a look at a Danbury Mint Figurine for our example.

Step One: Identifying Your Product

Lynn picked up eight statues of baseball players at a garage sale and spent $120 for all of them, or $15 each. They were all MIB with a COA. This is a test for you. What does that mean? That's right, mint in box with a certificate of authenticity. We will be looking at the Babe Ruth statue since it sold for the most money and Babe Ruth is a very popular sports hero.

A completed-auction search brought up several similar statues that had

Figure 16-5 This Babe Ruth Danbury statue in mint condition was purchased for $15 and sold on eBay for $100.

sold in the 2 weeks prior. The highest-price Babe Ruth had sold for $61.69, which is what we expected to sell this piece for.

Because we knew which one had been the most successful, we decided to list it in the same category on eBay: *Sporting Goods and Fan Shop>Fan Shop>Baseball-MLB>New York Yankees>Other Items #25145.*

Step Two: Choosing a Winning Title

Key words we wanted to use in the title were "Babe Ruth," of course, "Danbury Mint," for those who collect by manufacturer, "Statue," for those who collect by shape, and finally "Baseball," because baseball items are very collectible. The final three letters would be saved for the abbreviation MIB. The final title was: "Babe Ruth Danbury Mint Statue Baseball MIB!" We decided to sell this item in February, since it is pre–baseball season and still cold outside (meaning many people would be home using their computers).

Step Three: Photo Tips

We used two photos to list this item because the detail on the Babe's face was so incredible. We also decided to use two photos since we thought this piece would sell for more than $50. With more expensive items, serious buyers prefer to see more than one photo.

eBay TIP   A great listing tip when you have multiple items in the same series is to tell your buyers just that. In the listing we wrote, "We have eight of these baseball figurines/statues up for auction this week. Save on shipping with multiple purchases." People love to save money, and we hook buyers with that sentence.

Step Four: Pricing Strategies

Because this statue was made in quantity, like most collectibles, we thought that each piece would sell for the same price every time it was listed. From our research, we also had noted that the auctions that started at lower prices got more bids and sold for more money. The auction dynamic really seemed to work with these items. Since it had only cost $15, we started the auction at a low starting price of $9.99. It definitely helps to have multiple items in the same series up for auction at the same time. Consistently, we get more for these auctions because bidders are going for more than one in the series, which helps to drive up prices. This auction had 173 people look at it and sold for a cool $100, almost $40 more than our estimate!

FINAL ADVICE FOR THE *COLLECTIBLES* CATEGORY

It's smart to start keeping lists of your customers right away. Keep a list for who buys Royal Copenhagen, Bing & Grondahl, Enesco, and so forth. When you get a new piece in and it is going up for auction, e-mail those customers. Start "wanted" lists. Once customers have bought from you, e-mail them to say it has been a pleasure doing business with them and to ask if there are any particular collectibles they have had a hard time finding. Tell them you are constantly coming across new items and would like to help.

If you specialize in a certain collectibles category, such as *Precious Moments*, it would be worth your while to purchase key word banner ads on eBay. Also, get a link to your eBay Store and auctions on some of the many Web sites devoted to fans of these figurines.

17

The Future of Selling in Antiques and Collectibles

The antiques and collectibles business is cyclical. Items that are popular come in and go out of favor with the whims of the buying public. Just remember that there will always be value in high-quality items that were made with exceptional craftsmanship. Key things to remember: buy the best example you can afford and don't throw anything away just because they are not bringing a lot of money today. There is always tomorrow.

A great example in the collectibles market are the Ty Beanie Babies. Hold on to these, store them in a clean and safe area, and watch the market. The market will cycle, and the older ones will be popular again. Remember, as the years go by, the supply of perfect quality Beanies will diminish as people discard them and let their children play with them. Look for other things that fit this profile, and start stockpiling them also. Don't pay a whole lot, so you can afford to sit on them for several years.

STAY AHEAD OF THE CURVE

The buying public is a fickle bunch. It is very important to watch their changing demands and desires. Try to stay ahead of the curve. The best way to do this is to be constantly learning and reading. Make sure that all those subscriptions and books you have invested in actually get used! Spend several hours each week reading about antiques and collectibles. There are all sorts of good tips in periodicals like *Maine Digest* and the *Antique Trader*. Think about what was popular 10 to 20 years ago and start picking these items up. Lynn's grandmother always thought that stretch glass would become popular. It was produced by many different companies, but Imperial Glass made a lot of it. They called it Imperial Jewels. It was stretched after being made to create a crackly pattern in the glass. It came in lovely colors: vaseline, a brilliant turquoise blue, green, and pink. On a regular basis she placed ads in the *Antique Trader* that said "Wanted-to-buy: Stretch Glass." It came to her from all over the country, and she picked up pieces for $1 to $2 each. It turned out to be a great investment. The market demand for these pieces picked up in the 1980s and she saw her $100 to $200 total initial investment turn into thousands of dollars. Think ahead to the future by looking back into the past. All great collectibles started somewhere in history.

HAVE FUN AND GOOD LUCK!

At this point, you should feel very confident about selling antiques and collectibles on eBay. You have a solid knowledge base and are ready to give it a try. Don't worry if you make mistakes. We all do. Mistakes are what happens as we learn. Just remember not to spend too much money on items when you are starting out. The $5/$20 rule will save you from any big losses.

Practice with some things you find around your own house. Selling on eBay is a great way to clean up your home and life and make money at the same time! Look in your dining room for tableware that you aren't using anymore, check the kitchen for kitschy collectibles, and look around for furniture that is taking up space.

Think in terms of the five categories we have discussed as you begin shopping for treasures in the real world! Look for furniture, ethnographic items, pottery and glass, tableware, and decorative collectibles.

But most important, have fun! It is a blast to sell on eBay because you are your own boss. The joys of owning your own business, setting your own hours, and making an unlimited amount of money make it so wonderful.

We know you can do it! We want to hear your success stories. Please e-mail us at *allaboard@mail.com* for Lynn and *dlprince@bigfoot.com* for Dennis.

Index

About the Authors

Lynn Dralle grew up in Bellingham, Washington, where she spent her after-school hours, weekends, and summers working in her grandmother's antique store. Her grandmother, Cheryl Leaf, owned Cheryl Leaf Antiques & Gifts for 52 years. Cheryl Leaf was a very well known, respected, and knowledge-able dealer.

Lynn has an undergraduate degree in entrepreneur studies and a master's degree in business administration, both from the University of Southern California. In 1993 Lynn returned home to Bellingham to run her grandmother's store. The store was closed in 2002, and Lynn now sells on eBay full time as a PowerSeller.

Lynn has written many books, including two successful books on Beanie Babies and *iBuy* and *iSell*, an auction-tracking notebook system carried by eBay for three years in their online store. Her entertaining and inspiring chronicle of her eBay adventures, *The 100 Best Things I've Sold on eBay*, by the Queen of Auctions, is available in major bookstores.

Lynn lives in Southern California with her two children, an eight-year-old all-star baseball player and a five-year-old princess ballerina.

Dennis L. Prince is a well-recognized and long-trusted advocate for online auctiongoers who continues in his tireless efforts to instruct, enlighten, and enable auction enthusiasts and business owners, assuring his readers' success every step of the way. By continually mining and monitoring the trends and opportunities within the online auction business realm, he has maintained a vantage point to present fresh and immediately applicable methods to help online buyers and sellers get the most from their auction efforts. His advocacy of online auctioning and good business practices has earned him recognition as one of the *Top Ten Online Auction Movers and Shakers* by Vendio (formerly AuctionWatch). His insight and perspectives are regularly sought out by others covering the online auction industry. He has been featured in the nationally distributed *Entrepreneur* magazine (2003), *Access* magazine (2000), and and has been a guest of highly rated television and radio programs such as TechTV, BBC-Radio, and CNET Radio.

Dennis has been regularly commended for his unique insight, personable style, and fearless observations that have been celebrated as timely, truthful, and often "gutsy" in his readers' estimation. Besides his previous books about eBay and Internet commerce, his vast editorial contributions to industry stalwarts like Vendio, Krause Publications, Collector Online, and Auctiva have earned him a well-regarded reputation in his ongoing analysis of the online auction industry. He likewise maintains active interaction with his personal network of auction enthusiasts, PowerSellers, and passionate collectors, on-line and off-line.